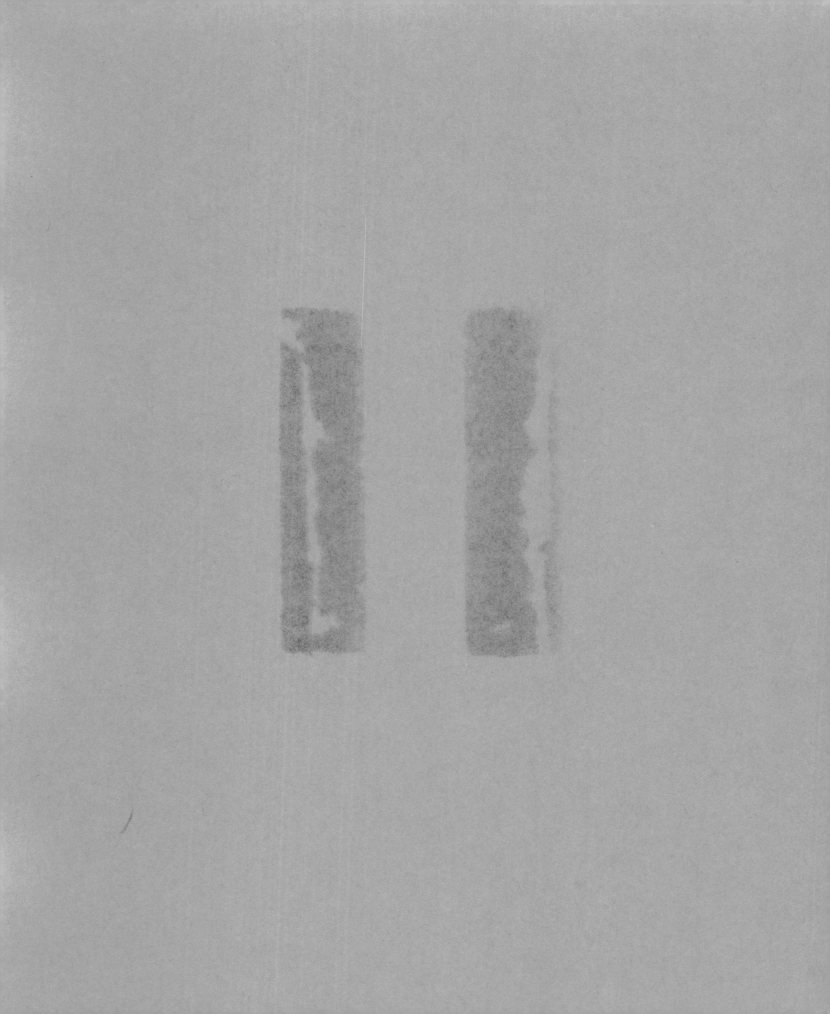

ART AND DESIGN
FROM THE
MERRILL C. BERMAN
COLLECTION

MAUD LAVIN *Series Editor*

GRAPHIC DESIGN

IN THE

MECHANICAL AGE

SELECTIONS

FROM THE

MERRILL C. BERMAN

COLLECTION

MECHANICAL

GRAPHIC DESIGN IN THE
MECHANICAL AGE

SELECTIONS
FROM THE
MERRILL C. BERMAN
COLLECTION

DEBORAH ROTHSCHILD

ELLEN LUPTON

DARRA GOLDSTEIN

YALE UNIVERSITY PRESS
NEW HAVEN *and* LONDON   *in conjunction with*

WILLIAMS COLLEGE MUSEUM OF ART

COOPER-HEWITT
NATIONAL DESIGN MUSEUM
SMITHSONIAN INSTITUTION

Printed in the United States of America
on Mead Moistrite® Matte, text,
and Mead, Signature®, cover

Library of Congress Catalog Card Number:
97-81268

ISBN 0-300-07494-8 (cloth: alk. paper)
ISBN 0-913697-23-0 (paper: alk. paper)

A catalogue record for this book is available from
the British Library.

The paper in this book meets the guidelines
for permanence and durability of the Committee
on Production Guidelines for Book Longevity
of the Council on Library Resources.
10 9 8 7 6 5 4 3 2 1

SPONSOR'S STATEMENT

Modern graphic design took shape in the 1910s and
1920s, when a revolutionary network of artists,
architects, poets, and typographers rethought the
traditional forms and functions of art and created a
dynamic new form of expression. Words and pictures
haven't been the same since.

The Mead Corporation is proud to sponsor
the exhibition *Graphic Design in the Mechanical Age:
Selections from the Merrill C. Berman Collection*. With
Williams College Museum of Art and Cooper-Hewitt,
National Design Museum, Smithsonian Institution,
The Mead Corporation celebrates the invention of
modern graphic design and its life today as one of the
most powerful art forms of our time. As a producer
of paper, the underlying medium of graphic design,
Mead welcomes the opportunity to promote excellence
and innovation in the art of design and printing.

We began our partnership with Cooper-Hewitt,
National Design Museum, as the primary sponsor
of the exhibition *Mixing Messages: Graphic Design in
Contemporary Culture* in 1996. Today we join two
major museums to offer *Graphic Design in the
Mechanical Age* as a gift to the public and as a grateful
acknowledgment to all who enliven our visual
landscape by rejecting mediocrity in search of new
and powerful ways to communicate.

JEROME F. TATAR
Chairman, President, and Chief Executive Officer
The Mead Corporation

DIRECTORS' FOREWORD

IN 1985 THE WILLIAMS COLLEGE MUSEUM OF ART organized *Art for the Masses: Russian Revolutionary Art from the Merrill C. Berman Collection*; Williams professor Darra Goldstein had proposed the exhibition and, in her capacity as guest curator, had contributed one of the two essays for the catalogue, which is now a collector's item. In the intervening years, the appetite for Russian avant-garde art between the wars has increased enormously, as has the appreciation for the extraordinary treasures of the Merrill C. Berman Collection. This collection, however, consists of far more than graphic designs by Russian avant-garde artists, and this current exhibition and publication can only begin to demonstrate the broad range and remarkable depth of Mr. Berman's artistic acumen. The 210 works of art included in the exhibition still represent just a small portion of his holdings, which now number more than 20,000.

Cooper-Hewitt, National Design Museum, Smithsonian Institution, has long included graphic design within the scope of its collections and exhibition program. As the only museum in the United States devoted exclusively to historical and contemporary design, the National Design Museum is committed to exploring the impact of all forms of design on daily life. The Merrill C. Berman Collection represents an exemplary effort to collect printed ephemera with an eye for both its aesthetic and its social significance. The collection is replete with masterpieces of graphic design created by some of the most influential artists of the century as well as with pieces by unknown designers whose work has been rescued from oblivion by Merrill Berman's keen eye. The Williams College Museum of Art and the National Design Museum are proud to have the opportunity to study and interpret this unequaled collection and make it available to the public through this exhibition and publication.

Merrill Berman studied history, politics, and government as a student at Harvard University. It was from this background, combined with his interest in the aesthetics of graphic design, that his passion grew for an area of art history that had received little scholarly attention. By area, we mean both medium and content. After all, artistic posters, commercial advertisements, and political propaganda are ultimately ephemeral—rarely intended to last beyond their immediate moment. It was a new concept to purchase, preserve, study, document, and exhibit examples of graphic design, much as had once been the case for photography. It is clear that Merrill Berman understood (and was exceedingly prescient about) not only the artistic value of these objects but also their cultural value for understanding our own lives and histories. These works of art appeal to our eyes and our minds, making vivid the unexpected links between avant-garde and commercial activity, shaped in an era of new technologies that was not unlike the electronic revolution of our own age. It is to Mr. Berman that we owe our first expression of gratitude; his generosity in sharing this extraordinary body of work is greatly appreciated, as has been his constant support and diligent oversight of this effort from the beginning.

The exhibition is scheduled to open at the Williams College Museum of Art; immediately following its run in Williamstown, Massachusetts, it will open at Cooper-Hewitt, National Design Museum, in New York City. The collaboration between the two museums has been productive, collegial, and immensely rewarding; this has been the case not only between the two of us but even more significantly among the three co-curators: Deborah Rothschild, Curator of Exhibitions at the Williams College Museum of Art; Ellen Lupton, Adjunct Curator of Contemporary Design, Cooper-Hewitt, National Design Museum, and co-chair of graphic design at Maryland Institute, College of Art, in Baltimore; and Darra Goldstein, Professor of Russian at Williams College. It should be noted that Ellen Lupton is also a practicing graphic designer, and her design for the book has sought to interpret the technological ambitions of the avant-garde in the context of contemporary publishing. The three curators have developed a close relationship with one another, founded on mutual respect and admiration for their respective skills, talents, and scholarly expertise. After three years of collaboration, it is all the more remarkable that their professional relationships have evolved into ongoing friendships, and we would like to express our gratitude to them for their outstanding devotion and creativity in so successfully realizing this project.

Added to this mix is the book's editor, Maud Lavin, whose introduction outlines the extensive parameters of the Berman Collection as well as its growth, especially in relation to Merrill Berman's intellectual and art historical interests. As content editor, her knowledge of both the Berman Collection and the cultural history of the period between the wars enhanced the cohesiveness of the essays.

Yale University Press has creatively and skillfully produced this book, bringing to bear all its incomparable strengths and resources. We would like to acknowledge the critical role that Judy Metro, Senior Editor at Yale University Press, played in seeing this production through to completion; it has been a complex project and she has been staunch in her commitment to it. She was aided by Mary Mayer, Production Controller, who ably oversaw the countless details involved in printing the book. Laura Jones Dooley, Assistant Managing Editor, did an excellent job editing the manuscript under tight time constraints, maintaining scrupulous attention to detail and a sense of humor throughout.

Photographer Jim Frank is responsible for the high quality of the reproductions in this book. To the daunting task of documenting the Berman Collection, Mr. Frank brought his informed awareness of the history of art and design, and his keen sensitivity and creativity as a photographer. He devoted attention to all aspects of the exhibition, from photographing works of art to researching, organizing, and identifying objects for reproduction and display. Kenneth Kramer, Mr. Berman's tireless assistant, was critical to assembling and preparing the works for exhibition.

On behalf of the curators, we would like to acknowledge the many individuals and institutions that assisted in the research and preparation of the exhibition and the publication. The curators would like to thank Deborah Rothschild's graduate assistant, Isabel Taube (Williams College Graduate Program in Art History, '97), and summer interns Jenny Raab and Ian Berry, all of whom worked diligently on the day-to-day administrative work of the exhibition as well as on researching and writing the artists' biographies. Ms. Rothschild would also like to express profound appreciation to Annie Elliott of the Williams College Graduate Program in Art History, '98, who has been an invaluable and resourceful assistant for two years. Ms. Rothschild is indebted to Wendy Kaplan and Marianne Lamonaca of the Wolfsonian Museum in Florida for information on their collection and to the staffs of the libraries at Williams College, Clark Art Institute, New York Public Library, and Museum of Modern Art. She expresses thanks also to Julie Martin in New York and Anne-Olivia Le Cornec in Paris for their help in locating photographs. She is extremely grateful to Brenda Niemand, who read her essay and, with a sensitive response to the material, helped to shape it. Dean Crawford also made valuable suggestions. David Rothschild has been constant in his support and encouragement.

On behalf of Ellen Lupton, we express our gratitude to her assistant, Eva Christina Kraus, who contributed to the design, writing, and research of this book from its inception to the final phases of production. Ms. Kraus was consistently helpful to all of the curators, and they would like to register their appreciation to her. Ellen Lupton also thanks her colleagues and students at Maryland Institute, College of Art, including Stephen Heaver, Jr., Hilary Lorenz, and Tracie Rosenkopf. She would like to acknowledge her many friends and associates in the field of design history, especially Jeremey Aynsley, Paul Carlos, Elaine Lustig Cohen, Leah Dickerman, Victor Margolin, J. Abbott Miller, and Teal Triggs.

Darra Goldstein would like to thank Ardath Weaver of the North Carolina Arts Council for her careful reading of the essay and astute suggestions. In Moscow, Marianna Shabat and Professor Dmitri Sarabianov provided valuable help with Ms. Goldstein's research. She is also grateful to Dean Crawford for his fine eye and editorial skills as well as for his faithful support.

It is a daunting prospect to acknowledge the many individuals within our museums who were instrumental in preparing the exhibition and publication. At Cooper-Hewitt, National Design Museum, we would like to single out Dorothy Dunn, Linda Dunne, Steven Langehough, Barbara Livenstein, Kerry Macintosh, Paul Makovsky, Christine McKee, Tracy Myers, Caroline Mortimer, Jen Roos, Cordelia Rose, Larry Silver, Susan Yelavich, and Egle Zygas; their characteristic dedication combined with their resourceful solutions to all challenges helped to ensure our success.

At the Williams College Museum of Art, Deborah Rothschild served as exhibition coordinator, working with Merrill Berman and managing a multitude of tasks associated with organizing the exhibition and publication. Diane Hart Agee, Scott Hayward, and Marion Goethals were key to the registrarial, preparatory, and administrative oversight of the organization and installation of the exhibition and its international tour. In orchestrating this complex effort, their attention to detail enabled us to feel confident that the special demands of this exhibition would be met thoughtfully and with unfailing professionalism. Working closely with Scott Hayward, designer Amy Reichert saw to it that the installation at the Williams College Museum of Art was appropriate to the innovative material on display.

After the showings in Williamstown and New York City, the exhibition is traveling internationally, and we would like to express our appreciation to the following museums for their interest in and commitment to *Graphic Design in the Mechanical Age: Selections from the Merrill C. Berman Collection*: IVAM Centre Julio González, Valencia, Spain; the Suntory and Kawasaki museums in Japan; and the Henry Art Gallery at the University of Washington, Seattle. Our colleagues at these institutions, Juan Manual Bonet, Josep Salvador, Hisa Ichikawa of Art Planning Rey, Richard Andrews, and Cheryl Conkelton, have shared our passion for this material, and it has been a pleasure to work with them.

No exhibition or related publication of this scale can take place without significant support, and we count ourselves most fortunate to have been able to turn to old and new friends who made it possible for us to realize this project in its full magnitude. *Graphic Design in the Mechanical Age* has been made possible by The Mead Corporation (Mead Coated Papers, Gilbert Paper, Zellerbach, Mead Coated Board, Mead Containerboard, Mead Packaging, Mead Pulp Sales, Mead School and Office Products, Mead Specialty Papers, and The Mead Corporation Foundation). This support represents a continuation of Mead's relationship with Cooper-Hewitt, National Design Museum, and a new relationship with the Williams College Museum of Art. We salute Hilary Strauss, Director of Specification Sales–Mead Coated Paper, whose ongoing commitment to the history of design played such an important role in securing this sponsorship.

The exhibition was made possible by additional support from the Curator's Grant Program of the Peter Norton Family Foundation, which supported the work of Ellen Lupton at Cooper-Hewitt, National Design Museum. The Andrew W. Mellon Foundation grants to the Williams College Museum of Art enabled Darra Goldstein's research and provided the necessary support for Ms. Goldstein and Ms. Rothschild to teach a course on twentieth-century graphic design together in the spring of 1997. We are also pleased to thank Christie's Fine Art Auctioneers, whose additional assistance is much appreciated. Catherine C. Vare, Vice President for Museum and Corporate Services at Christie's, was instrumental in securing this support.

Finally, it is to Merrill Berman and his wife, Dalia Berman, to whom we turn to extend our heartfelt thanks; without their loyal support, none of this would have been possible.

LINDA SHEARER, *Director*, Williams College Museum of Art

DIANNE H. PILGRIM, *Director*, Cooper-Hewitt
National Design Museum
Smithsonian Institution

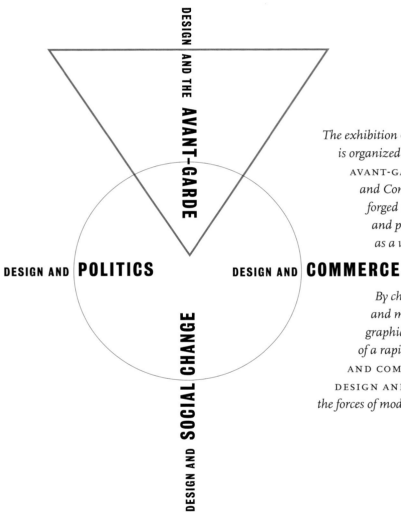

DESIGN AND THE **AVANT-GARDE**

DESIGN AND **POLITICS**

DESIGN AND **COMMERCE**

DESIGN AND **SOCIAL CHANGE**

The exhibition GRAPHIC DESIGN IN THE MECHANICAL AGE is organized into four main sections. The first, DESIGN AND THE AVANT-GARDE, focuses on such movements as Futurism, Dada, and Constructivism, which created new visual languages and forged new roles for the artist in the realms of mass media and public communication. The avant-garde can be viewed as a wedge that forced art into the arena of everyday life.

By challenging the conventional social functions of art and mobilizing the technologies of mechanical reproduction, graphic designers became the engineers, publicists, and prophets of a rapidly changing world. The exhibition looks at DESIGN AND COMMERCE, DESIGN AND SOCIAL CHANGE, and DESIGN AND POLITICS, showing how artists engaged and imagined the forces of modernity.

TENTS

Plate 1
HENDRIK NICOLAAS WERKMAN
The Next Call, No. 1
Magazine, Netherlands, 1926
Letterpress, 16 1/4 x 16 7/8 (open)

GRAPHIC DESIGN IN THE MECHANICAL AGE

WRITING A HISTORY

MAUD LAVIN

IN 1975, AS A YOUNG COLLECTOR, Merrill Berman was intrigued by a treasure trove of thirty early Soviet graphics he found in a Parisian art gallery. An unusual cache to appear in the French art market of the mid-1970s, posters and designs like these from the idealistic, nascent years of communism were commonly considered mere curiosities, dark and sullen in comparison to the more popular, graceful Art Nouveau posters. When these Soviet graphics surfaced in Paris with their heavy-handed messages and veiled elegance, they probably looked something like Greta Garbo's Soviet character in the comedy film *Ninotchka* when she first arrived, flat-footed, yet dedicated and secretly gorgeous, in the French capital. Not everyone could see their appeal. Berman though, a contrarian by personality and a political historian by education, was excited by the drama of these avant-garde designs and their function as historical emblems. He acquired the group, which included five major works by the then-unknown and now widely exhibited Gustav Klutsis. From this original group he has continued—with astounding aggression and dedication—to build his collection to its present size of more than twenty thousand works on paper. Because Berman's interests are political and historical as well as aesthetic, he has pursued a wide range of designs. And in his persistent devotion to collecting during the two-decade period when the scholarly field of design history was simultaneously emerging, he has had a direct role in shaping the history of graphic design.

Only since World War II has graphic design been categorized as a field worth knowing about and preserving, and most design collections have been narrowly defined. There are few extant archives of advertisements; some design collections only include political posters by established artists; other collections focus on such specific historical documents as election posters. Rigidly defined collections like these can foster pigeonholed concepts of design history. In contrast, Berman's ambitious reach as a collector, one that includes avant-garde graphics, anonymous political posters, and commercial advertisements, preserves graphics in a wide range to show how graphic designs paper our lives, not in isolation from one another, but all mixed together, part of the daily inundation of meanings and visual stimulation. Berman is an innovator in how he has categorized design—not exclusively as collectible, resalable art works or as mundane historical artifacts but as objects of art, politics, and cultural history.

The result is more than collecting as we commonly understand the word. For Berman, collecting does not simply mean amassing objects in a well-defined corner of the market, it means fashioning an archive, and, even more interesting, an "authored" archive—a personalized cut through twentieth-century visual culture. Berman's collection is as rooted in his political interests in liberal and leftist activism as his aesthetic ones in design innovation. Born in 1938, Merrill Berman collected even as an adolescent, buying political memorabilia. He came from a politically liberal family and was educated at Harvard, where he studied history, politics, and government. After graduate work in business, he went into investment banking and then ventured on his own, discovering young growth companies like H&R Block (little known at the time) for investment. There is an analogy between Berman's relation to finance and his collecting of graphics. In each case he relied on his own research and often-controversial judgment for successful outcomes.

Plate 2
THEO VAN DOESBURG
6e jaar, NB DeStijl, Dada, 1923
Postcard, Germany, 1923
Ink, watercolor, stamped and
printed letters, 3 1/4 x 5 3/8

When art collectors are written about in museum catalogs, the word "money" is rarely mentioned. This is in keeping with the tendency in art history to sanitize the field's evolution, upstaging talk about the funding of a collection with homage to the collector's eye. In Berman's case, though, both the funding and the intelligence of the collection are relevant and intertwined. Berman did not float his collecting enterprises on vast stores of inherited wealth. He earned the money for his collection, and his emotional investment is probably the deeper for it. He talks about the act of collecting as an antidote to the beatings he sometimes got in the market, although it was his market successes that supported his passion.

Berman is not extravagantly wealthy, and this also determined what he collected. He started out collecting paintings—valuable works from Post-Impressionism, Abstract Expressionism, Pop Art, and Photorealism—but when a financial downturn in 1973–74 forced him to sell that collection, he returned to graphics, his first love, with his acquired appreciation for art now melded with his early background in political history. Graphics, at least in the 1970s, were much more affordable than paintings. They were sold at book fairs as well as by such dealers as Elaine Lustig Cohen and Arthur Cohen at Ex Libris in New York and John Vloemans in the Netherlands. Berman remembers, for instance, acquiring a Jan Tschichold design for $325 early on that is now worth approximately ten times that price.

In collecting graphics of heroic modernism, as the work of the 1920s avant-gardes is sometimes called, Berman's interests grew with, and in some cases fed, certain trends in the design market. Since the 1970s, design has been an emerging field both in scholarship and in the art market. Collectors like Berman could thus influence its growth. There is also a generational component to Berman's influence. When he was helping to stimulate a market for modernist graphics in the 1970s and 1980s, the artists and designers who had come of age in the 1920s were dying and their archives were passing on to heirs. Because modernist design was not particularly in fashion at the time, nor were designers like Max Burchartz and Piet Zwart exactly household names (or even library ones), there was no certainty that these works would be treasured. By contributing to the demand, Berman was one of a few collectors who made a serious impact on what is now preserved as design history.

Of course, other factors in addition to individual collectors contributed to the growth of the design market. Pop Art encouraged a reconsideration of what art was and therefore what was collectible. So with the emergence of post–Pop Art, along with the market in photography, the market in graphic design also began to pick up. In Russian graphics, glasnost, followed by the end of the Cold War, prompted the sales of important graphics to the West. And, finally, art history, which broadened since the 1980s to include cultural history, now parallels Berman's interests; in recent years, Berman has loaned key works to such major exhibitions as the Walker Art Center's *The Twentieth-Century Poster: Design of the Avant-Garde*, the Guggenheim's *The Great Utopia: The Russian and Soviet Avant-Garde, 1915–1932*, and the Boston Institute of Contemporary Art's *Montage and Modern Life*.

Berman collects contemporary design, too, and Japanese graphics, and Viennese Secession posters, but the selection in this book and exhibition, *Graphic Design in the Mechanical Age*, is from one of his strongest suits, early modernist design. These are the graphics of the early twentieth-century avant-gardes whose aesthetics still strongly permeate our world and whose understanding of artistic values we still associate, sometimes unquestioningly, with design—beauty, clarity, innovation, attention-getting.

In the modernist area considered in *Graphic Design in the Mechanical Age*, Berman has acquired key pieces in avant-garde history like F. T. Marinetti's book *Les mots en liberté futuristes* and John Heartfield's first published political photomontage, "*Jedermann sein eigner Fussball.*" He has also collected rare and historically important activist works—anonymous political posters from the Spanish Civil War, from the American pre–civil rights race battles, from the Russian agitprop graphic artists, and from the German anti-Nazi left. In commercial graphics, a less idealistic but even more widely disseminated front, he has gathered advertisements whose early twentieth-century designs are so seductive that their styles are still being recycled today, such as an E. McKnight Kauffer ad for the London underground and another that reassures "Tea Drives away the Droops"; a Max Burchartz prospectus for the city of Bochum that idealizes its industries and railroads as only a technological romantic from the 1920s could have done; and a Piet Zwart virtuoso design for the Dutch postal and telephone service. Artists just now being

Plate 3
DESIGNER UNKNOWN
Demand Unemployment Insurance Relief.
Vote Communist.
Poster, USA, 1932
Letterpress, 22 x 17

Plate 4
EDWARD MCKNIGHT KAUFFER
Tea Drives Away the Droops
Poster, England, 1936
Lithograph, 29 x 19

revived are well represented in his collection, like the Russian Jewish artist Solomon Telingater and the Bauhaus metal journeywoman and designer Marianne Brandt.

There are financial risks involved in building a collection that includes anonymous design as well as graphics by famous avant-garde artists. "I don't follow a trail of names," says Berman. "If a piece is great aesthetically and it comes from the right historical context, it stands by itself." This is an unusual stance for a collector. It means building an archive somewhat independent of the preexisting name-driven art market, one that is inspired instead by the historical periods from which the collection draws. There is always the chance that such independence could be costly. Although anonymous designs are more affordable, and often significant historically, they are also of uncertain quality as investments. Without names attached the designs are certain only to be historical artifacts, and this hardly guarantees a high resale value. By the same token, however, if later a name is discovered and attached, this risk can yield financial profit. More certain, though, is the value of far-reaching collecting for design history. By "going against the grain of name-value collecting," Merrill Berman has opened up possibilities for the formation of a more inclusive canon, enabling scholars to delve into history and secure a place over the years for lesser-known designers.

The archival scope of Berman's collection is fertile ground for this book and exhibition. The curators, Deborah Rothschild, Ellen Lupton, and Darra Goldstein, have chosen visually delectable works that also tell of key chapters in the cultural history of early twentieth-century modernism in Europe, the Soviet Union, and the United States. In her essay, Rothschild looks at the artists' peer groups: expertly weaving avant-garde history and design history, she illustrates that some of design's most famous innovations came about when the avant-garde was promoting itself to itself (and to its select publics). Rothschild looks at the avant-garde's posters for its own events, its publications, and its announcements and reads this all as a visual trace of the furious networking going on, particularly in Europe, among avant-garde groups after World War I.

Ellen Lupton goes inside the world of design to reveal the production methods of the modernist designers and to explain why production itself was so highlighted in their works. Her essay reminds us of the early modernist values associated with industry—the dream that it could bring a more classless and, in some countries, democratic society. At the same time, her close look at the cottage-industry production in which most designers actually worked is a historical reality test—alongside newly rationalized industry with its well-organized assembly lines, the independent entrepreneur-designer still toiled with less technology at his or her disposal.

Darra Goldstein looks at the very different uses of persuasion in the Soviet Union, promoting the revolution and later the first five-year plan, and in Europe, selling objects. The collaboration between advertising and industry and the parallel mass dissemination of government propaganda that we take so for granted by now was born in the 1920s. Looking at the visual surface of these persuasions, and below it, allows us to question the uses of aesthetic appeal in these marketing efforts.

Berman's collection covers innovative design used in the politics of everyday life, in persuading consumers, in propagating for political causes, in redesigning ever-industrializing cultures, in papering modern and contemporary cities, in transmitting new ideas about art, and in promoting new modes of transportation and communication. The ambitious scope of the archive and of the curators' selections and theses can also prompt viewers to ask questions. For instance, what are the connections between graphic innovations and mass appeal? What can we see of early twentieth-century designs in advertisements of today? What are the visually seductive elements of persuasive graphics? How are the history of art and the history of industry intertwined? How did designers aesthetically combine elements of typography, photography, color, and composition? To whom were these designs speaking, and why do they hold our fascination today? Merrill Berman's landmark collection invites viewers to assemble their own understanding of the modernist visual culture that forms the groundwork of our contemporary, heavily designed world.

If this is a collection through which history is written, then it doesn't happen in a vacuum. In building this collection, Merrill Berman is at once engaging in a self-reflexive act, the healthy egotism of authorship, and an extroverted one, contributing to cultural history and inviting others to enjoy viewing the works and to enter into a dialogue—to question, to discuss, and also to write history.

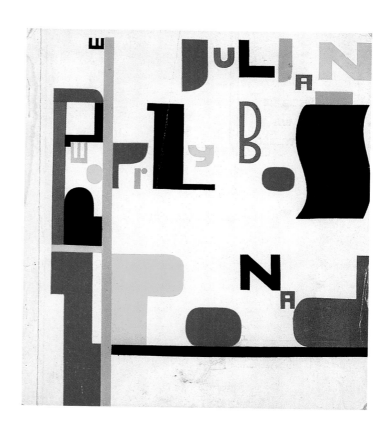

Plate 5
WLADYSLAW STRZEMINSKI
Ž Ponad (From beyond)
Book, Poland, 1930
Letterpress, 8 1/2 x 7 1/2

THE
BLINDMAN'S
BALL

For the BLINDMAN
A Magazine of *Vers Art*

Friday May 25ᵗʰ

at Ultra Bohemian, Pre-
Historic, Post Alcoholic

WEBSTER HALL 119 East 11ᵗʰ Street

DANCING EIGHT-THIRTY

Tickets $1.50 each in advance—$2.00 at the gate. Boxes not
requiring Costume, but requiring Admission tickets $10.00

Everything sold by the BLINDMAN

7 East 39ᵗʰ Street   Telephone Vanderbilt 3280

Figure 1.2
Marcel Duchamp, Francis Picabia,
and Beatrice Wood at Coney Island,
June 21, 1917
Photo: Collection of Francis M. Naumann

Figure 1.1
BEATRICE WOOD
The Blindman's Ball
Poster, USA, 1917
Letterpress, 28 x 10

DADA NETWORKING

HOW TO FOMENT A REVOLUTION IN GRAPHIC DESIGN

DEBORAH ROTHSCHILD

"THE BALL WAS A RIOTOUS AFFAIR. Marcel [Duchamp] climbed a chandelier and I performed a Russian dance." So begins Beatrice Wood's account of the 1917 Blindman's Ball, for which she designed the poster of a stick figure "thumbing its nose at the universe" (figs. 1.1, 1.2).[1] The ball celebrated the birth of the *Blindman,* a proto-Dada publication espousing artistic freedom from rules and conventions, a concept at the heart of the avant-garde movement.[2] Wood's defiant stick figure epitomizes just such unfettered expression. The advertisement—as well as the ball itself, billed as "ultra bohemian"—aimed at attracting an audience of progressive insiders and nonconformists while antagonizing upstanding members of the middle class.

Early in the century, modernists in cities throughout the West regularly directed experiments to an international community of like-minded artists, poets, and theorists. In spite of the many manifestos produced to "explain" new positions to the public, announcements produced for vanguard events, publications, and exhibitions were mainly pitched to those inside the fold and designed to irritate those outside it.[3] Like Beatrice Wood's nose-thumbing figure, the early avant-gardists were brazenly disrespectful. Their irreverence enabled them to defy artistic and social conventions and to innovate freely.

During the 1910s and 1920s in Europe and the United States there was an unprecedented give-and-take of new ideas and ways of seeing that took place among a small group of artist-designers of different nationalities, an interchange made possible in part by twentieth-century advances in travel and communication. This interchange was also in large part a reaction to the nationalism that led to World War I and the concomitant fresh belief that confreres, be they workers or artists, could form alliances across national boundaries. The result was not one homogeneous style but a variety of innovations in art-making, including design and typography, which were each inflected with national and personal accents.

1. Beatrice Wood writes, "Marcel suggested I make a poster advertising the event. Of the many I tried, he chose a stick figure thumbing its nose at the universe, and fifty years passed before I realized he liked it on account of the freedom it expressed." "Marcel," *Dada/Surrealism,* Duchamp issue (April 1988): 15. Another example of the poster, exhibited in *Making Mischief: Dada Invades New York* (New York: Whitney Museum of American Art, 1997; collection of Yale University Art Gallery, gift of Francis Naumann), is annotated by Wood: "This drawing chosen by Marcel—as final. B."
2. Wood, "Marcel," 14–15. Wood writes of the gestation of *The Blindman,* "The idea of freedom in art was so compelling to Marcel [Duchamp] and [Henri-Pierre] Roché, they thought there should exist a magazine dedicated to the cause. So they decided to publish one."

3. The manifestos themselves were often opaque to readers. Writing in 1914, the critic Roger Allard notes that a "special vocabulary" has been developed in programs and manifestos that offers a "means to disguise ignorance." See Jeffrey Weiss, *The Popular Culture of Modern Art: Picasso, Duchamp, and* *Avant-Gardism* (New Haven and London: Yale University Press, 1994), 60. Weiss provides an excellent account of public reaction to vanguard art.

This exhibition of graphic material from the Merrill C. Berman collection affords an excellent opportunity to trace that cross-fertilization of progressive ideas, in effect allowing us to look over artists' shoulders as they learn from one another and work collaboratively. The posters, announcements, and ephemera in the collection also provide a window onto those activities of the avant-garde that were transient in nature—the constant stream of performances, balls, demonstrations, manifestations, soirees, and exhibitions. The graphic art created to publicize them is often the only remaining record of these events, which involved a remarkable interaction of artists from all media, disciplines, and styles and from many countries. The Berman collection, with its great depth and scope, is a treasure trove that enables us not only to explore the history of the avant-garde's involvement in graphic art but also to experience some of the excitement that suffused its development.

It was largely through small magazines, reviews, and announcements that such movements as Futurism, Dada, and Constructivism became internationally known, and it was through them that innovations circulated. These little publications and the innovative graphics used on them created the face of the avant-garde. It was a look that signaled progressive ideas and unconventionality because it dispensed with the cardinal rule of graphic design: to take an idea and make it visually clear, concise, and instantly understood. Instead, graphics produced by the avant-garde exclusively for the avant-garde (as opposed to their advertising work), whether in magazines or posters, were usually difficult to decipher, ambiguous, and nonsensical. This overturning of convention, this assailing of standard graphic and typographic formats, was one aspect of a search for intellectual freedom. The impulse toward liberation enabled avant-gardists to break with easel painting for more egalitarian forms of expression as well as to see with fresh eyes untried possibilities for arranging and relating words and images on paper. Their experiments expanded the expressive potential of language, and with time their radical innovations were absorbed and modified, becoming a vital source for modern graphic design.

FUTURISM IN PARIS

We begin in the years around 1910 in Paris, where a group of boisterous Italians calling themselves Futurists loudly proclaim a passionate enthusiasm for technology, urbanism, advertising, and all that comprises the modern machine age. A key aspect of their rejection of the past is a desire to free language and form from confining literary and artistic conventions. *Parole in libertà* (Words in liberty) (see fig. 2.8), the work of the leader of the group, Filippo Tommaso Marinetti, is a cornerstone in the history of typographic invention. It is an aggressive call for a new graphic order in poetic work—one that thrusts language into the modern age of speed, industrialization, and publicity. In it, as well as in Fortunato Depero's *Depero futurista* and Ardegno Soffici's *BÏFʃZF+18, Simultaneità chimismi lirici* (see plates 10 and 11), words are manipulated in topsy-turvy arrangements with letterforms of varying size; compositions are imbalanced—cluttered in one place, empty in another; and standard syntax, diction, punctuation, and layout are flouted. Despite this, the works are readable, their vocabulary and references aimed at a broad public.[4]

A good example is the text of Marinetti's poem "CHAIRrrrrrRR," also titled "Lettre d'une jolie femme à un monsieur passeiste" (fig. 1.3), which serves as the cover for the mini-anthology of his collected writings and typographic experiments published in French in 1919 as *Les mots en liberté futuristes* (Futurist words in liberty). Mixing majuscules and minuscules in a variety of weights and fonts printed in red up the side of the page, the typography expresses the sardonic meaning of the poem—sex for sale hypocritically presented as love. The text, framed by endearments, lists in businesslike facts and figures the terms of the pretty woman's liaison with the outdated bourgeois man—three thousand francs per month, a large allowance of rubies and shoes in exchange for kisses, caresses, and fresh elegant beauty. The large CH does double duty for the salutation *Cher* and the word *chair* (flesh)—a punning summation of the exchange. Through unconventional typography and layout, Italian Futurist writing marries poetic content, visual form, and aural impression to create a multisensory experience. As Marinetti wrote, with typical Futurist emphasis on speed and militancy: "This new array of type, this original use of characters, enable me to increase many times the expressive power of words . . . . My reformed typesetting allows me to treat words like torpedoes and hurl them forth at all speeds."[5]

Figure 1.3
FILIPPO TOMMASO MARINETTI
Les mots en liberté futuristes: CHAIRrrrrrRR
(Futurist words in liberty: CHAIRrrrrrRR)
Book, Italy, 1919
Letterpress, 7 9/16 x 5 1/8

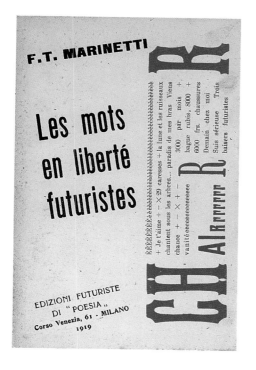

4. As Johanna Drucker notes, "Marinetti aimed for and achieved a readable public language, available to a wide public, communicative and consumable, streamlined and unburdened with arcane references and tropes." Futurism aimed at reaching the masses, hence its founder's constant courting of media attention. As part of his desire to be accessible, Marinetti rejected recherché language, private hermeticism, and metaphysical themes. *The Visible Word: Experimental Typography and Modern Art, 1909–1923* (Chicago: University of Chicago Press, 1994), 106ff.
5. Ibid., 117.

Futurist texts are filled with signs and phrases from the world of advertising and promotion. Many progressive artists fell prey to the lure of media hype; seeing its efficacy in reaching and manipulating countless citizens, they appropriated publicity and mass media tactics for their own work. Beginning with the bombastic Futurist manifesto announcing the birth of the movement, printed on the front page of *Le Figaro* on 20 February 1909, Marinetti and his fellow Futurists adopted hard-sell techniques by using the mass media and by making public spectacles of themselves.[6] Marinetti explained that reasonable behavior did not get attention: "It is because we want to succeed that we get straight to the point with exhibitionism."[7] Although this exhibitionism was impossible to ignore, it frequently obscured content: the yelps and noises with which Marinetti punctuated his reading of *Words in Liberty* at the Bernheim-Jeune Gallery in July 1913 caused critics to conclude that the verse held no artistic merit and was therefore merely a promotional strategy "concocted solely to attract notoriety."[8] As art historian Jeffrey Weiss demonstrates, the French press and the public at large perceived Futurism, as well as such other vanguard movements as Cubism and Dada, simply as novelty for its own sake accompanied by rampant self-promotion.[9]

Perhaps the novelty wore thin, for the Futurists were soon eclipsed in Paris by the emergence of the Dadaists. Dada, a movement christened in Zurich in 1916, was the creation of refugees from World War I living in neutral countries. Although Paris and Berlin became its dominant centers, the movement had adherents in cities as far flung as Rome, New York, and Moscow, as well as Warsaw, Prague, and Amsterdam. Dada was dedicated to destroying the status quo by irreverently lambasting pretension and authority. As one of its many manifestos states, "No more art! No more beauty! No more aristocrats! No more bourgeois! No more clergy! No more God! No more literature! No more music! No nothing, Dada, dada, tra la, la, la, la."[10]

The Cabaret Voltaire, where Dada began, was founded in Zurich in March 1916 by Hugo Ball and Emmy Hennings as an open house for artists and writers where art and culture could be presented like a "programme for a

THE ORIGINS OF DADA

6. The 1909 manifesto also appeared in other mass media publications and was translated into many languages. Drucker, *Visible Word*, 110.

7. Weiss, *Popular Culture of Modern Art*, 61. Marinetti interviewed in *Le Temps*, 1911.

8. Weiss, *Popular Culture of Modern Art*, 90.

9. Ibid., 51–105.

10. Recited by André Breton at the *Dada Matinée* of 5 February 1920 on the occasion of their inclusion in the Salon des Indépendants at the Grand Palais.

Figure 1.4
MARCEL JANCO
Galerie Corray
Poster, Switzerland, 1917
Linocut, 16 3/4 x 10 3/8

variety show." Initially there was an eclectic mix of Russian folk songs, modern "Cubist" dance and Negro music, costume performances, and a wide range of poetry. The first Dada review, *Cabaret Voltaire,* was similarly various, featuring examples of Expressionism, Cubism, and Futurism.

Ball and Richard Huelsenbeck, another cofounder of Zurich Dada, had been brought together by a shared interest in Marinetti's phonetic experiments. Their performances incorporated Futurist "noises" but went further by being totally illogical. "What we are celebrating is both buffoonery and a requiem mass," Ball wrote in his diary. And a month later he noted, "Every word that is spoken and sung here says at least this one thing: that this humiliating age has not succeeded in winning our respect."[11] Again Dada's metaphorical "nose-thumbing" at a society that had lost all claim to courteous treatment is evident.

A rare document from those early years is the first Dada poster, created by Marcel Janco to announce the inaugural Dada exhibition at the Galerie Corray in Zurich (fig. 1.4).[12] Although the lettering is uniform, Janco is already taking liberties with word spacing. "DADA" runs continuously around the border of the paper, and "Exposition" is hyphenated—rare in poster design—in order to keep within the rectangle of text. It is interesting to see that early in the movement the Dadaists were showing Cubism and African art; soon they would feature almost solely their own work.

The movement in Zurich coalesced and then devolved rapidly. Tristan Tzara took over and began planting Dada seeds in larger cities. By early 1917 both Ball and Huelsenbeck had left Zurich. Ball never returned to the fold, but Huelsenbeck helped to found Dada in Berlin.[13] Meanwhile, through Tzara, Dada was making itself known in Paris, rivaling Futurism in public malfeasance and attention-getting behavior.

11. Quoted in John Willett, *Art and Politics in the Weimar Period: The New Society, 1917–1933* (New York: Pantheon, 1978), 26.

12. Within two months the gallery was renamed Galerie Dada. The claim to Dada's paternity was a bitterly contested issue within the movement. Richard Huelsenbeck, Tristan Tzara, and Walter Serner said they found the name while thumbing through a dictionary. In Romanian "dada" means "yes, yes," in French it means hobbyhorse, and in German it's a sign of "foolish naiveté, joy in procreation, and preoccupation with the baby carriage." Dawn Ades, *Dada and Surrealism Reviewed* (London: Arts Council of Great Britain, 1978), 57.

13. Ibid.

ADVERTISING BOMBAST IN DADA ART

From the beginning, Dadaists in Paris, taking their cue from Marinetti and the Futurists, were enamored of commercial mass media and publicity. They were promotionally savvy and generated a prodigious amount of graphic material to attract attention for a constant stream of performance events and to advance their positions via books, tracts, and reviews. Both Futurists and Dadaists broke ground by appropriating for their publications and announcements the attention-getting mix of letters, images, and symbols found on broadsides, billboards, and newspaper ads. And although they cribbed from commercial advertisements, these avant-gardists created work that looked more chaotic and was certainly less legible than anything produced by the mass media. Moreover, in deliberately using commercial type that was as far removed as possible from good taste and elegance, these artists were thumbing their noses at all that was deemed aesthetically admirable.

In general, the public and press were disconcerted by works of art that looked loudly commercial but that sold no product. It was considered a violation of convention for high art to use the methods of lower commerce, trade, hype, and popular culture. When it did, the public's usual response was to dismiss the experiments as empty hucksterism.[14] This negative bias was exacerbated by Dada's penchant for attacking its audience—a tactic the Futurists did not use. Typical was Tzara's advice: "Punch yourselves in the face and drop dead."[15] Not surprisingly, the press and public recoiled.

For their part, the artists and writers in question not only expected negative critical reaction, they courted it. As is well known, Dada's avowed purpose was *épater le bourgeois*, to irritate the comfortable classes through shock tactics so that they would take a hard look at themselves. Instead of attempting to demystify or "explain" their work, Dadaists cultivated incomprehension by using the methods of modern advertising to put out baffling, often insulting announcements and reviews (see figs. 1.5, 1.9, 1.16, 1.24).

While denouncing the bourgeoisie, most of these artists mistakenly, and rather naively, believed that their work would speak directly to the masses and be embraced by them.[16] It is one of the avant-garde's many paradoxes that their adoption of nonelitist forms such as the vulgar language of advertising

14. Jeffrey Weiss documents the reaction of the popular press to avant-gardism and cites examples of ads that influenced modern artists. Weiss, *Popular Culture of Modern Art,* chap. 2.
15. Mark Polizzotti, *Revolution of the Mind: The Life of André Breton* (New York: Farrar, Straus and Giroux, 1995), 137.

16. The Futurists handed out leaflets on city streets, Berlin Dadaists tried to align themselves with factory workers and Communist revolutionaries, and French Dadaists posted announcements for events throughout Paris.

and the clattering brashness of variety theater brought these artists little acceptance among the laboring class, but only bemusement and hostility. But although reformers like Marinetti were habitually dismissed or derided by the common citizen, their work did strike a responsive chord among fellow experimenters in other cities. Indeed, many of these artists were active proselytizers, traveling widely to lecture and demonstrate, and pursuing an exchange of letters, poems, and magazines with as many progressives in different countries as they could locate.

French artists riding out World War I in New York, including Marcel Duchamp, Francis Picabia, and Jean Crotti, soon realized that their anti–"high art" position and linguistic experiments (self-published in journals such as the *Blindman, Rongwrong,* and *391*) shared affinities with Futurism as well as with the newer Dada movement. In 1916 Picabia, Duchamp, and their friend Marius de Zayas learned of the Zurich Dadaists then under Tzara's leadership.[17] Zayas wrote to Tzara in November 1916, "For some time now I have been trying to establish artistic relations between Europe and America, for I think that the only way to maintain the development and progress of modern ideas is through the exchange of ideas among all peoples."[18] Eager to collaborate, Tzara soon wrote to Picabia, "We could do beautiful things, because I have a mad and starry desire to assassinate beauty—the old kind, of course—with clarions and banners."[19] After the war Picabia traveled to Zurich, met with Tzara, and convinced him to come to Paris. There a group of young poets and critics associated with the review *Littérature,* including André Breton, Louis Aragon, Paul Eluard, and Philippe Soupault, disgusted by the war and consumed with nihilism, were making baby Dada noises. Like Marinetti and the poet Guillaume Apollinaire, who influenced them, they were searching for ways to liberate words from "centuries of syntactical accretions."[20] They thus shared an interest in phonetic, telegraphic, and typographic use of language. Having witnessed Futurist activities, they were also eager to destroy the status quo through scandal and media notoriety—but most of them were too inhibited to know how to begin. Enter Tristan Tzara, who arrived in Paris on 17 January 1920.

17. It is generally agreed that Tzara usurped the title of founder of Dada from Walter Serner, Hugo Ball, or Richard Huelsenbeck. All four, plus Marcel Janco and Jean Arp, were at the Cabaret Voltaire from its beginning in March 1916. The "international review," first called *Cabaret Voltaire* and then *Dada,* appeared in June 1916.

18. Zayas was affiliated with Alfred Stieglitz's gallery and publication *291,* and he enclosed several issues of the journal with the letter and included the suggestion to Tzara to exhibit American art in Zurich. Maria Lluisa Borras, *Picabia* (New York: Rizzoli, 1985), 198. I am grateful to Ian Berry for calling this quotation to my attention.

19. Quoted in Ades, *Dada and Surrealism Reviewed,* 143.
20. Dore Ashton, "The Other Symbolist Inheritance in Painting," in Anna Balakian, ed., *The Symbolist Movement* (Budapest: Akademiai Kiado, 1982), 513.

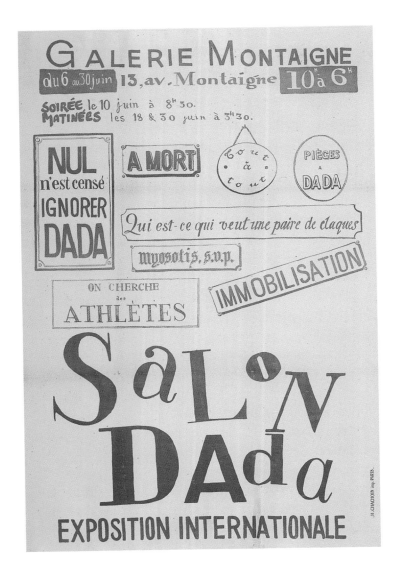

Figure 1.5
TRISTAN TZARA
Salon Dada, Exposition Internationale
Poster, France, 1921
Lithograph, 47 5/8 x 31 9/16

Figure 1.6
Installation view
Salon Dada Exhibition, Galerie Montaigne
Paris, June 1921
Photo: Roger Viollet, Paris

THE ART OF OUTRAGE

A born impresario adept at attracting scandal, Tzara promptly began organizing a series of events with the mission of destroying order, creating chaos, and becoming the talk of the town. Within twenty-four hours of his arrival, he had transformed the bland and sedate *Littérature*-sponsored matinees—lectures, poetry readings, music recitals—into outrageous events that had the audience jeering and throwing everything from their keys to beef cutlets. One manifestation drew a big crowd because advertisements falsely promised the appearance of Charlie Chaplin. At another, Breton carried a signboard bearing a bull's-eye and the slogan "Before you can love something, you have to have SEEN and HEARD it for a LONG TIME you heap of IDIOTS." It was signed "Francis Picabia." Tzara orchestrated these Dada performances, sprinkling them with the simultaneous reading of manifestos, the unbearable repetition of nonsense syllables, hammering on bells, and the hurling of insults and obscenities at the crowd.[21]

Tzara's poster for *Salon Dada,* an "international exhibition" that took place in June 1921, is a classic example of Dada graphic promotion (fig. 1.5). An irrational use of typefaces and sizes expresses instantly the unconventional nature of the enterprise. Why are certain letters capitalized and others not? Why different letterforms? The answer: no reason. A similar illogic is carried out in the little announcements that pepper the top half of the sheet. Under the location of the exhibition at the Galerie Montaigne and the dates of the show (6–30 June), are a number of asides and non sequiturs.[22] The rectangular box on the left reads, "No one is supposed to ignore Dada"; another box holds the phrase "to the death"; and yet others read, "Who wants a pair of claques?" "Looking for athletes," and "Immobilization."

The poster's promise of a disjointed and incoherent event was entirely fulfilled by the exhibition (fig. 1.6). To embody his anti-art position, Tzara had invited writers to make "pictures." The result was a host of befuddling works, bereft of pictorial craftsmanship, that in some ways anticipate contemporary installation art. A photograph of the exhibition shows a dummy in evening dress with a row of hanging neckties; a cello (also sporting a necktie) is suspended from the ceiling. On the wall are posters in German and French exclaiming "Dada Rules" and advertising a Dada ball.

21. Although Dada owed a great debt to Italian Futurism, Tzara felt no sense of loyalty—an outmoded notion to him in any case—and distributed a tract, "Dada soulève tout," in an effort to disrupt a lecture delivered by Marinetti in January 1921.

22. The exhibition did not enjoy its full run, and only the soiree on 10 June actually took place. Two matinees that were scheduled for 18 and 30 June were canceled, and the exhibition closed early because the Dadaists violently disrupted a performance by the Italian *bruitiste* Luigi Russolo, a wounded war veteran. The gallery owner felt this disrespectful act went too far and closed the exhibition on 18 June. See Georges Ribemont-Dessaignes, "History of Dada" (1931), in Robert Motherwell, ed., *The Dada Painters and Poets: An Anthology* (Cambridge: Belknap Press of Harvard University Press, 1951), 117.

Figure 1.7
IL'IA MIKHAILOVICH ZDANEVICH
Iliazd
Poster, France, 1922
Lithograph, 21 5/8 x 18 7/8

The *Salon Dada* poster exemplifies Tzara's random use of commercial signs and jargon. One of his goals was to subvert literary pretense and romantic ideas such as inspiration and genius by composing directly from newspapers and billboards. He demonstrates this method in his famous "recipe" for a Dada poem, which calls for cutting out the words of a newspaper article with scissors, putting them in a bag, shaking, and taking out each cutting one after the other—"Voilà, an infinitely original author of charming sensibility."[23] As Marinetti had done, Tzara cribbed the look, style, and language of advertising and publicity. But whereas Marinetti responded largely to the vitality and immediacy of these popular forms, Tzara saw them as a way of subverting "high art" and disorienting his public.[24] And whereas Marinetti's work makes sense—his poems are in effect verbal pictures—Tzara's usually does not. His aim was to use the dialect of hype and the appearance of public media, as well as affronts and nonsense, to undermine literary and artistic authority. He later wrote: "In 1916 I tried to destroy literary genres, I introduced into the poems elements which would ordinarily be judged unsuitable, such as sentences from the newspaper, sounds, and noises."[25]

23. Polizzotti, *Revolution of the Mind*, 145.
24. See Drucker, *Visible Word*, 193ff.
25. Quoted in ibid., 198.

THE RUSSIAN CONNECTION

Dada's dissatisfaction with the status quo overlapped with that of other experimental movements, including a group of Russian émigrés of Futurist and Constructivist tendencies. A link between the émigrés and the Dadaists was provided by the Russian Ilia Zdanevich. In Russia, Zdanevich was one of the practitioners of *zaum,* a style of verse that expressed the belief that the sound patterns of words are more important than their meanings. The zaum poets, sometimes called transrationalists, wanted to understand language at the fundamental level of sound, a problem that, as we have seen, also interested Italian Futurists and Dadaists. The zaum poets hoped to overthrow the pedestrian meaning of words in order to tap into states beyond language that were primal, universal, and purely emotional.[26]

While living in Paris, Zdanevich renamed himself Iliazd in 1922 and marked this "rebirth" with a public presentation. The poster for his "Birthday Eulogy" is bilingual, advertising the event in both Russian and French (fig. 1.7). It exemplifies his combination of zaum principles with Dada and Futurist tactics. The idea of dislocation, as in the shifting of letters and words, was central to zaum, an idea made literal in the rifts separating the map and the French and Russian texts, which were produced by reassembling a broken lithographic plate. Zdanevich injects typical Dada self-mocking ridicule into the text, which reads: "Iliazd. Eulogy by Ilia Zdanevich nicknamed the Angel, about himself, a stupid boor, coward, traitor, idiot, scoundrel and scabrous whore: on his birthday, triumphantly conceived." The Russian portion repeats the above and adds a strange biography mentioning such things as "three teeth, too curly hair, vices and prophets, something about trousers, secrets and illnesses, travel to Albania, a record of tenderness, sculptural activities, and inadmissible opportunities in the nursery."[27]

As he grew more interested in Dada, Zdanevich became friendly with Tzara. Both were foreigners living in Montparnasse, experimenting with language and performance, and in 1922 they began to meet and exchange ideas. It was a time of crisis in the Dada ranks in Paris, with the three leaders Picabia, Tzara, and Breton in perpetual disagreement. Picabia—feeling

26. Two important zaum essays, by Velimir Khlebnikov and Aleksander Kruchenykh, are "The Word as Such" and "The Letter as Such," of 1912 and 1913. See ibid., 69ff.
27. I thank Darra Goldstein for the translation from Russian.

hemmed in—had defected in 1921 but was using Dada tactics against his former colleagues.[28] Meanwhile, Breton and Tzara were not seeing eye to eye: Tzara considered Dada a loose association, without formal membership or leaders, while the more doctrinaire Breton wanted it to be a tightly knit group bound by a set of defined principles. Soon name-calling and put-downs were ricocheting in the pages of *Comoedia* and other magazines. The last straw was an article in which Breton accused Tzara of "intellectual larcenies" and referred to him as "a publicity-mad impostor." Shortly afterward, in early 1922, a meeting took place at the old café Cloiserie des Lilas, and the group decided to disband.

Dada as an official movement in Paris was dead, a victim of in-fighting and its own success. The ante had to be continuously raised as the public, expecting to be shocked and outraged, was increasingly immune to provocation. The constant pressure to perform and the need for new gimmicks had become tedious, especially in view of the continuous squabbling. The avant-garde, however, was alive and well, and the erstwhile Dadaists continued to create art and controversy.

In bitter response to the disintegration of Dada, Tzara published in April 1922 *Le coeur à barbe* (The bearded heart) (fig. 1.8), a "journal transparent" that contained violent attacks on Breton and his ill-fated symposium on modernism, the Congress of Paris. Those who sided with Tzara and wrote for the journal included Eluard, Georges Ribemont-Dessaignes, and Soupault. New contributors were Erik Satie and Marcel Duchamp (under the pen name Rrose Selavy). It is likely that Zdanevich designed the cover, employing irony by using quaint, antiquated imagery for a tract that was new and progressive. The words of the title are at first glance camouflaged by the old-fashioned printers' icons. For example, the *A* visually forms a unit with the pictograms of a man with his camera to its left and a tower to its right. The hand pointing to the balloon is a red herring—although it seems at first to be a meaningful part of the title, it leads nowhere.

**DADA IS DEAD.
LONG LIVE DADA.**

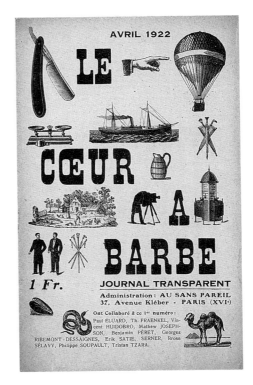

28. Picabia cut off his association with the movement by publishing in *Comoedia* a series of articles insulting not only Dada but those who had been his most devoted friends. Motherwell, ed., *Dada Painters and Poets*, 116–17. He also irritated Breton by associating with Dada's arch-enemy, the poet Jean Cocteau.

Figure 1.8
IL'IA MIKHAILOVICH ZDANEVICH
AND TRISTAN TZARA
Le coeur à barbe (The bearded heart)
Journal, France, 1922
Letterpress, 5 5/8 x 9

Figure 1.9
IL'IA MIKHAILOVICH ZDANEVICH
Soirée du coeur à barbe
(Evening of the bearded heart)
Poster, France, 1923
Letterpress, 10 1/4 x 8 1/8

A little over a year after the publication of *Le coeur à barbe,* Zdanevich and a group of his fellow Russian exiles who were associated with *Tcherez,* the review he edited, decided to organize a soiree using the name of Tzara's journal.[29] The *Le coeur à barbe* soiree was held at the Théâtre Michel on 6 and 7 July 1923. The program consisted of a showing of Man Ray's film *The Return to Reason;* a performance of Tzara's 1921 play, *Le coeur à gaz* (The gas-operated heart); a musical recital by Marcelle Meyer; and dances by Lizica Cordreno in costumes by Sonia Delaunay, which interpreted Zdanevich's zaum poems.

Zdanevich created the poster for this event (fig. 1.9). More advanced than his journal cover from the year before, the poster contains a sweeping arc in the form of the letters "organisée par Tcherez eo [part of *coeur*] ois [part of *soirée*]" that undermines the printer's grid structure. As a radical experiment in typography, the poster is comparable to El Lissitzky's *For the Voice* (see fig. 1.29) in its play of letterform sizes, the use of empty space, and asymmetrical layout. It also makes a bow to Marinetti's *Parole in libertà* in the autonomy given to individual letters as well as in the active, jumping movement that the assortment of different type sizes lends to the letterforms. One specific point of comparison is the V-shaped arrangement of "venDredI 6 et saMedi 7," the days of the soiree, which reverses Marinetti's *leger* and *lourd* from his "*Montagnes + vallées + routes + Joffre*" in *Parole in libertà* (see fig. 2.8). Marinetti, unlike Zdanevich, actually illustrates the meaning of the words *light* and *heavy* by printing the words to point up and down, respectively. Zdanevich's insistence on the visual properties of language and his separation of words into single letters that function as images at once look back to Futurism and Dada, parallel Russian Constructivism, and anticipate the experiments of the New Typographers, such as Piet Zwart and Paul Schuitema (see figs. 1.33, 2.22).[30]

29. Zdanevich was involved in a number of balls sponsored by the Union of Russian Artists. Among them were the *Bal Transmental* and the *Bal Banal,* which announced "the most banal surprises, the most traditional attractions, an ordinary cotillion, vulgar clowns, trivial pursuits, and a sentimental Pierrot." See *Iliazd* (Paris: Centre National d'Art et de Culture Georges Pompidou, Musée National d'Art Moderne, 1978), 53–61.

30. There is another less innovative poster advertising the *soirée du coeur à barbe.* It depicts an abstract heart handpainted by Robert Delaunay. The layout and typography are by Nachmann Granovsky. This poster is also represented in the Berman collection.

Figure 1.10
ANDRE LHOTE AND IL'IA MIKHAILOVICH ZDANEVICH
Fête de nuit à Montparnasse, Bal costumé
(Evening party at Montparnasse, costume ball)
Poster, France, 1922
Lithograph, 54 7/8 x 39 3/8

PUBLICIZING
BALLS AND THEATRICALS

Paris in the 1910s and 1920s was a cultural magnet for artists of every persuasion from many countries. The avant-garde who were drawn there created a steady flow of theatrical performances, balls, demonstrations, and exhibitions. The era's rich atmosphere of experimentation and international camaraderie fostered an exchange of ideas that led to innovations crossing disciplines and styles. André Lhote's poster for the Fête de Nuit (fig. 1.10), a gala costume ball held 30 June 1922 at the Bal Bullier, a Montparnasse dance hall, offers a glimpse onto the international mix of the Parisian art scene during the 1920s that belies the notion that artistic factions did not mingle.[31]

The poster announces the ball's sponsors in the lower right. It is as diverse a group as could be imagined. Cubist innovators such as Pablo Picasso, Juan Gris, and Fernand Léger are listed beside their epigones, the conservative so-called Right Bank Cubists, Jean Metzinger, Albert Gleizes, and Lhote himself. Marinetti, Picabia, Tzara, and Man Ray are present alongside the fashionable society painters Serge Ferat, Irène Lagut, and Kees Van Dongen. A wide range of literary tastes are also covered, and Russians expatriates are well represented (most eminently by the composer Igor Stravinsky). The Bullier was a favorite place for artists' organizations to hold benefit costume balls to raise money for poorer artists, and it is likely that this event benefited Russian émigrés.[32] Among them on the roster is Ilia Zdanevich. The poster's densely packed words at the bottom, the diagonal line that divides attractions from sponsors, and the "jumpy" lettering all bring to mind Iliazd's innovative graphics, particularly the "Birthday Eulogy" poster. Although he is not usually given credit, Zdanevich probably created the lettering for this poster, with Lhote supplying only the image of the harlequin.[33] It would be typical of Zdanevich to arrange for his name—last on the alphabetical list—to also read as a signature opposite Lhote's.

Lhote, a synthesizer of many trends, quite obviously cribs from Picasso's harlequins from the late 1910s. The profile of Lhote's figure suggests Picasso's 1917 painting *Harlequin and Woman with a Necklace* (Centre National d'Art et de Culture Georges Pompidou, Paris), but without the latter's psychological complexity.

31. The Bal Bullier, known since the 1850s for its "melange 'of games, sex, champagne and cancan,'" had been used during the war as a clothing depot for soldiers. When it reopened on 2 December 1921, it was a sign of recovery from the war. Billy Klüver and Julie Martin, *Kiki's Paris: Artists and Lovers, 1900–1930* (New York: Harry N. Abrams, 1989), 14, 64, 95.
32. Ibid., 95.
33. Zdanevich is listed with Lhote as artists for the poster only in Audrey Isselbacher, *Iliazd and the Illustrated Book* (New York: Museum of Modern Art, 1987), 85.

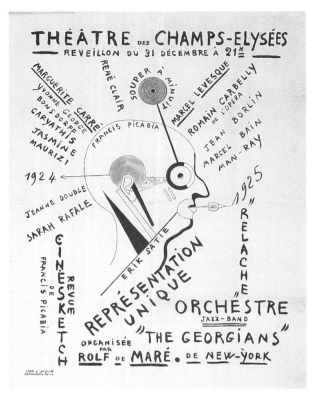

Figure 1.11
FRANCIS PICABIA
Cinésketch
Poster, France, 1924
Lithograph with watercolor
27 3/8 x 21

The attractions for the Fête de Nuit annotated on the lower left of Lhote's poster list "great stars of the dance, the circus and music hall," including "clowns, gymnasts, hindus, idiots, and jazz." Popular entertainment, especially the circus and music hall, not only was generally preferred over highbrow theatricals by the avant-garde during this period but was also a source of inspiration.[34]

As early as 1913 in his essay "In Praise of Variety Theater," Marinetti had called for a "new marvellousness" in theater through the adoption of such music-hall ploys as improvisation, topicality, and audience repartee.[35] He realized that popular entertainment had a vitality and broad appeal that such stuffy, tradition-bound forms as the ballet and opera could not rival. Similarly, Tzara used variety theater techniques in his Dada performances. Among the standard slapstick tropes he appropriated from the music hall were punctuating a verbal punch line with a bell, horn, or drum roll, engaging in banter and insults with the audience, and performing nonsensical skits in drag.

Francis Picabia was also a devotee of popular entertainment, especially the music hall and the relatively new cinema. Like Tzara, he delighted in confrontational theatricals and was known for ridiculing everyone and every-

34. See Kirk Varnedoe and Adam Gopnik, *High and Low: Popular Art and Modern Culture* (New York: Museum of Modern Art, 1990), and Varnedoe and Gopnik, eds., *Modern Art and Popular Culture: Readings in High and Low* (New York: Harry N. Abrams, 1990). See also Weiss, *Popular Culture of Modern Art,* and Deborah

Menaker Rothschild, *Picasso's "Parade" from Street to Stage* (London: Philip Wilson, 1991).
35. R. W. Flint, ed., *Marinetti: Selected Writings* (London: Secker and Warburg, 1972), 117–22.

Figure 1.12
Marcel Duchamp and Bronia Perlmutter
as Adam and Eve in Picabia's *Cinésketch*
Théâtre de Champs-Elysées
Paris, 31 December 1924
Photo: Courtesy Klüver-Martin Archives,
New York

thing, especially himself. The hallmarks of his art are provocation, self-mock-ery, sexual content, and disrespect for all forms of authority. Having lost his mother to tuberculosis when he was only seven, he was raised (and some say spoiled) by his wealthy Spanish father and uncle. This may account for his notorious personal and artistic restlessness, just as his mother's early death may have contributed to his infamous womanizing. A true Dada spirit throughout his life, Picabia advocated the primacy of individual expression over morality, loyalty, or acceptance.

After leaving Dada in 1921, Picabia continued to publish journals—now they were labeled "anti-Dada" but they can in no way be distinguished from his Dada periodicals—and also undertook a variety of other projects for stage and cinema. Among them was a plotless ballet entitled *Relâche* (Canceled) that Picabia created for Rolf de Maré's Les Ballets Suedois.[36] Opening at the Théâtre des Champs-Elysées in Paris on 4 December 1924, the ballet played just twelve times. The critics, the public, and even the troupe panned it.[37] After the closing performance, the discouraged and exhausted Maré dissolved his company.[38]

Before turning his theater into a music hall (where he recouped his losses by featuring the Revue Nègre with Josephine Baker), Maré allowed Picabia to put on a New Year's Eve spectacular entitled *Cinésketch*.[39] Picabia's poster advertising this gala event (fig. 1.11) lists the many participants in the show from all levels of entertainment—stage, screen, ballet, and music hall. The names of these collaborators surround a diagrammatic self-portrait bust of the artist—whose own name appears inside the cranium. Employing ves-tiges of his mechanomorphic style of the 1910s, Picabia gives the head in the poster a machinelike air by using geometric shapes that read as wheels and gears. A bar connects the circle around the eye to a disc of concentric circles rimmed by the words "supper at midnight."[40] The end of the old year is chart-ed by an arrow pointing out of the pink "brain" to 1924 written on the left, while the new year emerges from a pipelike object set in the mouth on the right. The words "Représentation Unique," referring to the event's sole per-formance, are written on the diagonal, mirroring the acute and obtuse angles of the names of participants.

36. The opening for *Relâche* was slated for 27 November 1924 but had to be canceled because the choreographer and lead dancer, Jean Borlin, was ill. Thus the promise of the title—*relâche* is commonly used on marquees during production changeover when the theater is closed—came true. Of course everyone was confused, not knowing if the 27 November opening, or the entire ballet, was a joke.
37. For more on *Relâche*, see Nancy Van Norman Baer, *Paris Modern: The Swedish Ballet, 1920–1925* (San Francisco: Fine Arts Museum of San Francisco, 1995), especially the essays by Lynn Garafola, "Rivals for the New: The Ballets Suedois and the Ballets Russes," and William Camfield, "Dada Experiment: Francis Picabia and the Creation of Relâche."
38. Maré later wrote: "Some of the members [of the troupe] declared that they would leave me if we insisted on doing ballets which neither the public nor the participants understood. Under these circumstances the risks and the costs surpassed my resources." Klüver and Martin, *Kiki's Paris,* 232.

39. See ibid., 137.
40. The disc is reminiscent of the ones Duchamp and Picabia used in their experiments with optics and movement. The film *Rotary Glass Plates (Precision Optics)* (1920) predates *Cinésketch* and *Relâche* (which also used discs as a leitmotiv). Duchamp and Ray's *Anemic Cinema* of 1926 postdates Picabia's theatricals.

The much-maligned *Relâche* had contained one element that was a critical and popular success: a cinematic interlude entitled *Entr'acte* (Intermission), directed by the young René Clair. Picabia used this recent film experience in *Cinésketch*. Working again with Clair, his aim this time was to bring film technique to the stage: "Until the present, the cinema has been inspired by the theater. I have tried to do the contrary in bringing to the stage the method and lively rhythms of the cinema."[41]

Cinésketch was a slapstick bedroom farce. The plot involved a sleeping bourgeois woman, her lover, his wife, a robber, the woman's husband, a maid, and a policeman. For it Picabia divided the stage into three sections—bedroom, hallway, and kitchen—from which the actors entered and exited in typical burlesque fashion, the husband just missing the lover, the robber leaving as the policeman enters, and so forth. A spotlight focused on one section, then cut over to another, achieving the effect of frames in a film. The well-known photo of a nude Marcel Duchamp and Brogna Perlmutter (who soon married René Clair) recreates their brief appearance in *Cinésketch* as the sleeping woman's dream—a tableau vivant of Lucas Cranach's famous painting of Adam and Eve (fig. 1.12).[42]

Cinésketch was well received. It was funny and unpretentious in the manner of music hall fare yet distinguished by Picabia's novel cinematic stage devices. It was neither as serious nor as insulting as most Dada productions. Instead it reflected Picabia's move away from Dada's stridency to an expression of his new philosophy of *vive la vie*—live life for the moment, enjoying the happiness of instants without thinking about tomorrow or yesterday.

This philosophy received graphic form in Picabia's publication of his appropriately short-lived *Instantanéisme* (October 1924), a movement that parodied the notion of all artistic movements in general. Subtitled "Journal of Instantaneism—for a while," it is a thinly disguised issue of *391* that notes on the cover, "There is only one movement—it is perpetual movement." On the title page, which carries a drawing that looks like a pipe-smoking Marcel Duchamp but is actually the boxing champion Georges Carpentier,[43] Picabia repeats the word "L'INSTANTANEISME" in identical majuscule type nine times followed by a colon and a definition, such as "Instantaneism: does not want yesterday. Instantaneism: does not want tomorrow. Instantaneism: wants liberty for all . . . believes only in life, . . . believes only in perpetual movement." The journal was another manifestation of Picabia's legendary restlessness and one-upmanship when it came to being avant-garde.

41. Paul Achard, "Picabia m'a dit . . . avant 'Cinésketch' au Théâtre des Champs-Elysées," *Le Siècle* (Paris), 1 January 1925, 4. Quoted in Williams A. Camfield, *Francis Picabia* (Princeton, N.J.: Princeton University Press, 1979), 213.

42. Camfield, *Francis Picabia*, 213. As Camfield notes, this scene is often wrongly attributed as coming from *Relâche*.

43. The likeness of Carpentier to Duchamp struck Picabia after he had made the drawing. Ades, *Dada and Surrealism Reviewed*, 154.

Figure 1.13
JEAN CROTTI
Poésie sentimentale
Painting with embossing
France, 1920
Gouache, ink
21 1/8 x 17 3/8

A DADA OFFSHOOT As Dada was beginning to disintegrate, it spawned a number of offshoots. Among the first was the short-lived Tabu, founded in 1921 by Jean Crotti and his wife, Suzanne Duchamp (sister of Marcel), who were its only practitioners. Crotti had become friendly with Marcel Duchamp and Picabia in 1915–16 in New York, where he took up their mechanomorphic style of painting. When he returned to Paris after the war, his friendship with Picabia led him and Suzanne (they were married in 1919) into involvement with Dada. Although they participated in movement activities, both Crottis were temperamentally more meditative and reserved than their Dada associates.

Poésie sentimentale of 1920 (fig. 1.13) is exemplar of Crotti's Dada style. Although it is not a poster or public announcement, the delicate drawing of watercolor, gouache, ink, and subtly embossed areas shares with Dada works an interest in letters, numbers, written titles, and machine imagery. The circles connected by lines recall the wheels and gears in Picabia's *Cinésketch* poster. However, the tone of *Poésie sentimentale* is quiet and intimate, the opposite of Dada's bombastic onslaughts. The letters and numbers cannot be deciphered into words as they can with Dada's jumbled typography. Instead they seem to hold to some cryptic personal symbolism. Circles are the main motif; the broken lines between them suggest invisible connections, and the ample amount of empty paper reinforces a feeling of infinite space.

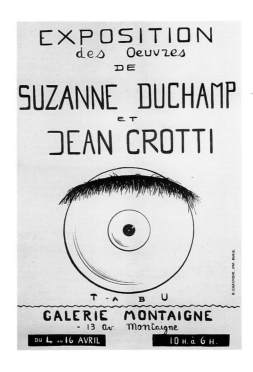

The mystical undercurrents in Crotti's work came to the surface the next year. On 12 February 1921, while visiting Vienna, he experienced a revelation. Shortly afterward he and his wife announced the birth of Tabu, a philosophic religion that aimed at liberation from matter. Basically a combination of Christianity and Buddhism, the name Tabu probably refers to a belief that the essential core of the universe is unknowable and therefore taboo.[44] Crotti, who had always been attracted to the mysterious and inexplicable, wanted to express the idea of forces that cannot be seen, touched, or understood.

On their return to Paris from Vienna, the Crottis began preparing for a show of their Dada work at the Galerie Montaigne. Although they had not created any Tabu art yet, they wrote the name of their new movement on the poster for the exhibition (fig. 1.14), marking its public debut. The exhibition, which was considered a major presentation of Dadaist art in Paris, occurred just two months before the important Salon Dada organized by Tzara (see figs. 1.5, 1.6) at the same gallery. Although the exhibition contained only Dada works, Crotti's impending defection is presaged in the preface to the catalogue, written by André Salmon, an anti-Dadaist, who sets Crotti apart from his "negative" (Dadaist) comrades.

The Tabu poster is dominated by a huge eyeball formed by Crotti's ubiquitous circles, topped with a shaggy eyebrow or eyelashes. The eye is his symbol for supernatural awareness, but the brow or lashes undercut any spiritual import and lend the image a comical Dada effect. Since 1916 glass eyes and circular forms had played a large part in Crotti's work, and he believed they "enabled him to see ultra-sensible wires linking his eyes to the generative bobbin of force, light and heat."[45] With Crotti we see Dada mutating into other forms. His work ties in to geometric abstraction as practiced by Wassily Kandinsky and others with its spiritual and cosmic overtones and also looks forward to Surrealism with its interest in interior states.

Figure 1.14
JEAN CROTTI AND
SUZANNE DUCHAMP
Exposition des oeuvres de Suzanne Duchamp et Jean Crotti
Poster, France, 1921
Lithograph, 46 1/2 x 31

44. Jean-Hubert Martin, "Tabu: Artistic Movement or Religion," in William A. Camfield and Jean-Hubert Martin, *Tabu Dada: Jean Crotti and Suzanne Duchamp, 1915–1922* (Bern: Kunsthalle, 1983), 88. Martin speculates that the spelling of Tabu with a "u" is a nod to the German birthplace of the movement as well as a reference to the Viennese Sigmund Freud's *Totem und Tabu*.

45. Camfield, "Jean Crotti and Suzanne Duchamp," in Camfield and Martin, *Tabu Dada*, 14.

DADA IN BERLIN

Figure 1.15
JOHN HEARTFIELD
Neue Jugend: Kleine Grosz Mappe
(New youth: Little Grosz portfolio)
Magazine, Germany, 1917
Letterpress, 25 1/4 x 20 3/8

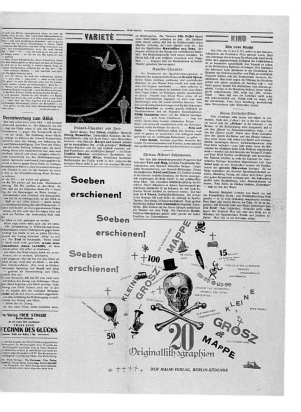

While Futurism and Dada flourished in Paris in the 1910s and 1920s, coexisting with and spawning other vanguard movements, there was simultaneous subversive art activity in other cities. Berlin, in spite of or perhaps because of the political upheavals that beset it, emerged at the end of World War I as the rival capital to Paris for avant-garde art in Europe. Surviving the defeat of Germany, the Revolution of 1918–19, the abdication of Kaiser Wilhelm, the brutal suppression by Friedrich Ebert and his Freikorps of the Spartakist uprising in Berlin, and the establishment of the Weimar Republic, Berlin in its madness was conducive to art that challenged normalcy, rationality, and convention. Dada's chaos and iconoclasm suited this city where many of the structures of life and culture had already been smashed, and its language of paradox, absurdity, irony, and nonsense seemed fitting indeed. In both Paris and Berlin the effects of the Great War in part bred Dada iconoclasm—the desire to shatter the prevailing order, and the forms of its verbal and visual languages—but events in Berlin led to a more overtly political Dada. While Parisian and American Dada are characterized by a general uninhibited zaniness, in Berlin the movement addressed specific targets for social and political change. As a result, a number of German Dada activities were suppressed by the government.

When Richard Huelsenbeck, one of the cofounders of the original Dada movement in Zurich, moved to Berlin in January 1917, he found a demoralized and half-starved nightmare city on the brink of political chaos. His poem-manifesto "The New Man," published in *Neue Jugend* for 23 May 1917 is a plea to keep sane in insane times while calling for the demise of "the burgher, the overfed Philistine, the overfed pig of intellectuality."[46]

Neue Jugend was published by Malik Verlag, run by the leftist Wieland Herzfelde. Huelsenbeck had met Herzfelde and his brother, John Heartfield, through the artist George Grosz, who had attended Huelsenbeck's first Dada lectures in Berlin. Both Grosz and Heartfield, who had changed their names as a protest against German nationalism during World War I, were instantly sympathetic to Dada's angry rejection of petit-bourgeois values.[47] In June 1917 *Neue Jugend* published Heartfield's advertisement for Grosz's portfolio *Kleine Grosz Mappe* (fig. 1.15). The ad, which Heartfield called a typo-collage, is an astonishingly advanced example of avant-garde typography. It surpasses other

46. Ades, *Dada and Surrealism Reviewed*, 80.
47. Heartfield's given name was Helmut Herzfeld. Grosz anglicized his name by adding an "e" to Georg. Grosz and Heartfield shared a studio beginning in 1916.

Figure 1.16

Dada graphics of the time in terms of its anarchistic arrangement of slanting, curved, crooked, and overlapping words and images printed in a variety of typefaces.

Heartfield was expert at grabbing a reader's attention. Using three colors—red, green, and black—he announces with each of them "Soeben erschienen!" (The portfolio has just come out!). He places a large skull and crossbones at the center of the composition, then scatters banal icons from the printer's tray throughout, undercutting here and emphasizing there the macabre nature of the image. Thus it appears as if the skull is wearing a top hat while a hot air balloon, a little ballerina, and a gramophone hover around it. Twelve crosses strewn throughout the ad, as well as two more skulls and crossbones both much smaller than the main one, reinforce the impression that the portfolio is a grim affair, though perhaps leavened by gallows humor. Made five years before Zdanevich's cover for *Le coeur à barbe,* Heartfield's advertisement far exceeded typographic invention at the time.

PHOTOMONTAGE AND COLLAGE

Heartfield and Grosz did not become fully involved in Dada activities until 1919.[48] That year is the date usually credited with the invention of photomontage, the art form associated with Berlin Dada and the group's main contribution to Dada graphics. Hausmann, Heartfield, Grosz, and Hannah Höch are generally cited as photomontage's earliest practitioners. In actuality, by 1919 photomontage was commonly used in both advertising and commercial photography. What was new was its appropriation by avant-gardists who had been on the brink of abstraction. The new form, which differed from commercial photomontage in its complex compositions and self-referential content made an early appearance in the journal *Der Dada,* which Hausmann edited.[49]

The third number of *Der Dada,* appearing in April 1920, was edited collaboratively by Hausmann, Heartfield, and Grosz. The indicia playfully reads, "Editors: groszfield, hearthaus, georgemann." For the cover Heartfield created a photomontage (fig. 1.16)—a vibrant mix of newspaper cutouts of consumer products and logos. The cover has an active, fragmented look and a staccato rhythm that mirrors modern city life. The composition is dominated by a photo of Hausmann's face caught mid-scream—perhaps in the midst of reciting one of his sound poems that he was known for performing at Dada

48. Grosz did sign the Dada Manifesto read by Huelsenbeck at an April 1918 meeting. Other signatories included Tzara, Franz Jung, Marcel Janco, Gerhard Preiss, Raoul Hausmann, and Walter Mehring.

49. The multitalented Hausmann was initially a painter and sculptor working in an Expressionist style. But by 1917 he renounced fine art in favor of a thoroughgoing iconoclasm. Moving from one discovery to another, he experimented with collage, photomontage, sound, and light.

He invented his own brand of sound poetry that relied solely on letters instead of words, for which he developed a system of notation where the letter's size reflected its sound level. He often "danced" these poems in Dada performances.

events. The same photo of the artist appears in Höch's major collage, *Cut with the Kitchen Knife Dada Through the Last Weimar Beer-Belly Cultural Epoch of Germany* (1919–20, collection Nationalgalerie, Staatliche Museen zu Berlin), where it surmounts a small sausage-armed robot body.[50] Like Höch's giant collage, Heartfield's cover uses wheels at different angles to suggest motion. A toothbrush, iron, and metal piping added to disparate lettering lend the collage a chaotic, urban feel. As is obvious by now, Dada posters are almost always self-obsessed, and this cover is no exception. The word "dada" is repeated several times in different typefaces, and the names of members, including Hausmann, Johannes Baader, and Grosz, are incorporated into the jumble of collaged print.

The exchange of ideas among Grosz, Heartfield, Hausmann, Höch, and Baader is amply demonstrated by works in the Berman collection. Grosz's collage *The Dance of Today* (fig. 1.17) shares with Heartfield's cover for *Der Dada* no. 3 snippets of printed logos and captions collaged upside-down and sideways over one another. Both also employ the echoing of objects—shoes (suggesting dancing feet) and bank notes in Grosz's tiny collage, and wheels and logos on Heartfield's cover. Grosz's collage is also self-referential in a way

50. The same photo of Hausmann is also used in his own collage, *ABCD* (1923), where those letters are pasted between his teeth.

Figure 1.17

Figure 1.16
JOHN HEARTFIELD, RAOUL HAUSMANN, AND GEORGE GROSZ
DER dADa 3
Journal with reproduction of collage by Heartfield
Germany, 1920
Letterpress, 9 1/8 x 6 3/16

Figure 1.17
GEORGE GROSZ
The Dance of Today
Collage, Germany, 1922
Printed letters, photographs, paste, handwriting, stamped letters, label, postage stamps, 5 1/2 x 3 1/2

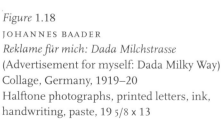

von dem ich richte das Erdall nach

Figure 1.19

JOHANNES BAADER AND
RAOUL HAUSMANN
Dada Milchstrasse (Dada Milky Way)
Poster with letter, Germany, 1918
Lithograph with handwriting in ink
19 5/8 x 12 1/8

Figure 1.18

JOHANNES BAADER
Reklame für mich: Dada Milchstrasse
(Advertisement for myself: Dada Milky Way)
Collage, Germany, 1919–20
Halftone photographs, printed letters, ink,
handwriting, paste, 19 5/8 x 13

that is typical of Dada. Here Grosz has cut up his own etching, *Café*, from 1916 and pasted it in three blue sections and in an orange circle. He shows only parts of the etching, but the full scene depicts a woman whispering to a man about someone at another table while a third party looks on. Their gossip relates to the fragmentary phrases, printed in English, reading "with opinions by" and "free information." In the upper right Grosz includes a photo of himself on which he pastes his name, next to that of a woman with a collaged oversized child's head, labeled Maud, the nickname of his wife, Eva.[51] This is a private one-of-a-kind work, not a Dada poster, and as such, it is allusive and personal. The postal stickers reading "registered letter" and "printed matter" and the dates ranging from 26 May 1922 to 31 June 1929 haphazardly stamped on the paper, as well as the repeated shoes and English phrases, conjure up the idea of a mail-order bride or long-distance romance.

Johannes Baader's collage *Reklame für mich: Dada Milchstrasse* (Advertisement for myself: Dada Milky Way) of 1919–20 (fig. 1.18) is also a unique work. Like Heartfield's and Grosz's collages, it makes use of photographic portraiture and overlapping printed text from newspapers and magazines. Baader had a talent for garnering personal publicity, but he was delusional and some think insane: dubbing himself the Oberdada, he elected himself president of the universe. In this collage he pastes a postcard, an envelope, photographs, and printed self-propaganda onto a poster he had designed for a performance with Hausmann (the two often performed together in Dada manifestations). The poster for this event, *Dada Milchstrasse* (Dada Milky Way), which is also represented in the Berman collection (fig. 1.19), serves as a ready-made base for the collage, with part of the trumpetlike form and starting time of the performance visible at the top and bottom right.[52]

The photograph at the lower right of the collage shows Baader facing forward and Hausmann in profile, an image not nearly as strange as the one in which both are head to head and topless (fig. 1.20). Another photographic self-portrait pasted onto the collage depicts Baader's disembodied head floating over a fragment of a star and Dada typography that is recycled from *Der Dada* no. 2, where it appeared with the caption "illustration for *Dadako* [sic]:

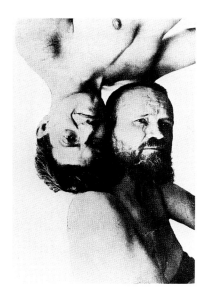

Figure 1.20
RAOUL HAUSMANN
The Dadasoph and the Oberdada:
Hausmann and Baader
Photomontage, Germany, 1920
9 3/4 x 6 1/4
Photo: Courtesy Private Collection, Milan

51. The collaged couple brings to mind Hannah Höch's painting *The Bride* of 1927 (Berlinische Galerie, Landesmuseum für Moderne Kunst), in which a similar large child's head is grafted onto a woman's body and paired with a stiff-looking man.

52. The letter as reprinted at bottom left on Hausmann and Baader's *Dada Milchstrasse* poster roughly translates, "Dear Tzara, [printed upside down], I'm curious if nhhaaums [Hausmann] will be able to hire the German press of the ninth of April. You need big guns to get those businessmen. I think I will die.

It happened yesterday evening; people give away these messages to the press; losing this of the last of it is more hurtful because B was just ready to go to Zurich where the dadaists and Tzara are at the peak. I wanted to give the biggest Dada soiree on April 9 where the dead should have been welcomed officially as the

[cont.]

This is the vision of the Oberdada in the clouds of heaven."[53] At the top left of the collage Baader announces, "Reklame für mich"—as if there were any doubt—and pastes below it the article from the same *Der Dada* no. 2 spread. The copy begins, "There is only one historical name and it is Baader. Those men in power hang forever like marionettes which I direct. They forget the war was lost." The postcard in the center of the collage reads, "In my thoughts there is room for all of you. Why are yours so small?" A postscript mentions telegramming the government in China to see if they would welcome a Cosmic World Congress to Peking in "the year of the sky." Baader also includes a letter to the editor of a newspaper, responding to a lecture by the president of the university in Berlin entitled, "What Jesus Christ Means to Us." His answer: "Nothing." Finally, pasted vertically up the right side of the collage is a biblical fragment, "from which I judge the entire universe."[54] Hausmann had been friends with Baader since before the war and liked to perform with him (probably because he was so outrageous). Other Berlin Dadaists, however, felt that he was not loyal to the movement and was using Dada for personal, megalomaniacal ends.

In June 1920 the various members of Dada came together to exhibit for the first and last time at the big Berlin *Dada Fair* (or *Dada-Messe*). Among those exhibiting were the Berlin contingent—Grosz, Hausmann, Heartfield, Baader, Herzfelde, Otto Dix, and Höch, as well as Picabia, Hans Arp, Max Ernst, and Johannes Baargeld. An indication that Russian Constructivism, with its foundation in collectivism and technology, had infiltrated Dada—ideologically if not aesthetically—is the fact that at least four works referred to Vladimir Tatlin, the epitome of the new socialism's artist-engineer. In Germany's unstable political climate, Tatlin's *Monument to the Third International* struck a responsive chord in the hearts of Berlin Dadaists through its antinationalism as well as its use of agitprop and machine technology. A poster pinned to the wall read, "Art is dead. Long live the new machine art of Tatlin." The effigy of a pig-faced dummy in army uniform led to a police raid of the exhibition and the prosecution of Grosz and Herzfelde for "insulting the armed forces."

international Oberdada. Why don't I appear in Dada 4–5. I insist on participation of the brain tumor. [signed] pustule." I thank Eva Kraus for the translation from the German.

53. *Dadaco* was an unpublished anthology from 1920.

54. I thank Eva Kraus for the translation.

DIVERGING FROM DADA

Figure 1.21
JOHN HEARTFIELD
"Jedermann sein eigner Fussball"
("Every man his own soccerball")
Magazine, Germany, 1919
Letterpress, 16 7/8 x 11 11/16

As had happened in Paris, before too long the Berlin Dada group began to splinter, with the aggressive and iconoclastic Hausmann in the role of Tzara and with Huelsenbeck playing the rigid part of Breton. Amid the infighting, some Berlin Dadaists moved toward Constructivism, some further toward political activism. Throughout the Dada years Grosz, Heartfield, and Herzfelde had been involved with the Workers' Communist Movement, and they had been producing small political journals through Malik Verlag. Among them is the famous *"Jedermann sein eigner Fussball"* ("Every man his own soccerball") of February 1919 (fig. 1.21). Adeptly using photomontage on its cover, Heartfield ridicules German government leaders by pasting their photos on a fan and posing the question, "Who is the prettiest?" The potency of the image is indicated by the fact the government immediately confiscated the journal.

Heartfield was above all an activist who used political satire as a tool for social change. As such, his images are clearer, simpler, and more readily understood than standard Dada fare. He and Grosz were initially attracted by the movement's denunciation of "high art" and promotion of revolutionary action. But by 1922 they had both become more engrossed in reaching a mass public through the press or large print editions and their involvement with Dada ended. Over the next years Heartfield became a master of the new form of photomontage, creating riveting images for the Communist Party and scathing indictments of Hitler's Third Reich (see plate 97). Through the popular press, such as the newspaper *Arbeiter Illustrierte Zeitung,* he achieved his aim of being a force for political change and, later in exile, an annoying thorn in the side of the fascist regime.

Some artists, such as Tzara, Picabia, and Hausmann, were Dadaists by nature. Their life and work remained true to Dada long after the movement officially ended. Others had a more fluid association. Hannah Höch, for example, became involved with Dada through Hausmann, who was her partner from 1915 until 1922. Her collages, like his, use ready-made materials, especially photographs of friends and pictures from popular magazines. But unlike most of the other Dadaists, she was primarily interested in showing what the modern world around her was like, particularly with regard to the changing

Figure 1.22
HANNAH HÖCH
dada
Collage, Germany, 1922
Printed letters, postage stamp,
cut paper, paste
18 5/8 x 24 7/8

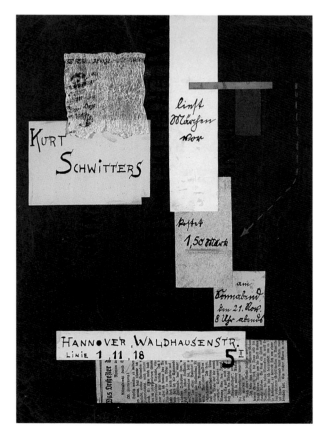

Figure 1.23
KURT SCHWITTERS
Kurt Schwitters liest Märchen vor
(Kurt Schwitters reads fairy tales)
Collage, Germany, c. 1925
Printed letters, printed wrapper,
handwriting, cut paper, paste
13 1/2 x 9 1/8

role of women.[55] More important, she diverged from Dada in that she never renounced the value of art.[56] In contrast to the anti–fine art beliefs of her colleagues, she continued to attend the School of the State Museum of Applied Arts throughout the Dada years (1918–20) and to participate in the Novembergruppe, an artists' organization that was the frequent target of Dada ridicule.[57] Her collage *dada* (fig. 1.22) provides an excellent example of her abiding respect for aesthetic values. Unlike the deliberately slapdash and disorganized works we have seen, Höch's piece adheres to a neat rectilinear grid where color and form are carefully balanced. Black vertical and horizontal rectangles mark intervals in the composition, with similar forms in shades of peach, green, and yellow harmonizing and creating a rhythmic syncopation. Letters and word fragments unobtrusively enliven the surface, with the word "dada" slightly off-center and quietly prominent.

Höch's *dada* collage, in its use of a rectilinear scaffolding on which scraps of torn paper are layered, shares affinities with the work of Kurt Schwitters, such as his *Kurt Schwitters Reads Fairy Tales* collage of around 1925 (fig. 1.23). Indeed, Höch confirmed that "in 1922 I began to try my hand at *Merzbilder* . . . I mean at the same kind of collages as those of my friend Schwitters."[58] Merz was the name of the one-person movement that Schwitters founded after being rejected from Club Dada in 1918. Although Schwitters shared with Dada a disrespect of convention, a love of nonsense and spontaneity, he was not anti-art. Rather he believed that art was a primal, inexplicable force, the basis of human achievement, and as such should be disciplined but unfettered by rules.

Living his philosophy, Schwitters was a ceaseless source of multifaceted creative expression. He used "Merz" as a term to cover all his artistic activities, including and often combining sound poetry, prose, stage design, architecture, painting, sculpture, collage, construction, and graphic design. Because he believed that art could be made from anything, he did not buy materials but found them in rubbish heaps and dustbins. What was important to him was the selections and choices the artist made in creating a formal composition. The collage *Kurt Schwitters Reads Fairy Tales* exemplifies Merz philosophy, with its bits of crumpled wrapping, printed letters, and handwrit-

55. From a 1959 interview with Edouard Roditi in Lucy Lippard, ed., *Dadas on Art* (Englewood Cliffs, N.J.: Prentice-Hall, 1971), 68–79.
56. For recent studies on Höch, see Maud Lavin, *Cut with the Kitchen Knife: The Weimar Photomontages of Hannah Höch* (New Haven and London: Yale University Press, 1993), and Maria

Makela, Peter Boswell, and Carolyn Lanchner, *The Photomontages of Hannah Höch* (Minneapolis, Minn.: Walker Art Center, 1997).

57. Her poster for the Spring Fair of the Applied Arts Group of the German Lyceum Club, c. 1925, is also represented in the Berman collection.
58. Roditi quoted in Lippard, ed., *Dadas on Art*, 76.

ten words on scrap paper carefully arranged over an old book cover bearing the title "Monuments of Ancient Painting." The irony of associating discarded refuse with great paintings of the past no doubt delighted Schwitters, but the formal soundness of the work tempers its humor. Note how the faded red tonality of the book cover's letters are picked up by a thin strip of salmon-colored paper that connects the top layer of white to the back layer of blue. A broken line in the same pinkish color points to the information "1,50 Mark," also underlined in light red. The collage appears to be an announcement for a reading of fairy tales that notes date, time, and place.[59]

59. Printed versions of this unique collage have not turned up, and it is possible the fairy tale reading was either fanciful, a small affair for just his son and other children, or simply an event that was never realized.

Figure 1.24
KURT SCHWITTERS AND
THEO VAN DOESBURG
Kleine Dada soirée (Little Dada evening)
Poster, Germany, 1923
Lithograph, 11 7/8 x 11 3/4

DADA MEETS CONSTRUCTIVISM

Figure 1.25
Theo and Nelly van Doesburg with
Kurt and Helma Schwitters at the time of
the *Kleine Dada soirée*, The Hague, 1923
Photo: Roger Viollet, Paris

Schwitters was an individualist who lived and worked in Hanover, but he was one of those artists, like Picabia and Tzara, who thrived on the exchange of ideas. After 1920 he participated in Dada activities and traveled incessantly promoting Merz. In 1921 he came in contact with a kindred spirit, Theo van Doesburg, the founder of the Constructivist and purely abstract De Stijl movement. Both Schwitters and Doesburg were zealous promoters of progressive art who saw that, despite differences, avant-gardists shared common theoretical interests. Chief among them was the fundamental ideal of universal elemental forms of expression that were unburdened by the past and its rules of propriety and reason.[60]

Doesburg and Schwitters promoted their ideas in lectures and performances, organized conferences and international meetings, and sent their publications to artists and publishers throughout Europe. In 1923 they collaborated on a tour through Holland of Dada-Merz evenings. The flier for the event, *Kleine Dada soirée*, is a little masterpiece of Dada-Merz ephemera (fig. 1.24). In a horror vacui composition, with letters of different sizes and styles fitting together like a jigsaw puzzle, the reader needs time to make sense of who, what, when, and where is being advertised. One thing that is clear is that this is Dada. Bold red capitals announce "DADA" with insistent diagonal force beneath the black type. In tiny letters at the upper left we see "Kleine Dada soirée"; next to it is "Programma," with its last two letters making a sharp right turn up the side. Beneath the pointing hand is printed "Théo van Doesburg," and below that, "Great Glorious Revolution in Revon," the title of Schwitters's poetic recitation for the evening ("Revon" comprises the last letters of "Hanover," reversed), followed by his name.[61] Underneath the word "Pauze" is written, "Poetry from abstract lyric to Urlaut" (primary sounds). One word that does stand out clearly is "Banalitäten" printed in block letters and outlined in black. Schwitters's fondness for the banal is demonstrated by the verses sprinkled around the flier, such as "For rheumatic toothache and headache usually 2–3 Revon tablets suffice—specifically on the belly," or "And then she looked in the bag, there were red cherries in there, then she closed the bag, then the bag was closed." Quotations from Tzara and Picabia in French also appear, such as "Dada is against the future, Dada is dead, Dada is

60. An example of this interest in elemental forms is Schwitters's *Ursonate*, a composition of primal sounds and repeated baby noises that he frequently performed. A recording of Schwitters reciting the *Ursonate* has been found and is now available on a disc on the Wergo label.

61. The word *door*, Dutch for "by," precedes the names of the participants in the soiree, Schwitters, Doesburg, and Vilmos Huszar (a member of De Stijl and also represented in the Berman collection). Nelly van Doesburg, sometimes referred to as Petro van Doesburg, also participated in the performance, but she is not listed on the flier.

Figure 1.26
THEO VAN DOESBURG
Mécano No. Bleu, Blauw, Blau, Blue, 1922
Journal, Netherlands, 1922
Letterpress, 6 1/2 x 5 1/8

idiot, Long live Dada!" and "Every morning I slip on my boots." Like Tzara's poster for *Salon Dada*, this flier adequately reflects the tenor of the *Kleine Dada soirée*. Behind the scenes the Schwitters and Doesburg ménages had a reputation for high spirits, which continued onstage (fig. 1.25). At the first performance, while Doesburg paused in his explanatory lecture about Dadaism, Schwitters began to bark like a dog. After that the rest of the tour sold out.[62]

Doesburg played a pivotal role in the network linking Constructivism to Dada. The De Stijl movement that he founded with Piet Mondrian and others in 1917 was initially driven by spiritual Theosophic values. Nonetheless, it shared with Russian Constructivism an emphasis on geometric purity and planar abstraction, as well as a nascent "faith in technological progress as a cornerstone of societal improvement."[63] Although wholly dedicated to the ordered and severe rationalism of De Stijl (exemplified in this exhibition by the work of Bart van der Leck and Vilmos Huszar; see plates 6–9, 38–39, and fig. 2.19), Doesburg was also a closet Dadaist who wrote Dada poems under the pseudonym I. K. Bonset (*Ik ben sot* means "I'm crazy" in Dutch slang). In 1921 he invited Tzara, Hausmann, and others to publish in the periodical *De Stijl*, and in the next year he came out with his own Dada magazine, *Mécano* (fig. 1.26). The *Mécano* logo, a saw blade, occurs in both Dada and De Stijl publications as an emblem of destruction and mechanization. In content *Mécano* has a mocking, Dada tone; advertised as "the international magazine of mental hygiene and Neo Dadaism," it pokes fun at the solemnities of the Bauhaus and the utilitarianism of Russian Constructivism. But in style it betrays its De Stijl origins—primary colors identify each issue (this one is blue), and the text is set at right angles without Dada clutter, arcs, or dueling diagonals.

62. For an account of the Dada-Merz tour and a tribute to Doesburg, see Kurt Schwitters, "Theo van Doesburg and Dada" (1931), in Lippard, ed., *Dadas on Art,* 108–10.
63. Lavin, *Cut with the Kitchen Knife,* 62.

BRIDGING
DADA AND CONSTRUCTIVISM

Figure 1.28
EL LISSITZKY
(LAZAR' MARKOVICH LISITSKII)
AND VLADIMIROVICH MAIAKOVSKII
Pro 2 kvadrata (Of two squares)
Book, Germany, designed 1920,
published 1922
Letterpress, 11 1/8 x 8 7/8

In October 1922 Doesburg organized a Constructivist Congress at Weimar (home of the Bauhaus) and invited several Dadaists to attend and to perform, among them Schwitters and Tzara (fig. 1.27). Some purists walked out because "they felt Dada was a destructive and obsolete force in comparison with the new outlook of the Constructivists."[64] But the Congress was an important step in establishing an international modernist community. One of the key participants there was the Russian Constructivist El Lissitzky, who having assimilated Dada's unconventional typography and abstract Suprematism into accessible commercial graphics became a link between avant-gardism and modern graphic design.

Trained as an engineer and architect, Lissitzky was imbued with the new Soviet goal of training artists to benefit the state and society rather than the individual. He was adamant about renouncing private and elite forms of art-making, such as oil painting, for work that was egalitarian, affordable, and comprehensible to the masses. "The innovation of easel painting made great works of art possible, but it has now lost its power. The cinema and the illustrated weekly have succeeded it," he wrote in 1926.[65] Thus to reach the masses he turned to printed forms such as posters and books that could be mechanically reproduced in great numbers. His book *Of Two Squares* (fig. 1.28), designed in the Soviet Union in 1920 but published in Berlin two years later, was a reading lesson for children in which, he said, "the action unrolls like a film." For it he developed a visual language of abstract symbols with which children could directly interact.

The next year he published in Berlin *For the Voice*, a book of typographic illustrations and settings of poems by the heroic poet-activist Vladimir Maiakovskii. The physical form of the book is innovative, incorporating a thumb index to enable the reader to find the poems easily. Typographically it is

Figure 1.27
A group of artists at the Constructivist Congress in Weimar, September 1922. Tristan Tzara is kissing Nelly van Doesburg's hand. Theo van Doesburg is between them wearing a white suit and a paper hat. El Lissitzky, wearing a plaid cap, stands behind him. Max Burchartz holds a boy on his shoulders, László Moholy-Nagy is at the top right in a dark suit, and Hans Arp is at the far right.
Photo: Instituut Collectie Nederland, Amsterdam

64. The quotation is from László Moholy-Nagy, who attended the congress (see fig. 1.27). He goes on to write, "Doesburg, a powerful personality, quieted the storm and the guests [Dadaists] were accepted to the dismay of the younger, purist members, who slowly withdrew and let the congress turn into a dadaistic performance." Moholy-Nagy, *Vision in Motion* (Chicago: Paul Theobald, 1947), reprinted in Motherwell, *Dada Painters and Poets*, xx.
65. Quoted in Marc Dachy, *The Dada Movement, 1915–1923* (New York: Skira, 1990), 179.

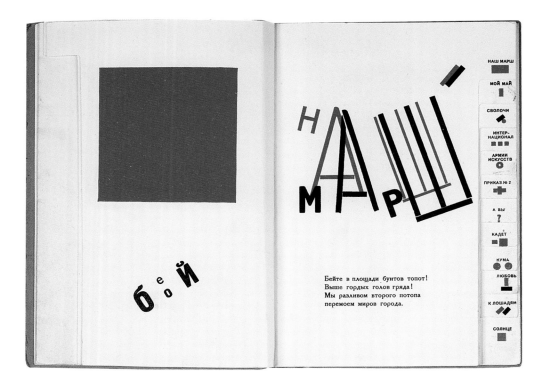

a tour de force of advanced graphic design. Using only the resources of the typographer's case he created active designs that bring Maiakovskii's words to life. For example, in the poem "Our March" (fig. 1.29), the letters forming the word "March" actually seem to walk on the page. Lissitzky's mixing of different typefaces, sizes, and weights, his sharing of letters between words, and the use of diagonals and free-form arrangements of words were nothing new—all were used by Futurists and Dadaists before him. But Lissitzky ordered and uncluttered these earlier advances so that they retain their liveliness but become more legible. His work in effect tames Dada for public consumption and serves as a bridge from Dada to Constructivism and the New Typography.

Lissitzky acted as a catalyst to the existing interest in Europe in the Bolshevik Revolution—especially among the international community of artists in Germany. By 1920, in the wake of the emotional excesses of Expressionism and in the aftermath of Germany's own political upheavals, these artists turned increasingly to Russian Constructivism, embracing its technology-based aesthetic and its ideal of a collective of designer-engineers working to produce objects that improved life for everyone. Russian Constructivism practiced by Tatlin, Aleksandr Rodchenko, Varvara Stepanova, Lissitzky, and others generated an international movement characterized by sobriety, utility, practicality, and objectivity.[66]

Figure 1.29
EL LISSITZKY
(LAZAR' MARKOVICH LISITSKII)
AND VLADIMIR VLADIMIROVICH
MAIAKOVSKII
Dlia golosa (For the voice), "Our March"
Book, Germany, 1923
Letterpress, 7 7/16 x 10 1/4 (open)

66. See Willett, *Art and Politics,* chaps. 5–8. Among other factors contributing to the new sobriety was the emergence of the New Objectivity in German art and culture.

Lissitzky settled temporarily in Berlin in the autumn of 1922 and became good friends with the sociable and genial Schwitters. The influence on Schwitters was profound; his work became neater, sparer, and more ordered (his *Kurt Schwitters Reads Fairy Tales* collage probably reflects this). Schwitters learned much about typography and layout from Lissitzky and recruited him to contribute to Merz design and publications. The 1924 program that Lissitzky designed for Schwitters's *Merz-Matinéen* (fig. 1.30) is a good example of the way Lissitzky maintained a Dada feeling within a structured framework. The pointing hand—a Dada staple—wittily touches the ovoid form above to read as a head in thought with finger to chin. The flier announces the Merz program by Schwitters and Hausmann that includes lectures (*Vortrag*) on the laws of sound, two manifestos, phonetic poems, dance (*Tänze*) including the Typsi-step, and the Wang Wang Blues performed by the Raynbows. An arrow points from Kurt Schwitters's name inscribed within the "head" to his two phonetic poems, "Revolution in Revon" and "Anna Blume." Lissitzky uses the letters "REVO" to do double duty for "Revolution" and "Revon" and then makes the idea of the sound poems visual by arranging the letters "TATA, Ti La La La," and "tui Ei" in rhythmic formation below. Black bars or rules divide and organize the space so that information is compartmentalized and easy to read, despite the fact that it is written vertically as well as horizontally.

Figure 1.30
EL LISSITZKY
(LAZAR' MARKOVICH LISITSKII)
Merz-Matinéen
Broadside, Germany, 1923
Letterpress, 9 x 11 1/8

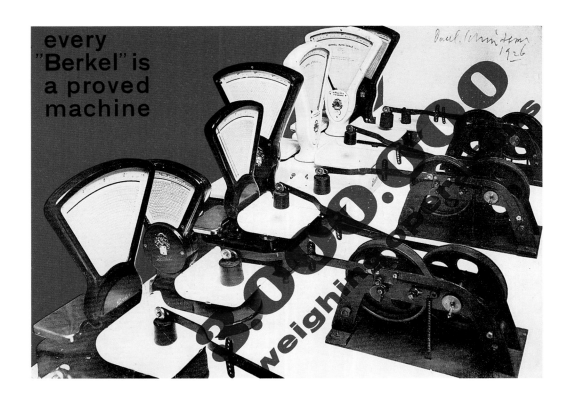

Figure 1.32
PAUL SCHUITEMA
Every Berkel Is a Proved Machine
Advertisement, Netherlands, 1926
Letterpress, 8 1/4 x 11 1/2

Figure 1.33
PAUL SCHUITEMA
Toledo Berkel 85000
Advertisement, Netherlands, 1926
Letterpress, 11 9/16 x 8 1/4

THE NEW TYPOGRAPHY

Figure 1.31
PAUL SCHUITEMA
Superior Dutch Ham
Poster, Netherlands, c. 1925
Lithograph, 19 3/4 x 19 7/8

Simultaneous with his avant-garde activities, Schwitters in the late 1920s and 1930s executed typographic designs for mainstream design clients.[67] In 1928 he formed the Circle of New Advertising Designers (Ring "neue werbegestalter") with Willi Baumeister and Jan Tschichold, further disseminating the assimilation of Dada and Russian Constructivism. The Ring, or NWG, as they called themselves, was a pan-European group whose others members included Walter Dexel, César Domela, Georg Trump, Robert Michel, Piet Zwart, and Paul Schuitema (all well represented in the Berman collection). Their style is characterized by active yet clean compositions with shapes, letters, and numbers that seem to move forward and back in space. The group was adamantly against any preconceived arrangement of type, insisting that form follow function—that "visible form develop out of the functions of the text."[68] In the late 1920s, the Ring became a chief vehicle for the New Typography, linking Dada and Constructivism to commercial production. Unlike the French Dadaists, whose graphics promoted their own events and publications, members of the Ring served paying clients.[69] Paul Schuitema's graphics for the Berkel Company provide a good cross-section of the range of New Typography design. In the red, yellow, and blue ad for Superior Dutch Ham (fig. 1.31) he uses plain geometric forms in an arrangement that is distinctively De Stijl. In the poster *Every Berkel Is a Proved Machine* (fig. 1.32) he uses the red, black, and white palette as well as the photomontage technique common to Russian Constructivism. Finally, Schuitema's advertisement for *Toledo Berkel 85000* (fig. 1.33) also uses photomontage, yet in a much more Dadaist composition; it jampacks many photos in a cluttered Dada way but then restores order through the repetition of circular forms.

In addition to the network established by Schwitters, Lissitzky's ideas and Russian Constructivism spread further through his association with the Bauhaus and De Stijl. The relations Lissitzky established during the Weimar Constructivist Congress with Doesburg and László Moholy-Nagy were among the closest made between Constructivist circles. Moholy-Nagy, an extremely influential teacher, was instrumental in altering the Bauhaus curriculum from craft-based instruction that resulted in one-of-a-kind objects to one that taught industrial design employing machine technology and mass production. Adopting Lissitzky's ideas on graphic design, Moholy-Nagy, in his book

67. In Hannover in 1924 Schwitters founded the advertising agency Merz Werbezentrale. For Schwitters's typographical activity, see Werner Heine, "'Futura' Without a Future: Kurt Schwitters' Typography for Hanover Town Council, 1929–1934," *Journal of Design History* 7, no. 2 (1994): 127, 140.

68. Jan Tschichold, *The New Typography,* trans. Ruari McLean, intro. Robin Kinross (Berkeley: University of California Press, 1995), 66–67.

69. See Maud Lavin, "Photomontage, Mass Culture, and Modernity: Utopianism in the Circle of the New Advertising Designers," in Matthew Teitelbaum, ed., *Montage and Modern Life, 1919–1942* (Cambridge, Mass.: MIT Press, and Boston: Institute of Contemporary Art, 1992).

Figure 1.34
JOOST SCHMIDT
Staatliches Bauhaus Ausstellung
(Bauhaus exhibition)
Poster, Germany, 1923
Lithograph, 27 x 19

Figure 1.35
FRITZ SCHLEIFER
Staatliches Bauhaus Ausstellung
(Bauhaus exhibition)
Poster, Germany, 1923
Lithograph, 39 3/8 x 28 3/4

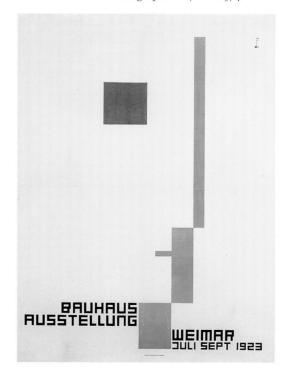

Malerei photografie film (1925), exhorts typographers to abandon the old concentric order for a new dynamic but eccentric balance, a page design more interesting to the eye than the old, centered, reductive layout.[70]

A few years later, in 1928, Jan Tschichold's book on the New Typography elaborates these ideas and traces their beginnings in Futurism and Dada (see fig. 2.12): "It is to a 'non-technician,' the Italian poet F. T. Marinetti, the founder of Futurism, that the credit must be given for providing the curtain-raiser for the change-over from ornamental to functional Typography." After citing Marinetti's manifesto, Tschichold goes on to write of Dada, "In typography it broke completely with tradition and made uninhibited use of every kind of typographic material. . . . Dada's uncompromising shapes had a far-reaching influence in almost all fields, particularly in advertising."[71] There is a measure of irony in the fact that the highly ordered and rational New Typography traced its lineage to Futurism and Dada.

The ideas expressed by the New Typographers, among them an insistence on clarity, functionalism, and asymmetry, are also incorporated into Bauhaus graphic design. By 1922 the Bauhaus school was another outpost of Soviet-inspired Constructivism, characterized by the same rationalism and faith in machine technology. The poster Joost Schmidt designed for the Bauhaus exhibition of 1923 (fig. 1.34) exemplifies the Bauhaus style of the early 1920s in the clear and strict use of geometric abstraction enlivened by asymmetry and open space. Fritz Schleifer's poster (fig. 1.35) advertising the same event is even more reductive, restricted to blue rectangular rules and a red square to create the famous Bauhaus profile logo.[72]

By the late 1920s, commercial and cultural patrons steadily increased their commissions for advertisements by practitioners of the New Typography. Modernist aesthetics had an immediate and far-ranging influence on mainstream advertising, with designers such as Schwitters, Tschichold, and Zwart attracting major clients like Pelikan Ink, Phoebus-Palast Cinema, and PTT (the Dutch Telephone and Telegraph Company). The experiments in typography and layout that had once alienated the general public were by the mid-1920s sufficiently tamed so as to be deemed acceptable to progressive corporations and their clientele.

70. Marc Dachy, *The Dada Movement, 1915–1923* (Geneva: Skira, 1990), 172.
71. Tschichold, *New Typography,* 53, 56, 36.
72. The profile logo was designed by Oskar Schlemmer.

CONSERVATIVES RESPOND

Of course, not all advertisers approved of the New Typography; the reaction on the part of the conservative advertising press was, more often than not, out-and-out rejection. In the 5 November 1926 issue of the London-based *Advertising Display,* Machiel Wilmink, an editor of the Rotterdam advertising journal *De Reclame,* illustrates his article "Twentieth-Century Type Problems: Jazz Effects in Dutch Printing and Some Reasons for Their Failure" with Piet Zwart's De Stijl design (fig. 1.36).[73] Wilmink writes, "Freakish type will never be the best way to address the community." Describing Zwart's advertisement for Vickers House, he notes, "It needs a Sherlock Holmes to decipher. . . . It endeavors to sell saws, braces, files, by using an allegorical representation of these tools, three sets of teeth, by four holes, and a series of squares. I wonder what carpenter or works manager will tumble to it. Sometimes N stands for N, but this is not so in the first case—in fact, a false scent is given to make the search more difficult." Wilmink ends by warning designers, "Don't be crazy to be modern. The first necessity of any message is to be understood."[74]

Objection to modern graphic design persisted in many advertising periodicals published throughout the 1920s and 1930s in Europe and the United States, such as *International Advertising Art, Advertiser's Weekly, Publicité,* and *De Reclame.*[75] A few years after Wilmink's article, an essay in *Advertising Display* of July 1929 entitled "The Keynote of Good Poster Design," took criticism against modern graphic design further. The author writes:

> Modernist art in its many weird forms and under its many pseudo-scientific names has invaded the commercial studio. Many commercial artists have welcomed it with open arms. They find it so interesting and so exciting; they get such great fun from experimenting in new manners and along new lines that they often forget that it is their job to sell goods and not either to satisfy their own aesthetic sense or to educate the public in aesthetics. Their attitude toward their work is understandable, but it is nevertheless wrong.
>
> In the advertising of what are known as "Class" products there is, of course, room for modernist art, though seldom for merely abstract design, but poster advertising is almost exclusively used to sell low-priced goods to the masses; and here I say that abstract design, pure pattern, symbolism, distortion of the human figure, defiance of the laws of perspective and all the other mannerisms of the modernist artist are thoroughly bad commercial practice. What is wanted is realism.[76]

Figure 1.36
PIET ZWART
Advertisement for N.E.T.H.M.I.J.
Page from *Advertising Display,*
England, 1926
Letterpress
Photo: Science, Industry and Business Library; The New York Public Library; Astor, Lenox and Tilden Foundations

73. This work by Zwart is also represented in the Berman collection.
74. Wilmink does mention with regard to Zwart's ad: "One redeeming feature which will interest the printer—no blocks are used, all the illustrations(?) are built up out of type material" (142).

75. Articles in which authors express admiration for progressive design occasionally appear in these periodicals. For example, H. J. B. Morris, in "The Continent Suggests," *Advertising Display* (July 1929): 8–11, singles out Francis Bernard's poster *Gaz* (fig. 3.5) as masterful. The February 1939 issue of *La publicité* contains a witty essay by

former Dadaist Marcel Janco describing idiosyncrasies of American advertising entitled "L'aspect général et les facteurs de la publicité américaine" (85–90).
76. C. T. Williamson, "The Keynote of Good Poster Design," *Advertising Display* (July 1929): 48–51.

The posters the author offers as paradigms of good design that "give no offence to the lowbrow" are not only forgettable but by today's standards look retardataire and dated (fig. 1.37). In contrast, the type of work he condemns has become the common coin of graphic communication. Typography and layout that use abstract design, pattern, and symbolism surround us today on the Internet, on television, in movies, on billboards, and in magazine and newspaper advertisements.

The radical experiments of Dadaists, who in the wake of World War I felt that destroying old forms of art and literature was the only answer to a world gone mad, laid the foundations for an art production that would correspond to the needs of a newly industrialized society. Over time, their innovations were tempered and reconfigured into graphic design that could be widely and cheaply produced and distributed. What these artists helped to generate was a thorough aesthetic renewal of all kinds of printed matter—from the designs of books, reviews, posters, and advertisements to newspapers and documents of practical use, such as bills and stationery.

In examining the fruitful exchange and interaction among members of various vanguard groups, so comprehensively represented in the Berman collection, it becomes clear that ideas and innovations were attached to active personalities. The Dadaists and other innovators were tireless in their efforts at communication and exchange—via letters, poems, magazines, pamphlets, fliers, conferences, and manifestos—with other progressives around the world. It was largely through their networking, which magnified and enhanced the impact of their movements, that modern artists and designers were able to create new art forms that ultimately shaped the face of modern art and graphic design.

Figure 2.1
ALEKSANDR MIKHAILOVICH RODCHENKO
Kino Glaz (Kino eye)
Poster, USSR, 1924
Lithograph, 36 1/2 x 27 1/2

DESIGN AND PRODUCTION

IN THE MECHANICAL AGE

ELLEN LUPTON

TAKE A LOOK at Aleksandr Rodchenko's 1924 film poster *Kino Glaz* (Kino eye) (fig. 2.1). A boy, his image doubled by a pair of movie cameras, is depicted from below, an extreme perspective borrowed from the cinema. The boy looks up at a single giant eye whose monocular stare—both arrested and arresting— appears fixed upon some imposing spectacle. The images of boy and camera look as if they have been flipped and copied, like prints made from a photographic negative. The pictures are set into a field of massive sans serif letters whose geometric silhouettes reject the organic modulations of classical lettering. The boys squint against a harsh light; naturalistic shadows flood their faces. Do they stare into the sun or into the riveting glare of a new technology?

Although the poster's style and symbolism celebrate the mechanization of vision, the images and letters all have been drawn by hand. Rodchenko used a lithographic crayon rather than a halftone screen to approximate the tonality of the photographic print. By rendering shades of pale green and black and combining them in layers, he produced a depth of tone often lacking in photomechanical reproductions. He chose to build his letters with a ruler, compass, and brush—employing the tools of the engineer alongside those of the artist— rather than rely upon the manufactured characters available in a printer's type shop, which would likely have lacked the scale and mass he required. Rodchenko's hand-constructed letters convey the *idea* of technology more vividly than the machine-made yet traditionally designed fonts typically stocked by commercial printers.

Rodchenko's poster is a striking instance of how modern designers, working in the ambitious decades between the two world wars, aimed to emphasize and transform the conditions of reproduction; they sometimes buried the evidence of one technology in order to objectify another. Mass manufacturers in the nineteenth century had proven that industrial production could replicate the work of traditional artisans; modern designers sought instead to express the techniques of production in the form and appearance of the object. They sought to expose technology and loosen its constraints, viewing the processes of manufacture not as neutral, transparent means to an end but as devices equipped with cultural meaning and aesthetic character.

By the 1920s, industrial production had accrued diverse cultural meanings, holding forth the utopian promise of social transformation as well as the ominous threat of war and destruction. In Europe in the early twentieth century, the American factory became a paradigm for economic and social planning. There was a growing adherence to Taylorism, a theory of management that, by advocating the objective analysis of human labor, promised to maximize profits while enhancing the lives of workers. Fordism, named after Henry Ford and his mass-produced Model Ts, crossed the Atlantic to Europe, bringing the concepts of the assembly line and the creation of vast markets for low-cost, standardized goods. The administrators of this freshly mechanized civilization were the engineers, professionals equipped to apply scientific methods to the organization of people, procedures, and environments. The new production experts helped the factory shed its image as a squalid site of exploitation and emerge into the healthy light of efficiency and rationality.[1]

Artists and designers saw industrial modes of production as vehicles for moving art into life. In the Soviet Union, the decision to take art "into production" marked a commitment to modern technology and a utopian mass culture. The critic Osip Brik, describing his friend Rodchenko as the prototypical production artist, wrote in 1923, "Rodchenko knows that you won't do anything by sitting in your own studio, that you must go into real work, carry your own organising talent where it is needed—into production."[2] In the Soviet Union, many artists championed the industrial artifact—generated mechanically and consumed collectively—over the singular work of aesthetic contemplation. Although the utopian desire to transform the aesthetic innovations of the avant-garde into a popularly understood language ultimately crashed against the rocks of Soviet political reality, this new approach to art helped spawn the modern profession of graphic design.[3] As a practice rooted in the experiments of the avant-garde, graphic design emerged as a socially engaged, technologically critical discourse involving the reproduction of texts and images, a domain that now extends from the printed page to the Internet.[4]

1. See Charles S. Maier, "Between Taylorism and Technocracy: European Ideologies and the Vision of Industrial Productivity in the 1920s," *Journal of Contemporary History* 5, no. 2 (1970): 27–61.

2. Osip Brik, "Into Production," in David Elliott, ed., *Rodchenko and the Arts of*

Revolutionary Russia (New York: Pantheon, 1979), 130–31; first published in *Lef* 1 (March 1923).

3. Leah Dickerman has studied the phases of Soviet graphic design in relation to the political transformation of the USSR in *Building the Collective, Soviet Graphic Design, 1917–1937:*

Selections from the Merrill C. Berman Collection (New York: Princeton Architectural Press, 1996). Victor Margolin's book *The Struggle for Utopia: Rodchenko, Lissitzky, Moholy-Nagy, 1917–1946* (Chicago: University of Chicago Press, 1997) situates the work of Rodchenko and Lissitzky within the political and economic context of the Soviet Union; Margolin analyzes Moholy-Nagy's attempts to deploy Constructivist theory within the culture of Weimar Germany.

4. See Ellen Lupton, *Mixing Messages: Graphic Design in Contemporary Culture* (New York: Cooper-Hewitt, National Design Museum, and Princeton Architectural Press, 1996).

For graphic designers, *production* consists of the process of planning and assembling a poster, book, or other document before its manufacture by a printer. In their drive to celebrate the machine age, modern designers delved into the system of mechanical production in order to reveal and transgress its limits. This stance aligned them with modern architects and industrial designers, who also believed that expanded factory production was a cornerstone of an improved society and the key to a new language of construction.

Most critical literature on graphic design looks past the question of production, approaching the printed surface as a smooth and glassy plane on which float disembodied marks and images. It is typical, for example, for historians to use the term "typography" in reference to any manipulation of the printed word. Understood from within the narrower perspective of production, however, *typography* is the organization of prefabricated letters—produced by a metal or wood relief, paper stencil, photographic negative, or digital signal—while *lettering* includes the construction of characters with pen, brush, or cut paper. The indifference to production among historians of design is bolstered by the very technological apparatus that gave birth to our field of study. Since the late nineteenth century, photomechanical reproductions have been the dominant source of information, for scholars and the public, about the visual arts. Our bottomless appetite for images has been fed with printed pictures, whose uniformity of surface and flexibility of scale obscure the differences among physical artifacts. Compounding this problem, many books about graphic design feature poor illustrations distanced by multiple generations of reproduction from the works they document.

Merrill C. Berman's vast collection of twentieth-century graphic design has given the authors of this book an unequaled opportunity to study artifacts of design firsthand and view them as the result of physical processes. The Berman collection includes maquettes, drawings, and original photomontages as well as printed pieces created by some of the most influential designers of the twentieth century. The collection is staggering in both range and depth, constituting a premiere repository of primary documents of modern design.

This essay considers the role of production within the ideologies and aesthetics of modernism. How did techniques of making shape the meaning of design? What conflicts emerged between the ideal of mass production and the conditions of the print shop and designer's studio? In this transitional period of modernism, many artists relied on hand processes and cottage-scaled industries to execute their visions of a technologically enhanced, rationally constructed future. The language they created outpaced the technologies of the time; the implications of this work continues to unfold today, in an era when the tools of visual communication are becoming ever more powerful, pervasive, and accessible.

Figure 2.2
GEORG TRUMP
Ausstellung Kunstgewerbeschule
Bielefeld
(Exhibition at the School of
Applied Arts, Bielefeld)
Design for poster, Germany, 1927
Gelatin silver print, cut paper
letters, pencil, paste, 23 1/8 x 18

FROM LETTERPRSS TO LITHOGRAPHY

During the first decades of the twentieth century, artists drew from a mix of old and new technologies, using the tools of printed media to overhaul the established codes of poetic and public address. Two major printing technologies dominated the commercial graphic arts: letterpress and lithography. Each accommodated distinctive manners of generating images and texts for reproduction. Technological features had interacted with visual conventions to yield the entrenched vernacular styles of the nineteenth-century printing trades. Working within and against the established frameworks of production, avant-garde artists and designers forged new approaches to layout, lettering, typography, and illustration.

The letterpress system, introduced in the fifteenth century, consists of relief surfaces that are inked and pressed against a sheet of paper. Individual characters made from lead or wood are assembled into blocks of copy. The relief letters are stored in gridded cases, which also hold rules, ornaments, and blank bars and spacers used to adjust the distance among characters. The traditional aesthetic of letterpress is governed by a battalion of gridded structures, from the printer's archive of prefabricated forms to the rectangular support of the "chase," a frame in which parallel lines of type are locked together, hemmed in by blank blocks of "furniture" that establish margins and open spaces (figs. 2.2, 2.3).[5]

While letterpress printing was invented to create multiple copies of *texts,* other techniques were devised to reproduce *images,* including woodcut,

Figure 2.3
PIET ZWART
Handzetsel
Advertising catalogue
Netherlands, c. 1930
Letterpress, 6 7/8 x 17 1/2 (open)

5. On the role of letterpress technology in shaping modern Western ways of thinking, see Walter Ong, *Orality and Literacy: The Technologizing of the Word* (London: Methuen, 1982).

etching, engraving, and lithography. For commercial printers, the most important of these methods was lithography. Invented in Germany in 1796, lithography involves marking a smooth stone with a water-resistant substance;
when the surface is bathed in water during the printing process, the treated
areas accept ink, and the resulting image prints onto paper. In offset lithography, which employs a flexible metal plate rather than a rigid stone, the inked
image is "offset" from the plate to a rubber cylinder, which then prints the
image onto paper. The offset method, introduced in the early twentieth century, proved more conducive to automation than stone lithography.[6]

Lithography enabled artists to draw images for reproduction in a direct
and spontaneous manner with a crayon or brush, either directly on the stone
or—to ease the awkwardness of drawing a flipped image—on transfer paper.
Unlike letterpress, lithography is organized by no a priori grid. The stone is
smooth, seamless, unmarked; it is not figured in advance by a matrix of horizontal elements and prefabricated characters. A lithographic design is built on
open ground, not assembled out of rigid pieces. The early masters of the modern poster, such as Jules Cheret and Henri de Toulouse-Lautrec, were celebrated for their ability to command the entire surface with their gestural images.

Although offset lithography would become dominant after World War
II, printing from metal type was the principal means for reproducing text in
the first half of the century, while lithography was the preferred medium for
replicating images. Yet neither technology was confined to conveying solely
words or solely pictures. The rise of magazines and advertising in the mid-
nineteenth century encouraged the mixing of text and image. Letterpress
printers inserted woodcut illustrations into their typographic grids, while lithographers created organic, freeform lettering, sometimes densely ornamental,
using the tools of illustration. Letterpress printers used images as typographic
elements, while lithographers treated words as pictures (figs. 2.4, 2.5).

Photography, invented in 1839, was quickly exploited by commercial
printers. By the 1850s, the literature of the printing trades was replete with
texts devoted to photomechanical reproduction.[7] Because neither letterpress
nor lithography can reproduce shades of gray, photographic techniques served
primarily to copy "line" images, or illustrations consisting of pure black and

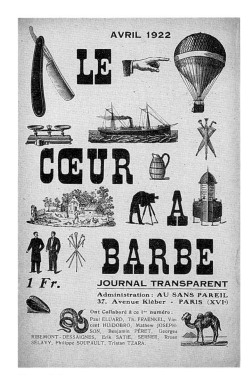

Figure 2.4

Figure 2.5

6. See Bamber Gascoigne, *How to Identify
Prints: A Complete Guide to Manual and
Mechanical Processes from Woodcut to Ink Jet*
(London: Thames and Hudson, 1986).

7. Numerous texts on photographic processes
are referenced in Gavin Bridson and Geoffrey
Wakeman, *Printmaking and Picture Printing:
A Bibliographical Guide to Artistic and Industrial
Techniques in Britain, 1750–1900* (Oxford:
Plough Press, 1984).

Figure 2.4
IL'IA MIKHAILOVICH ZDANEVICH
AND TRISTAN TZARA
Le coeur à barbe (The bearded heart)
Journal, France, 1922
Letterpress, 5 5/8 x 9
The mix of woodcut illustrations with
typography recalls nineteenth-century
vernacular advertising. Illustrations are
treated as typographic material.

Figure 2.5
SENCO
2e mostra della radio
(Second radio exposition)
Promotional card, Italy, 1930
Lithograph, 9 1/2 x 6 3/4
The letterforms have been drawn with
the lithographic crayon; they are handmade
illustrations, not readymade types.

Figure 2.6
XANTI SCHAWINSKY
1934—Year XII of the Fascist Era
Poster, Italy, 1934
Letterpress, 37 11/16 x 28 1/4
The artist has enlarged the halftone dot,
treating it as an expressive element rather
than as a transparent, barely perceptible
screen.

white tones, such as an ink drawing, a logo, or a line of lettering or type. The halftone process, invented around 1884, translated the continuous tones of photography into a pattern of black and white dots, which could be engraved into metal or transferred to a lithographic stone or plate (fig. 2.6). Photographs could now be printed simultaneously with typography; the conditions for the birth of the modern newspaper and magazine had been created.

Not only were photographs a special mode of representation—detailed and depersonalized—but the new halftones were cheaper to produce than drawings. The photographic image quickly became a ubiquitous mass medium; halftone reproductions of photographs and wash illustrations were a routine feature of newspapers and magazines by the 1890s. Some journalists and intellectuals were alarmed by the insurgence of the image enabled by the new technology, citing the mass-produced picture as an obstacle to clear thinking and the camera as an invasion of personal privacy.[8] In contrast to such responses of fear and dismay, one writer dryly commented in 1900 that the halftone had managed to penetrate modern life without calling attention to itself—despite its omniscience, few readers had troubled to discern its structure. The halftone process was deliberately discreet; it sought to obscure its own presence, operating at the threshold of perception.[9]

8. On diverse responses to the rise of the illustrated press, see Neil Harris, "Iconography and Intellectual History: The Half-Tone Effect," in John Higham and Paul K. Conkin, eds., *New Directions in American Intellectual History* (Baltimore: Johns Hopkins University Press, 1979), 196–211.
9. The printer and historian Charles W. Gamble wrote in 1900 that few members of the public had stopped to examine the character of the halftone, despite its enormous impact on their environment. Gamble, "A Wonderful Process," in James Moran, ed., *Printing in the Twentieth Century: A Penrose Anthology* (London: Northwood, 1974), 85–96.

Figure 2.6

The avant-garde artists and designers of the 1910s and 1920s, many of whom were born in the 1880s and 1890s, grew up with halftone photography delivered to them through the ubiquitous media of letterpress and lithography. The halftone, absorbed into the vernacular codes of commercial printing, became an indigenous texture of daily life, especially in Europe, Britain, and the United States, where a flood of images passed through its radically unobtrusive mesh. Although industrialization was less advanced in Russia, all the major graphic arts technologies, including photomechanical reproduction, were in place there by 1895.[10]

The modernists didn't *invent* new technologies but rather devised new ways to *use* them, ways that often sought to emphasize technology itself. The means of production became a tangible presence, infusing the printed page with the taste—bitter, metallic, invigorating—of the mechanical age. This celebration of the machine was sometimes achieved through contradictory processes. As in Rodchenko's *Kino Glaz,* one technique could aggressively broadcast its status while another was striving to cover its tracks.

10. On the Russian printing trades, see Elena Chernevich, Mikhail Anikst, and Nina Baburina, *Russian Graphic Design, 1880–1917* (New York: Abbeville, 1990).

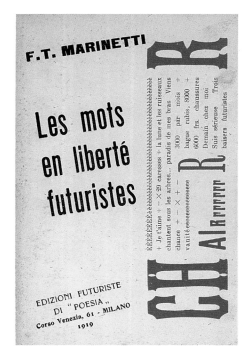

Figure 2.7
FILIPPO TOMMASO
MARINETTI
Les mots en liberté futuristes:
CHAIRrrrrrrRR
(Futurist words in liberty:
CHAIRrrrrrrRR)
Book, Italy, 1919
Letterpress, 7 9/16 x 5 1/8

DECOMPOSING THE GRID

FUTURISM AND DADA

Breaking the grid of letterpress while at the same time asserting it as the framing condition of mechanical reproduction was a recurring challenge for avant-garde typographers. Consider F. T. Marinetti's poem "CHAIRrrrrrRR," first published in 1912 (fig. 2.7). The poem rejects the linear stream of conventional writing, in which words follow one another like beads on a string. The enlarged letters bracketing the ends of the poem cut through the rows of characters that oscillate furiously between them. "CHAIRrrrrrRR" deviates from conventional composition while rendering emphatically visible the grid underlying letterpress typography.[11] Once it had been produced within the letterpress system, however, the poem stabilized as an image, which was photomechanically reproduced in various contexts across its life, from Marinetti's own publications to manuals of design and histories of art.

Other Futurist poems sought to obliterate the technological framework of letterpress typography. Marinetti's *"Montagnes + vallées + routes + Joffre"* (1915), a textual journey through a mountainous landscape, was produced by cutting apart scraps of printed matter, pasting them onto a page, and creating additional marks by hand (fig. 2.8). This collage, submitted to a printer for reproduction, was then photographed as a line image, consisting of pure tones of black and white. The resulting line engraving could then be printed letter-

11. Johanna Drucker interprets Futurist poetry from a typographic perspective in *The Visible Word: Experimental Typography and Modern Art, 1909–1923* (Chicago: University of Chicago Press, 1994), 91–140. Marinetti's poem "CHAIRrrrrrRR" was reproduced as a line image on the cover of Marinetti's own *Les mots en liberté futuristes* (1919 [fig. 2.7]) and in Jan Tschichold's *Die Neue Typographie* (1928).

Figure 2.8
FILIPPO TOMMASO
MARINETTI
*Parole in libertà:
Montagnes + vallées +
routes + Joffre*
(Words in liberty:
Mountains + valleys +
roads + Joffre)
Journal, Italy, 1915
Letterpress
13 5/8 x 9 3/4

press. Thus the printer treated the poem as an illustration, not as "typography" in the technical sense, composed from individual characters locked together in a chase. By incorporating a collage of letters as an overall picture, the letterpress system was able to accommodate free-form compositions cut loose from the strictures of the typographic grid.

Marinetti's "CHAIrrrrrrRR" and *"Montagnes + vallées + routes + Joffre"* represent two distinct approaches to producing visual poetry, even though both pieces ultimately were printed letterpress. The first approach actively acknowledges the constraints of typography as a mechanical system—at once fighting and confirming the grid—while the other confronts the page as an unstructured field. Poems generated within the system of letterpress typography (rather than through the technique of collage) were composed from manuscripts marked up with directions to the printer, who would select characters whose size and spacing might not exactly match the poet's sketch.[12] In contrast, the collage, assembled at the poet's work table, was photomechanically reproduced by the printer in a relatively neutral way.

Dada artists and poets also used the technologies and conventions of commercial printing to attack the institution of art. To construct poems, posters, and invitations, Tristan Tzara and Ilia Zdanevich (Iliazd) lifted slogans from advertising and journalism and borrowed typographic conventions from commercial printing, such as mixed fonts and shifting scales of type.[13] In a 1923 poster for a Dada soiree (fig. 2.9), Iliazd assembled a motley assortment of typographic elements—letters large and small, ornaments and dingbats, wood-engraved illustrations, an oversized exclamation mark—in a composition whose stacked forms and curved and angled lines aggressively eat away at the structural grid of letterpress. Yet the grid, ragged and bruised, remains intact, its orthogonal pressures bracing together the elements of the printed page. Each letter and ornament is a fabricated object, a rigid readymade, locked into place with spacers and blank blocks of printer's furniture.

Tzara's lithographic announcement for the 1921 *Salon Dada* expresses a similar aesthetic of commercial quotation (fig. 2.10). Various slogans, written in a tone of abject defeat ("Nobody is supposed to ignore Dada. . . . Forget me not, please"), are depicted as street signs casually littered across the surface

Figure 2.9
IL'IA MIKHAILOVICH ZDANEVICH
Soirée du coeur à barbe
(Evening of the bearded heart)
Poster, France, 1923
Letterpress, 10 1/4 x 8 1/8

---

12. During the early twentieth century, compositors increasingly were expected to produce designs specified to them from freelance designers or from "layout men" working in a separate department in the printing firm. Herbert Simon and Harry Carter described the layout process in a 1931

manual: "The lay-out is a sketch of the typesetting to serve as a guide to the compositor. . . . Written directions for the kind of type and amount of spacing between the lines are added in the margin. Considerable latitude should be left to the compositor, who will often be able to improve on the rough sketch." See *Printing*

Explained: An Elementary Practical Handbook for Schools and Amateurs (Leicester: Dryad Press, 1931), 122. A. G. Sayers and Joseph Stuart also discussed the role of the "layout man" in *The Art and Practice of Printing*, vol. 1: *The Composing Department* (London: Sir Isaac Pitman and Sons, 1932).

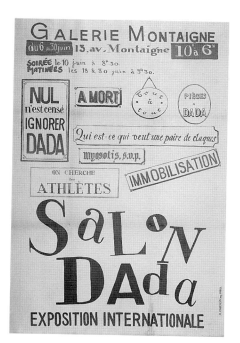

Figure 2.10
TRISTAN TZARA
Salon Dada, Exposition Internationale
Poster, France, 1921
Lithograph, 47 5/8 x 31 9/16

of the poster. Although the elements resemble industrial artifacts, every mark and letter has been drawn by hand. The design is infused with the accidental aesthetic of the found commercial object, yet it has been executed with conventional drawing tools. To create the poster, the artist probably worked directly on lithographic transfer paper, unaided by any photomechanical processes.

Kurt Schwitters, famous for his pasted paper collages and his outrageous public performances, led a double life: alongside his Dada activity, he operated an advertising agency that created logos, stationery, posters, and other ephemera. Although the obscure references of his collages suggest a hermetic bent, in his graphic design Kurt Schwitters embraced a philosophy of functional communication. He belonged to an international vanguard of modern graphic designers who leapt without hesitation from the abrasive experiments of Futurism and Dada to a commercial design practice—at once rationally organized and emotionally charged—aimed at enlightened clients and consumers.[14]

In a letterpress booklet promoting his services (1930), Schwitters diagrammed two paradigms of typographic composition (see fig. 2.11). One page, titled *Orientierung* (orientation), features a tightly packed, strictly gridded space; the other, titled *Werbung* (advertising), frames an open field where forms soar and collide. Modernist advertising drew its energy from Dada and Constructivism, while the upright structures of information design reflected the *Neue Sachlicheit*, or new objectivity, coursing through the visual culture of Weimar Germany. Together these two impulses—so vividly diagrammed by Schwitters in his own promotional brochure—fueled the founding of modern graphic design, a profession built on the conflicts between free expression and technological precision, between consumer culture and social critique, between the deliberately opaque experiments of the avant-garde and the New Typography's dream of a transparent language.

13. On Dada typography and poetry, see Drucker, *Visible Word*, 168–222.
14. On the graphic design of Kurt Schwitters, see Serge Lemoine, "Merz, Futura, Din, and Cicero," in *Kurt Schwitters* (Valencia: IVAM, Centre Julio Gonzalez, 1995): 507–10. On Schwitters and his circle, see Maud Lavin, "Photomontage, Mass Culture, and Modernity: Utopianism and the Circle of New Advertising Designers," in Matthew Teitelbaum, ed., *Montage and Modern Life, 1919–1942* (Cambridge, Mass.: MIT Press, and Boston: Institute of Contemporary Art, 1992), 37–59.

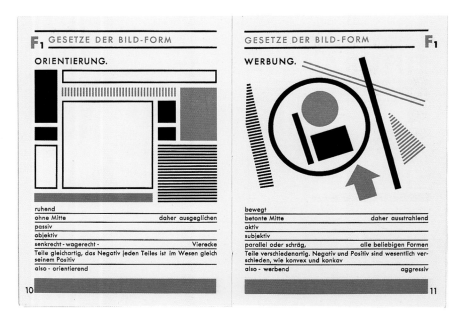

Figure 2.11
KURT SCHWITTERS
Die Neue Gestaltung in der Typographie
(The new design in typography)
Booklet, Germany, c. 1930
Letterpress, 5 7/8 x 8 3/8 (open)

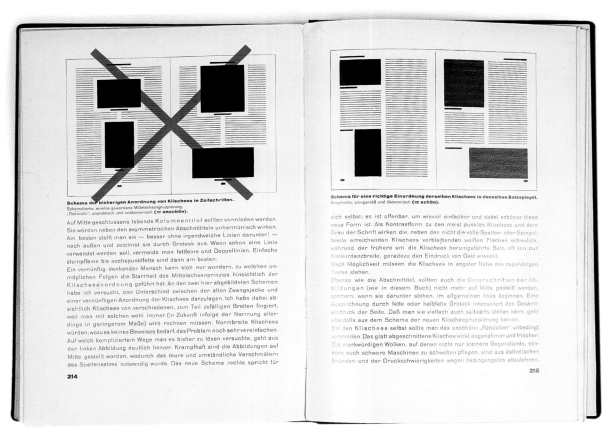

Figure 2.12
JAN TSCHICHOLD
Die Neue Typographie (The new typography)
Book, Germany, 1928
Letterpress, 8 5/6 x 11 7/8 (open)

REGULATING THE INFINITE

FROM CONSTRUCTIVISM TO THE NEW TYPOGRAPHY

By emphasizing the visual character of the printed word, Futurism and Dada freed letters from their subservience to the visual and verbal conventions of literature, just as Cubism and Suprematism had cut loose the elements of painting from the laws of perspective. The turbulent poetics of the avant-garde, which playfully manipulated commercial techniques and imagery, were retooled by proponents of functional communication in the 1920s. In his manifesto *Die Neue Typographie,* published in Berlin in 1928, Jan Tschichold placed Tzara and Marinetti among the founders of modern functional design. He attacked the centered compositions of the classical book and the florid individualism of Art Nouveau and Jugendstil in favor of asymmetrical layouts, uniform page sizes, sans serif letterforms, and the division of texts into functional parts (fig. 2.12). Whereas Futurism and Dada had cultivated chaos and contradiction, the New Typography claimed to be rational and coherent, capable of giving "pure and direct expression to the contents of whatever is printed; just as in the works of technology and nature."[15]

A bridge from the disruptive experiments of avant-garde painters and poets to the functional philosophy of the New Typography had been built in the Soviet Union, where artists, sparked by the energy of the young communist state, sought to enter the realm of industrial production and public communication. In 1920 El Lissitzky published his tract "Suprematism and World Reconstruction," which challenged artists to plunge the abstract art of Kasimir Malevich into the broader social realm.[16] Lissitzky proclaimed that Malevich, by collapsing the history of painting into a black square, had staked a flag at the edge of a "new planet," marking an alien landscape to be explored by the artists of the future. Malevich had created a radically reduced object whose promise of infinite transformation was hemmed in by the social and physical limits of easel painting. Lissitzky's PROUN compositions (from Project for the Affirmation of the New) of the late 1910s and early 1920s elaborated a space at once architectural and abstract. The PROUNs attempted to ground the mystical sublime of Suprematism in the physical world.

Lissitzky's text "Suprematism and World Reconstruction" was a founding document of Constructivism, a theory and practice that flourished into an international movement during the 1920s. Constructivism was positioned

15. Jan Tschichold, *The New Typography,* trans. Ruari McLean, intro. Robin Kinross (Berkeley: University of California Press, 1995), 67.
16. El Lissitzky, "Suprematism in World Reconstruction, 1920," in *Russian Art of the Avant-Garde: Theory and Criticism,* ed. John Bowlt (New York: Thames and Hudson, 1988), 151–58.

from the outset in relation to the technologies of production. Lissitzky wrote: "Those of us who have stepped out beyond the confines of the picture take rulers and compasses . . . in our hands. For the frayed point of the paintbrush is at variance with our concept of clarity and if necessary we shall take machines in our hands as well because in expressing our creative ability paint-brush and ruler and compasses and machines are only extensions of the finger which points the way."[17] Against the "frayed point of the paintbrush," Lissitzky promoted the ruler and compass as instruments of precision and economy that could transport the artist beyond the "confines of the picture." Yet even the brush, worn to the point of exhaustion, could be put in the service of society, because any tool was considered a life-affirming celebrant of labor.

The goal of the new art was not just to create objects but to change the way the public perceives and acts in the world.[18] In "Suprematism and World Reconstruction," Lissitzky observed the subordination of discrete houses, streets, and squares to decentralized patterns of electrical wires, radio signals, and subway systems. Looking at an urban landscape transformed by industry, he applauded the dissolution of the individual citizen and the isolated object and the triumph of the modern town as a network of energies. For Lissitzky, industrialization was embodied not in the machine-as-object but in diffused social and technological relationships.

Indeed, the interaction of technology with new social forms already had yielded powerful cultural tools. Such was the achievement of the poster project launched by ROSTA, the Russian Telegraph Agency, between 1919 and 1922. With ROSTA, crude production methods became central features of a sophisticated medium of communication. Known as "ROSTA windows" because they sometimes were installed in empty storefronts, these posters translated into a concise visual form news announcements and political directives that were conveyed across the telegraph wires. Originating in Moscow and Petrograd, ROSTA agencies soon appeared across the Soviet Union. The posters usually were produced overnight, sometimes in less than an hour.[19]

Vladimir Maiakovskii was the leader of ROSTA's Moscow division, where he wrote copy for hundreds of posters. Maiakovskii would compose a text announcing news or information and then give it to an artist for visual

Figure 2.13
VLADIMIR IVANOVICH KOZLINSKII
Nesmotria na trekhletnie usiliia
(Despite three years of effort)
Poster, USSR, 1920
Linocut, 28 1/8 x 19 5/8

organization in *The Bolshevik Poster* (New Haven and London: Yale University Press, 1988). See also Leah Dickerman, *ROSTA Bolshevik Placards,* exhibition catalogue (New York: Sander Gallery, 1994); Darra Goldstein, *Art for the Masses: Russian Revolutionary Art from the Merrill C. Berman Collection,* exhibition catalogue(Williamstown, Mass.: Williams College Museum of Art, 1985). Maria Gough provides a critical interpretation of ROSTA's relationship to the broader communications infrastructure in the Soviet Union in "Switched On: Notes on Radio, Automata, and the Bright Red Star," *Building the Collective,* 39–55.

17. Ibid., 157.
18. Leah Dickerman has written that "Constructivism can best be characterized by its understanding of artistic practice as a form of technology—as the manipulation of artistic elements according to their material character to produce an object, serving a

more or less defined social function. For the Constructivists, this 'function' was always, ultimately, the production of a revolutionary subjectivity or consciousness." *Building the Collective,* 27.
19. Stephen White describes in detail the technical and social organization of the ROSTA

Figure 2.14
VARVARA FEDOROVNA STEPANOVA
Smert' Tarelkina (The death of Tarelkin)
Poster, USSR, 1922
Letterpress, 27 1/16 x 41 1/4

interpretation. In Moscow, the ROSTA posters typically were printed from cardboard stencils, from which an edition of three hundred posters could be generated in two or three days. The workshops were cold and cramped, but the artists were paid regularly and commanded a degree of professional respect. Production methods varied from city to city: lithographs in Smolensk, linocuts in Petrograd (fig. 2.13). In Odessa, texts and images were painted on sheets of plywood that were then washed down and reused, plywood being more plentiful than paper. Maiakovskii described the posters as "'telegraphic bulletins, instantly translated into poster-form, decrees immediately published as rhymes. The vulgar character of the poetry, the coarse character— this is not only due to the absence of paper, but the furious tempo of the revolution with which printing technology could not keep pace.'"[20] Although the ROSTA windows were crudely made, they reflected a sophisticated convergence of social systems and production methods. Simple means proved a more expedient response to the demand for immediate communication than the more polished techniques used by commercial printers.

Writing in 1926, Lissitzky recalled that the books of the Russian avant-garde in the 1910s had been produced largely by hand, "written and illustrated with the lithographic crayon, or engraved in wood."[21] During the reconstruction of the Soviet Union beginning in 1922, artists increasingly had access to letterpress and commercial lithography. Lissitzky wrote, "Comrades Popova, Rodchenko, Syenkin, Stepanova, and Gan devote themselves to the book. Some of them work in the printing-works itself, along with the compositor and the machine."[22] Varvara Stepanova's 1922 announcement for the theatri-

20. Quoted in Dickerman, *ROSTA*, 8.
21. El Lissitzky chronicled the history of Russian graphic design from the viewpoint of production in his essay "Our Book, 1926," in Sophie Lissitzky-Küppers, ed., *El Lissitzky: Life, Letters, Texts* (London: Thames and Hudson, 1967), 358–59.

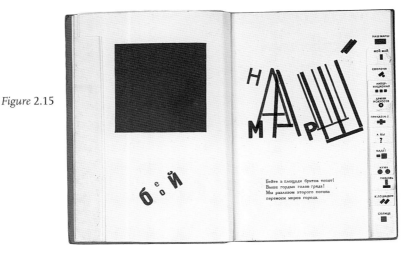

Figure 2.15
EL LISSITZKY
(LAZAR' MARKOVICH LISITSKII)
AND VLADIMIR VLADIMIROVICH
MAIAKOVSKII
Dlia golosa (For the voice), "Our March"
Book, Germany, 1923
Letterpress, 7 7/16 x 10 1/4 (open)

Figure 2.16
ALEKSANDR MIKHAILOVICH RODCHENKO
U.R.S.S. L'Art décoratif Moscou-Paris 1925
Book, USSR, 1925
Lithograph, 10 1/4 x 7 7/8

Figure 2.17
ALEKSANDR MIKHAILOVICH RODCHENKO
AND VARVARA FEDOROVNA STEPANOVA
LEF No. 2 Prospekt
Prospectus for magazine, USSR, 1924
Letterpress, 9 1/8 x 6 1/8

cal production *The Death of Tarelkin* (see fig. 2.14) reveals the tentative entry of Suprematist forms into the mechanical framework of letterpress: geometric shapes jostle among a mix of printed letters whose mismatched styles reflect the arbitrary inventory of the metal type shop.

In 1920, the same year he wrote "Suprematism and World Reconstruction," Lissitzky applied Suprematist theory to the design of the book *Of Two Squares;* this landmark work would not be published until 1922 in Berlin, where Lissitzky could exploit "the high standard of German technology."[23] In 1923 Lissitzky published *For the Voice* (fig. 2.15), also in Berlin, a typographic interpretation of a poem by Maiakovskii. *For the Voice* was a triumph of letterpress composition that resulted from careful collaboration between designer and printer.[24] By combining typographic elements with geometric forms, Lissitzky compressed the exploded spaces of his PROUN constructions into the functional mechanics of the printed page. Describing his method, Lissitzky wrote, "The spatial arrangement of the book, by means of the type matter and according to the mechanical rules of printing, must express the strains and stresses of the contents."[25] Lissitzky approached letterpress as a system of elements that could visually translate the meaning of a text.

While Lissitzky was actively exploring the structure of letterpress typography, Rodchenko approached the printed letter as an object to be constructed with the tools of the geometer and engineer. Drafting techniques had become familiar to Rodchenko as an art student in the early 1910s, when he performed painstaking exercises in descriptive geometry using the compass, pen, and ruler.[26] Against the open spaces of Lissitzky's books, pierced with typographic elements, Rodchenko built broad, massive forms that tend to fill and flatten

22. Ibid., 359.
23. Ibid., 358.
24. On Lissitzky's work in Berlin and its links to Suprematism, see Roland Nachtigaeller and Hubert Gassner, "3 x 1 = Veshch, Objet, Gegenstand," introduction to reprint of *Veshch/Objet/Gegenstand* (Baden: Lars Müller, 1994). See also Philip B. Meggs, "For the Voice," *Print* 44, no. 5 (1990): 112–19, 148–49.
25. El Lissitzky, "Topography of Typography, 1923," in Lissitzky-Küppers, ed., *El Lissitzky*, 355. This passage was quoted in Tschichold, *New Typography*, 60.
26. Rodchenko was a student at the Kazan School of Art, 1910–14. See Alexander Lavrentiev, "Alexander Rodchenko: An Introduction to His Work," in *Rodchenko and the Arts of Revolutionary Russia*, ed. David Elliott (New York: Pantheon, 1979), 26–31.

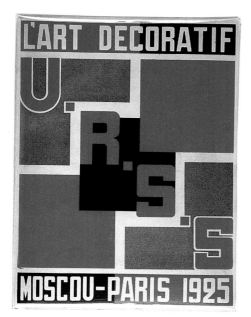

Figure 2.16

Figure 2.17

the surface.[27] On Rodchenko's lithographic catalogue cover for the Soviet Pavilion at the *Exposition de l'Art Decoratif* in Paris (1925), letters take shape as negative forms inscribed into fields of color (fig. 2.16).[28] Rodchenko's distinctive manipulation of large-scale letters was well-suited to the drawing-based medium of lithography. In contrast, his letterpress designs for the journal *Lef* (fig. 2.17) were crudely produced—the large-scale letters appear to have been carved in linoleum or cut quickly out of paper and photographed. The rawness of Rodchenko's *Lef* covers may reflect the journal's limited economic resources as well as the nature of letterpress production.[29]

Rodchenko and Maiakovskii had been close collaborators in the Moscow division of ROSTA. They joined forces in a second enterprise with the founding of Lenin's New Economic Policy (NEP) following the end of the civil war in 1922. The NEP sought to revitalize the Soviet economy by allowing limited free enterprise, making state-owned businesses healthier by forcing them to compete with private companies. Rodchenko and Maiakovskii formed an advertising agency that produced posters, packages, and billboards for Soviet businesses, from GUM, the state department store, to Dobrolet, the state airline. Maiakovskii wrote avant-garde sales copy that reveled in alliteration, rhythm, and repetition; Rodchenko converted these texts into frontal assaults on the eye. Maiakovskii saw no contradiction between the shift from ROSTA's campaigns of news and propaganda to the product solicitations he created with Rodchenko: "'Advertising,'" he proclaimed in 1922, "'is industrial, commercial agitation.'"[30]

As Rodchenko recounted, the Maiakovskii-Rodchenko advertising agency was organized along professional lines. The designer was assisted by two students from the VKhUTEMAS, an art school similar to the Bauhaus, who worked with him through the nights to complete his designs.[31] This support staff may have provided the meticulous execution seen in several of Rodchenko's original advertising designs, preserved in the Berman collection.

27. On Rodchenko's distinctive typographic style, see Selim O. Khan-Magamedov, *Rodchenko: The Complete Work* (Cambridge, Mass.: MIT Press, 1987), 131.
28. An artist could incorporate mechanically printed letters into a lithographic design by having galleys typeset by a letterpress printer; the galleys would then be photomechanically reproduced by the lithographer. See Georg Fritz, *Photo-Lithography*, trans. E. J. Wall (London: Dawbarn and Ward, 1895), 22–23.
29. Victor Margolin documents the limited circulation and financial marginality of *Lef* in *The Struggle for Utopia*, 105.
30. Quoted in Christine Lodder, *Constructivism* (New Haven and London: Yale University Press, 1983), 199.
31. Khan-Magamedov, *Rodchenko*, 134.

Figure 2.18
ALEKSANDR MIKHAILOVICH RODCHENKO
Stolovoe maslo (Vegetable oil)
Design for poster, USSR, c. 1923
Gouache, ink, pencil, cut paper, paste, 33 x 23

In a 1923 design promoting Mosselprom vegetable oil (fig. 2.18), the lettering, illustrations, and geometric background were painted entirely by hand; the only readymade element is a pair of small printed seals pasted toward the bottom of the poster. This hand-painted design would then have been photographically separated into plates for color lithography. Exploiting the character of the lithographic medium, Rodchenko's design dominates the surface of the poster with its field of flat broad stripes and its heavy black rectangles filled with white letters: at the center floats the product, stark and pristine. By collaborating with Maiakovskii as well as employing technical assistants to create prototypes for reproduction, Rodchenko eschewed the role of the solitary creator and entered the realm of production for industry; his working methods anticipated those of the post–World War II art director.

Constructivism was instrumental in bringing the radical typographic poetics of Futurism and Dada into the commercial realm. Lissitzky traveled extensively during the 1920s, making Berlin his European outpost; his lectures, publications, and exhibitions had an enormous impact on design internationally.[32] Kurt Schwitters's decision to work in advertising design was inspired, in part, by his contact with Lissitzky. Italian designers learned from Lissitzky's Soviet propaganda exhibitions of the late 1920s; they adapted his use of architecturally scaled photomontage to create extravagant environments promoting the fascist revolution.[33] Graphic design in the Netherlands also collided productively with Lissitzky's work, taking cues from his spatial reconception of letterpress typography.[34]

Working within the framework of De Stijl, the Dutch artists Theo van Doesburg, Vilmos Huszar, and Bart van der Leck began constructing alphabets out of heavy perpendicular slabs in the late 1910s. Huszar's logo for N. V. Hollandsche Deurenfabriek (fig. 2.19) consists of a dense cluster of horizontal and vertical elements; Huszar exploited the technological grid of letterpress as an analogue for the transcendental grids of De Stijl painting. Working in the more decorative context of the Amsterdam School, Hendrikus Wijdeveld built geometric letterforms out of the elements of the printer's type case; he converted the constraints of letterpress into the vocabulary of a new aesthetic.

32. See Stephen Bann, "Russian Constructivism and Its European Resonance," in *Art into Life: Russian Constructivism, 1914–1932*, exhibition catalogue, Henry Art Gallery, University of Washington, Seattle (New York: Rizzoli, 1990), 213–21.

33. On Italian exhibition design, see Sergio Polano, *Mostrare: L'allestimento in Italia dagli anni Venti agli anni Ottanta* (Milan: Edizioni Lybra Immagine, 1988). See also Benjamin H. D. Buchloh, "From Faktura to Factography," *October* 30 (Fall 1984): 82–117, on Lissitzky's influence on Fascist exhibitions.

34. See Kees Broos and Paul Hefting, *Dutch Graphic Design: A Century* (Cambridge, Mass.: MIT Press, 1993), and Alston W. Purvis, *Dutch Graphic Design, 1918–1945* (New York: Van Nostrand Reinhold, 1992).

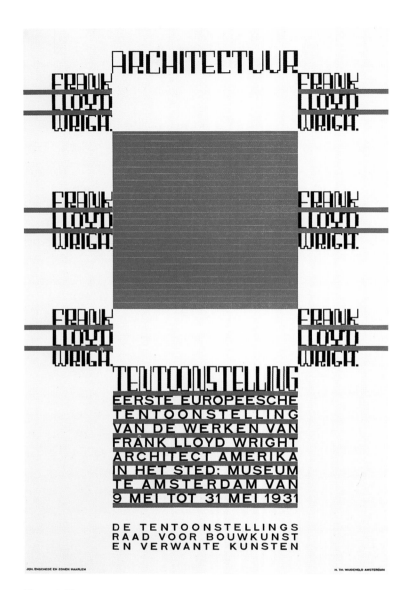

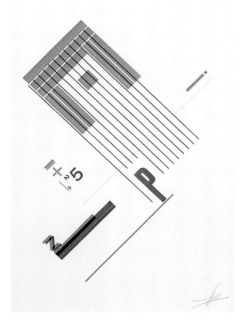

Figure 2.21
PIET ZWART
Homage to a Young Woman
Typographic experiment, Netherlands, 1925
Letterpress, 9 1/2 x 6 11/16

Figure 2.20
HENDRIKUS THEODORUS
WIJDEVELD
Architectuur Tentoonstelling
(Architecture exhibition)
Poster, Netherlands, 1931
Letterpress, 30 1/4 x 19 1/4

Figure 2.19
VILMOS HUSZAR
N. V. Hollandsche Deurenfabriek
(Dutch Door Factory)
Envelope, Netherlands, c. 1920
Letterpress, 4 1/8 x 9 1/2

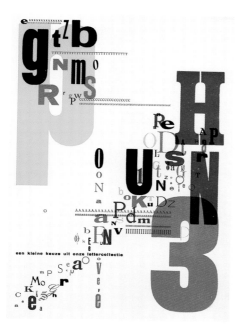

Figure 2.22
PIET ZWART
Drukkerij Trio (Trio printers)
Page from booklet, Netherlands, 1931
Letterpress, 11 5/8 x 8 3/16

Wijdeveld's 1931 poster *Architectuur Tentoonstelling* (fig. 2.20), for an exhibition about Frank Lloyd Wright, embodies the austere yet ornamental style Wijdeveld developed for the magazine *Wendingen*, published from 1918 to 1931.[35] Printed letterpress, Wijdeveld's poster is pieced out of typographic rules, molecular elements that form chains of delicate geometric letters. The broad red square occupying the center has been built from horizontal strips of lead, whose visible seams manifest the poster's means of manufacture.

Several Dutch designers pushed past the heavily orthogonal systems of Wijdeveld and De Stijl in the early 1920s, reflecting the impact of Lissitzky's visit to the Netherlands in 1923 as well as the excitement generated by the Bauhaus, Kurt Schwitters's Circle of New Advertising Designers, and various publications and exhibitions promoting modern art and design.[36] Piet Zwart, in a letterpress experiment of 1925 (fig. 2.21), assembled letters and typographic rules around a diagonal thrust reminiscent of Lissitzky's PROUNs; the ruled lines are tightly locked together, reflecting the mechanical framework of letterpress. Zwart's work quickly became more free and organic, as seen in a 1931 design in which a swarm of letters rushes from background to foreground (fig. 2.22). Zwart deliberately mixed the contents of the printer's archive, printing the elements in successive layers of color. The gridded quality of letterpress asserts itself behind the soaring freedom of the design; although the letters appear to shift forward and backward in space, each retains the upright orientation of classically printed text.

Zwart, who worked for industrial clients as well as producing typographic experiments, became a major figure in the New Typography, a movement linking designers in Holland, Switzerland, Germany, Czechoslovakia, Poland, Hungary, and the Soviet Union. Jan Tschichold's 1928 manual *Die Neue Typographie* was illustrated with work by an international cast of artists and designers from Iliazd and El Lissitzky to the German designers Willi Baumeister, Max Burchartz, and Walter Dexel. These designers codified the avant-garde experiments of the 1910s into a design methodology suited to corporate and commercial communication. The New Typography claimed to be international and objective, providing a technological framework for a universal language of vision. This language was made complete by the incorporation of another technology—the photograph—into the domain of the printed text.

35. See Hans Oldewarris, "Wijdeveld Typografie," special issue of *Forum* 25, no. 1 (1975).
36. Lissitzky's work also reached the Dutch avant-garde with the publication of his project *Of Two Squares* in van Doesburg's magazine *De Stijl* 5, no. 10/11 (1922). On the impact of Lissitzky on Dutch graphic design, see Kees Broos, "From De Stijl to a New Typography," in Mildred Friedman, ed., *De Stijl, 1917–1931: Visions of Utopia* (Minneapolis, Minn.: Walker Art Center, 1982), 147–63.

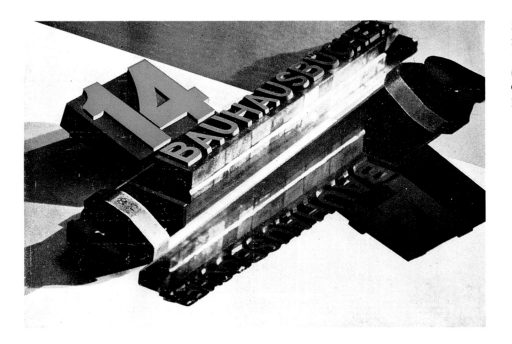

Figure 2.23
LASZLO MOHOLY-NAGY
14 Bauhausbücher
(Fourteen Bauhaus books)
Catalogue, Germany, 1927
Letterpress, 5 5/16 x 8 1/4

Figure 2.24
LADISLAV SUTNAR
Státni grafická škola v Praze
(Prague State School of Graphic Arts)
Brochure, Czechoslovakia, 1933
Letterpress, 8 1/4 x 5 7/8

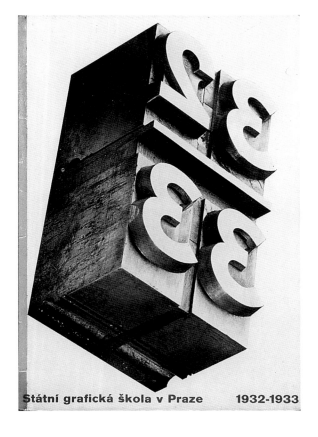

EDITING REALITY

FROM TYPE TO MONTAGE

Before the publication of Tschichold's landmark book, the phrase "new typography" was used by various other designers, including the Hungarian artist László Moholy-Nagy, whose essay "The New Typography" was published at the Bauhaus in 1923. Moholy-Nagy focused on the integration of photography with text, heralding the halftone process as the catalyst of a communications revolution. In his view, the mechanical eye of the camera had reformed the arbitrary subjectivity of the written word: "What the Egyptians started in their inexact hieroglyphs whose interpretations rested on tradition and personal imagination, has become the most precise expression through the inclusion of photography into the typographic method. . . . The objectivity of photography liberates the receptive reader from the crutches of the author's personal idiosyncrasies and forces him into the formation of his own opinion."[37] Moholy-Nagy would later name this merging of text and image "typophoto," a medium made possible by the halftone process. In Moholy's view, photography could cleanse the printed page of its troublesome ambiguity and yield a universally accessible language of the eye: "The hygiene of the optical, the health of the visible is slowly filtering through."[38]

Moholy-Nagy and other designers at the Bauhaus, including Herbert Bayer and Joost Schmidt, explored ways that typography and photography could intersect, from the layering of text and image to the photographic representation of letterpress technology itself. For the cover of a 1927 *Bauhausbücher* prospectus (fig. 2.23), Moholy-Nagy photographed a block of metal type bearing the title of the catalogue, a self-reflexive act performed by several other designers around this time as well, including Ladislav Sutnar (fig. 2.24). Whereas Moholy-Nagy's prospectus documents the horizontality of the letterpress process, in which heavy chunks of lead lie together on the flat "bed" of the press, Sutnar's metal characters are liberated by the photographic medium, enabled to float, assembled in formation, through the void of the page.

Phrases akin to Moholy-Nagy's "typophoto," which celebrated the merging of text and image, had been used to name the halftone process in general since the rise of the technique in the 1880s. In its early years of ascension, there was no single term for the technique of converting the continuous tones—or "half tones"—of a photographic image into a pattern of black and

37. László Moholy-Nagy, "The New Typography," in *Moholy-Nagy,* ed. Richard Kostelanetz (New York: Praeger, 1970), 75; orig. publ. in *Staatliches Bauhaus in Weimar, 1919–23* (Munich, 1923). Lissitzky used the phrase "new typography" in his essay "Our Book" in 1926.

38. László Moholy-Nagy, *Painting, Photography, Film* (Cambridge, Mass.: MIT Press, 1969), 38; orig. publ. 1925 as Bauhausbücher ser., vol. 8; 2d ed., 1927.

On the language of vision as a Bauhaus ideology, see Ellen Lupton and J. Abbott Miller, *The ABC's of ▲■●: The Bauhaus and Design Theory* (New York: Cooper Union and Princeton Architectural Press, 1991).

Figure 2.26

Figure 2.27

Figure 2.28

Figure 2.26
GEORG TRUMP
Das Lichtbild (The photographic image)
Poster, Germany, 1930
Lithograph with pasted paper correction
23 9/16 x 32

Figure 2.27
WALTER DEXEL
Fotografie der Gegenwart
(Contemporary photography)
Poster, Germany, 1929
Linocut, 33 1/16 x 23 7/16

Figure 2.28
JAN TSCHICHOLD
Der Berufsphotograph
(The professional photographer)
Poster, Germany, 1938
Letterpress, 25 1/8 x 35 13/16

Figure 2.25
DESIGNER UNKNOWN
Film und Foto
Poster, Germany, 1929
Offset lithograph, 33 x 23 1/8
The German Werkbund's exhibition
Film und Foto presented work by several
photographers who were also graphic
designers, including László Moholy-Nagy,
El Lissitzky, and Piet Zwart.

white dots. In France at the turn of the century, the formal name for the process was *la photo-typogravure à demi-teintes,* although the expressions *simili* and *similigravure* were more common.[39] A technical article published in England in 1888 used the term "typo-photography" to name the halftone process: "typo-photography dissolves a given colour area . . . in its fundamental colours, black and white, not by the hand of the engraver, but according to laws of nature."[40] As such terms as *"photo-typogravure"* and "typo-photography" reveal, printers valued the new method for allowing the photograph to print simultaneously with text: that is, the power to convert the photograph into typographic material.

The integration of text and photographs was an important issue for the proponents of the New Typography. As Tschichold proclaimed, "We today have recognized photography as an essential typographic tool of the present."[41] The New Typography developed in tandem with the "New Vision" in photography, which promoted the camera as a technological extension of the eye (fig. 2.25). Moholy-Nagy was fascinated with long exposures, extreme close-ups, X-rays, and other specialized applications of photography because they explored unknown forms of vision.[42] In an article titled "Production-Reproduction," published in *De Stijl* in 1922, Moholy-Nagy denigrated conventional uses of the camera as mere "reproduction"; in contrast, "productive" uses of a tool allow it to assert its own identity and extend the sense perceptions of human beings.[43]

Many graphic designers mastered the camera alongside the tools of illustration, layout, and lettering. In three posters announcing photographic exhibitions, the medium of photography became a subject for interpretation by graphic designers: Georg Trump's *Das Lichtbild* (1930), Walter Dexel's *Fotografie der Gegenwart* (n.d.), and Jan Tschichold's *Der Berufsphotograph* (1938). Although these posters share a common theme—the photographic negative—each was produced with a different method. Trump's poster is a lithograph, Dexel's is a linocut, and Tschichold's is letterpress. In Trump's lithograph (fig. 2.26), type and image blanket the surface; the lettering has been built, rather crudely, with a ruler and triangle, supplying an abundance of mechanical enthusiasm in place of subtle typographic forms. In Dexel's

39. Gamble, "Wonderful Process," 86.
40. C. A. Muller, "Theory of Typo-Photography," *British and Colonial Printer* 20 (1888): 129–30, 145–46; first published in *American Lithographer and Printer.*
41. Tschichold, *New Typography,* 92.
42. Moholy-Nagy included a portfolio of such pictures, drawn from various photographic archives, in his book *Painting, Photography, Film.*
43. Victor Margolin discusses this article by Moholy-Nagy in *The Struggle for Utopia,* 63–64, 139–41.

linocut, all the letters have been carved by hand out of linoleum, despite their thematic reference to a photomechanical process (fig. 2.27). In contrast to the broadly filled fields of the lithograph and linocut, Tschichold's letterpress poster features precisely articulated elements that punctuate the page: the mechanical bite of the press is felt in the design. Tiny letters pierce the surface like tight black stitches, while the larger headline contains a rainbow of colors, printed with a single pass of the press (fig. 2.28).[44]

Although Moholy-Nagy's term "typophoto" named an issue that was central to modern graphic design, it failed to supplant the term "photo-montage," which survived as the dominant tag for the role of the reconfigured photograph in avant-garde art and design.[45] Unlike typophoto, the concept of photomontage emphasizes the juxtaposition of images over the mixing of images with text. The origin of photomontage was disputed among members of the avant-garde. The Dadaist George Grosz argued that he and John Heartfield had invented "'photo-pasting montage'" in 1915; Raoul Hausmann claimed that he and Hannah Höch had invented the technique in 1918.[46] The art historian Tim Benson has reviewed these many claims, placing the first avant-garde uses of photomontage in 1919.[47]

In place of the assertion that montage was an avant-garde invention, Lissitzky identified it with the birth of the "highly developed technique of the process block" and its subsequent impact on American advertising.[48] Locating montage in the realm of commercial communication and mechanical repro-duction, he described the technique as the combining of text and image in the service of printed media: "Most artists [in the Soviet Union] make montages, that it is to say, with photographs *and the inscriptions belonging to them* they piece together whole pages, which are then *photographically reproduced for printing.*"[49] Lissitzky thus identified montage as the fabrication of a prototype for industrial manufacture, not the making of a unique work of art.

Preserved in the Berman collection are numerous photomontages cre-ated by the Soviet designer Gustav Klutsis, whose work bears witness to the mounting political pressures on progressive artists in the Soviet Union during the 1920s and early 1930s. In a series of postcards commemorating the Moscow Spartakiada athletic competition in 1928 (fig. 2.29), Klutsis deployed

Figure 2.29
GUSTAV GUSTAVOVICH KLUTSIS
Spartakiada Moscow 1928
Three postcards, USSR, 1928
Letterpress, approx. 6 x 4 1/2 each

44. Tschichold's poster commonly is misidentified as a lithograph; careful examination of the print reveals the indentations left by the letterpress process. Robin Kinross's introduction to *The New Typography* (vx–xliv) points out that unlike other prominent modernists of the period,

who began their careers as painters or architects, Tschichold was formally trained as a typographer.
45. For a comprehensive study of photomontage, see Teitelbaum, ed., *Montage and Modern Life.*
46. Dawn Ades, *Photomontage* (London:

Thames and Hudson, 1976), 19.
47. Timothy Benson, *Raoul Hausmann and Berlin Dada* (Ann Arbor, Mich.: UMI Research Press, 1987), 109–16.
48. Lissitzky, "Our Book," 357.
49. Ibid., 359; emphasis mine.

Figure 2.30
GUSTAV GUSTAVOVICH
KLUTSIS
K mirovomu oktiabriu
(Toward a world October)
Design for poster, USSR, 1931
Gelatin silver prints,
halftone photographs,
gouache, ink, paste
11 1/8 x 8 1/8

starkly silhouetted photographic images in abruptly shifting scales, creating unstable spaces that recall the sublime voids of Malevich's Suprematist compositions and Lissitzky's PROUNs. The Spartakiada postcards, singled out in a 1931 attack on the cultural legitimacy of avant-garde abstraction, were condemned as "'inundated with mechanistically assembled material.'"[50] Klutsis's montages in the early 1930s began to respond to the dominance of social realism and the demand for romanticized, heroically scaled depictions of individuals, as seen in the 1931 photomontage *Toward a World October* (fig. 2.30), in which gigantic figures of Stalin and Lenin, linked in a fictitious conversation, loom over an industrialized cityscape. In place of the synchronized, depersonalized athletes of Spartakiada are the imposing figures of two larger-than-life individuals.[51]

As revealed in the original maquette for "Toward a World October," Klutsis freely retouched his images, working by hand with brush, paint, and ink as well as scissors and knife. Although Lissitzky had denigrated the "frayed point of the paintbrush" as an outdated technology, the lowly brush was a crucial if anonymous player in the system of photographic reproduction. Since the rise of the halftone process, printers had been faced with photo-

50. Quoted in Hubertus Gassner, "Heartfield's Moscow Apprenticeship, 1931–1932," in Peter Pachnicke and Klaus Honnef, eds., *John Heartfield* (New York: Abrams, 1992), 256–89.
51. Leah Dickerman analyzes the transformation of Klutsis's work in response to political pressure in *Building the Collective*, 33–34.

See also Vasilii Rakitin, "Gustav Klucis: Between the Non-Objective World and World Revolution," in Jeanne D'Andrea and Stephen West, eds., *The Avant-Garde in Russia, 1919–1930: New Perspectives* (Los Angeles: Los Angeles County Art Museum, 1980), 60–63.

graphic "originals" lacking in sufficient detail and contrast for halftone reproduction, a process that tends to dull and soften the image. Used for retouching photographic prints, the paintbrush effaced its own identity in the service of the mechanically made image. Employed commercially, the retoucher's brush could heighten detail, sharpen focus, and soften the edges between objects; as a tool of propaganda and censorship, it could be used to eliminate unwanted individuals and simulate the conjunction of people and events.

Printers and designers used various techniques, from cropping and framing to retouching and silhouetting, to hone the impact of raw photographic material. Charles W. Gamble, writing from the perspective of a commercial printer in 1933, explained,

> In a large branch of photographic work, particularly that which comes under the head of commercial, a certain amount of hand-work . . . is quite necessary. . . . There are cases where the object itself is of a very rough character, and the photograph must be "smoothed up" to meet the taste of the buyer of photo engravings. These cases occur particularly with photographs of machinery. . . . It is frequently necessary to emphasize some part of the object, as some feature in a machine, in order particularly to draw the observer's attention to that part. Now, the photographer's power in giving the *kind of emphasis* that an engineer, say, might require to be given to a certain part of the machine, is practically negligible.[52]

As Gamble noted, retouching routinely was used by printers to accommodate flaws in photographic prints. The camera, valued for its ability to capture the specificity of products with its supposedly objective eye, rotely recorded the details of context; the retoucher could silhouette the subject and remove it from its setting, a technique commonly employed in catalogue work.

Figure 2.31
MIKHAIL IOSIFOVICH RAZULEVICH
Kabel' i ukhvaty (Cables and tongs)
Design for book cover, USSR
Gelatin silver prints, hand lettering, gouache, ink, paste, tracing paper, colored paper, pencil, 6 3/16 x 9 9/16

Figure 2.32
MIKHAIL IOSIFOVICH RAZULEVICH
Kabel' i ukhvaty (Cables and tongs)
Book cover, USSR
Letterpress, 8 1/2 x 13 1/4
The cut and painted edge that is visible in the original design disappears in the photomechanical reproduction.

52. Charles W. Gamble, *Modern Illustration Practices: An Introductory Textbook for All Students of Printing Methods* (London: Sir Isaac Pitman and Sons, 1933), 96–97.

Modernist designers were attracted to the camera's seemingly unprejudiced depiction of objects, its ability to represent the modern commodity as an enlightened, demystified icon. Working with hand illustrations, as in Rodchenko's posters for vegetable oil, an artist could depict a product weightless and alone, unencumbered by a physical setting. Working with photographs, as in the Soviet artist Razulevich's book cover *Cables and Tongs* (figs. 2.31, 2.32), a designer could use scissors or knife to excise the object from its surrounding tissue; brush and gouache masked the sutures between the object and the blank new world of the page. Liberated from its background by cutting and painting, the product could float as a starkly industrial presence.

The silhouetted image, freed from the clutter of context, becomes a symbol: a repeatable, prototypical mark removed from a specific time or location. The placeless, isolated figure occupies the page like a letter or logo—flat, self-contained, frozen in time, ready to be combined with typographic elements. The transformative power of editing is seen in Werner David Feist's 1928 poster *Städtische Bäder* (figs. 2.33, 2.34), in which the flexed body of a diver flies against a smooth blue void, his figure interchangeable with diagonal red bars of typography. In the photograph that Feist created as raw material for this poster, the diver's body lies firmly on the ground, anchored by the horizontal pull of gravity. His clothes and shoes rest casually on the lawn behind him, quotidian remains of a world that would be cut away by the designer.

Whereas modernist designers favored a sharp break between the object and the page, producers of mainstream commercial catalogues often used the airbrush to wrap the object in a hazy vignette. The airbrush, a device that sprays a fine mist of ink across a surface, allowed professional retouchers to produce shades as gently gradated as those in a photographic print. As

Figure 2.33
WERNER DAVID FEIST
Städtische Bäder (Municipal pools)
Poster, Germany, 1928
Offset lithograph, 23 9/16 x 31 5/16

Figure 2.34
WERNER DAVID FEIST
Diver
Photograph, Germany, 1928
Gelatin silver print, 3 5/16 x 4 5/8

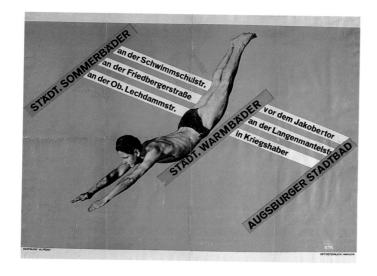

Gamble explained, the humble paintbrush always "proclaimed what had been done," but the airbrush could perfectly simulate the tones of photography.[53] Retouchers used the airbrush to refine facial features, soften or enhance details, and increase tonal contrast. Among the members of the avant-garde to use the airbrush was John Heartfield, who often employed it to ease the transitions among photographic elements and to create a sense of atmosphere in otherwise flat, blank backgrounds. The airbrush is a mechanical device that demands great manual skill; Heartfield did not perform retouching by himself, preferring to engage the same technicians who serviced the commercial printing industry.[54] Heartfield appropriated for his own political ends techniques of photographic manipulation that commonly were used in the context of state propaganda and censorship (fig. 2.35).

Heartfield gave the caption or headline a crucial conceptual role in many of his montages, yet he often deployed typography in a neutral way, rejecting expressive, flamboyant form in favor of a cool, journalistic appearance. In 1936 the Soviet writer Sergei Tretyakov recalled Heartfield's comment, "'A photograph can, by the addition of an unimportant spot of color, become a photomontage, a work of art of a special kind.'"[55] Tretyakov continued, "We should not forget that a montage is not necessarily a montage of photographs. No—it may be a photo and a photo, a photo and a text, a photo and paint, a photo and a drawing."[56] Heartfield could transform the significance of an image with the introduction of an alien element, interrupting its seemingly natural meaning with a witty caption or a jolt of color. Klutsis also defined montage as a mixed medium: "'One must not think that photomontage is the expressive composition of photographs. It always includes a political slogan, colour and graphic elements.'"[57] Although the juxtaposition of images is the focus of most art historical accounts, montage is also the editing of images through silhouetting and other framing devices, and the combination of photography with text. Montage renders the photograph discursive, thrusting it into a new context, turning it into a component of a larger structure. No longer appearing as a smooth, transparent image of reality, the photograph is a part that interlocks with other parts, a phrase whose meaning must be actively extracted by the reader.

53. Ibid., 97.
54. See Ades, *Photomontage*, 49.
55. Quoted in Sally Stein, "The Composite Photographic Image and the Composition of Consumer Ideology," *Art Journal* 41, no. 1 (Spring 1981): 40.
56. Sergei Tretyakov, "Montage Elements,"
1936, in Pachnicke and Honnef, ed., *John Heartfield*, 291.
57. Quoted in Lodder, *Constructivism*, 187.
58. Walter Benjamin, "The Author as Producer" (1934), in Peter Demetz, ed., *Reflections: Essays, Aphorisms, Autobiographical Writings* (New York: Schocken Books, 1978), 230; emphasis mine.
59. On Rodchenko's complex relationship with consumerism and his attempt to reconcile commodity culture with socialism, see Christine Kiaer's essay "Rodchenko in Paris," *October* 77 (Winter 1996): 3–35.

Figure 2.35
JOHN HEARTFIELD
AIZ: Der Sinn des Hitlergrusses;
Kleiner Mann bittet um große Gaben
(AIZ: The meaning of the Hitler salute;
Little man asks for big gifts)
Advertising poster, Germany, 1932
Rotogravure, 18 3/8 x 13

FROM DESIGNER TO PRODUCER

Heartfield's practice matched the criteria for a new kind of author delineated in Walter Benjamin's 1934 text "The Author as Producer." Benjamin argued that artists and photographers could transform the system of publishing by learning one another's skills: "What we require of the photographer is the ability to give his picture the caption that wrenches it from modish commerce and gives it a revolutionary useful value. But we shall make this demand most emphatically when we—the writers—take up photography. Here, too, therefore, technical progress is for the *author as producer* the foundation of political progress."[58] Benjamin claimed that to bridge the divides between author and publisher, author and reader, poet and popularizer is a revolutionary act because it challenges the economic categories upon which the institutions of "literature" and "art" are erected.

Benjamin's essay was inspired, in part, by artists in the Soviet Union who sought to go "into production," creating prototypes for mass manufacture and mass consumption. Their goal was to transform the institutions of art and commerce and to create revolutionary objects.[59] Artists and designers tapped the cultural energy of the machine, viewing industrial production as a catalyst of utopian social change. The visual languages of the avant-garde ultimately were suppressed in the Soviet Union but were allowed to grow in the West, where graphic design emerged as a discipline that continues today to translate new technologies into compelling visual forms. Modernist objects and advertisements aspired to a state of demystified transparency, yet they left intact the commodity form. Modernism fetishized the very means of manufacture, using the systems of mechanical reproduction to build a mode of design that openly endorsed its technical origins. The ruler and compass, the camera and halftone block, the tools of the letterpress shop and the offset press: these were technologies charged with meaning, their presence heroically narrated in the visual forms they served to produce.

The designers who carried modernism into the post–World War II era approached their trade as a service to industry, embracing the world of commerce as a democratic arena in which to serve the masses. In rare instances did designers grasp the tools of authorship, as had Lissitzky with his experimental books and Heartfield with his critical photojournalism. Instead, they became suppliers of form to the existing apparatus of publishing and promotion. With the rise of digital typography and on-line communication in the closing decades of the twentieth century, designers and authors have received new opportunities to become producers, in Walter Benjamin's sense: taking control of the tools and systems of publishing and thus moving production beyond the look of the artifact to transform its dissemination and use.

DESIGN AND THE
AVANT-GARDE

Plate 6
BART VAN DER LECK
Delftsche Slaolie (Delft Salad Oil)
Design for poster, Netherlands, 1919
Gouache, 34 1/4 x 23 1/8

Plate 7
BART VAN DER LECK
Delftsche Slaolie (Delft Salad Oil)
Design for poster (state 1), Netherlands, 1919
Charcoal, pastel, 39 1/8 x 28 1/2

Plate 8
BART VAN DER LECK
Delftsche Slaolie (Delft Salad Oil)
Design for poster (state 2), Netherlands, 1919
Gouache, pencil, charcoal, 34 1/4 x 23

Plate 9
BART VAN DER LECK
Delftsche Slaolie (Delft Salad Oil)
Design for poster (state 3), Netherlands, 1919
Gouache, pencil, 39 1/8 x 28 3/4

Plate 10

Plate 11

Plate 10
FORTUNATO DEPERO
Depero Futurista (Depero the Futurist)
Book, Italy, 1927
Letterpress, 9 5/8 x 11 5/8

Plate 11
ARDEGNO SOFFICI
BÏF∫ZF+18, Simultaneità chimismi lirici:
Treno-Aurora
(The simultaneity of lyrical chemical reactions)
Book, Italy, 1919
Letterpress, 7 3/4 x 11 3/8 (open)

Plate 12
GIACOMO BALLA
TI TA TO One Step
Music sheet, Italy, 1918–20
Lithograph, 13 3/8 x 9 1/2

Plate 13
FORTUNATO DEPERO
Secolo XX (Twentieth century)
Magazine cover, Italy, 1929
Letterpress, 15 5/8 x 11 9/16

Plate 12

Plate 13

Plate 14
FILIPPO TOMMASO MARINETTI
Almanacco Italia veloce (Almanac of fast Italy)
Cover, Italy
Letterpress with handwriting, 9 x 11 5/8

Plate 15

Plate 16

Plate 17

Plate 15
LIUBOV' SERGEEVNA POPOVA
Da zdravstvuet diktatura proletariata!
(Long live the dictatorship of the proletariat!)
Placard, USSR
Ink, watercolor, pencil, cut paper, paste
7 15/16 x 9 13/16

Plate 16
LIUBOV' SERGEEVNA POPOVA
Prozodezhda aktera No. 7
(The magnanimous cuckold: Actor no. 7)
Costume design, USSR, 1921
Pencil, gouache, cut paper
13 1/2 x 9 11/16

Plate 17
NATAN ISAEVICH AL'TMAN
Krasnyi student (Red student)
Design for journal cover, USSR, 1923
Ink, crayon, 15 3/8 x 11 1/2

Plate 18

Plate 19

Plate 18
SOLOMON BENEDIKTOVICH TELINGATER
Vytiazhka (Stretching)
Collage, USSR, 1920s
Ink, watercolor, crayon, decorative paper, halftone
photographs, printed letters, printed illustrations,
paste, 13 3/4 x 9

Plate 19
SOLOMON BENEDIKTOVICH TELINGATER
Slovo predostavliaestsia Kirsanovu
(Kirsanov has the floor)
Book, USSR, 1930
Letterpress, 8 x 3 1/8

Plate 20
VASILII VASIL'EVICH KAMENSKII
Tango s korovami (Tango with cows)
Book, Russia, 1914
Letterpress on wallpaper, 7 7/8 x 16 1/8 (open)

Plate 20

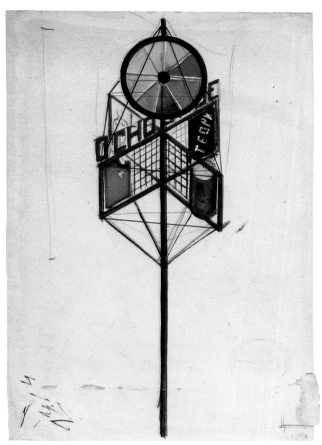

Plate 21

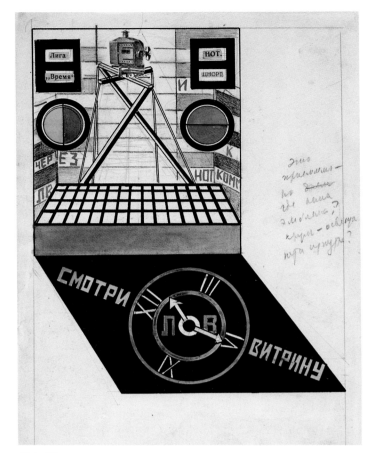

Plate 22

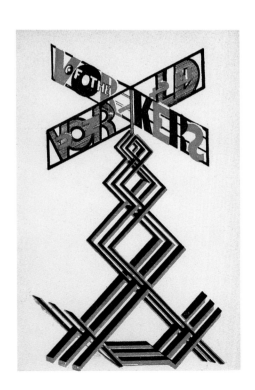

Plate 23

Plate 21
GUSTAV GUSTAVOVICH KLUTSIS
Osnovanie (Fundamentals)
Design for stand, USSR, c. 1926
Pencil, ink, gouache, 7 1/16 x 4 13/16

Plate 22
GUSTAV GUSTAVOVICH KLUTSIS
Smotri v vitrinu (Look in the shop window)
Design for window display, USSR
Pencil, ink, gouache, 10 1/8 x 7 7/16

Plate 23
GUSTAV GUSTAVOVICH KLUTSIS
Workers of the World Unite
Design for propaganda stand, USSR, 1922
Linocut, 9 1/4 x 5 5/16

Plate 25

Plate 24

Plate 24
HENRYK BERLEWI
1ᵃ *WYSTAWA PRAC MECHANO = Fakturowych*
(First exhibition of Mechano-Faktur works)
Design for poster, Poland, 1924
Gouache, 24 3/4 x 19 3/8

Plate 25
FARKAS MOLNAR
MA—Aktivista Folyoirat
Design for cover, Hungary, 1924
Gouache, ink, pencil, cut paper
12 1/16 x 12 1/8

Plate 26
HENRYK BERLEWI
Neo Faktur 23
Theoretical exercise, Germany, 1923
Gouache, pencil, 21 x 16 5/8

Plate 26

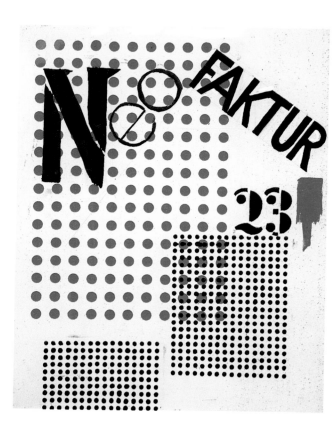

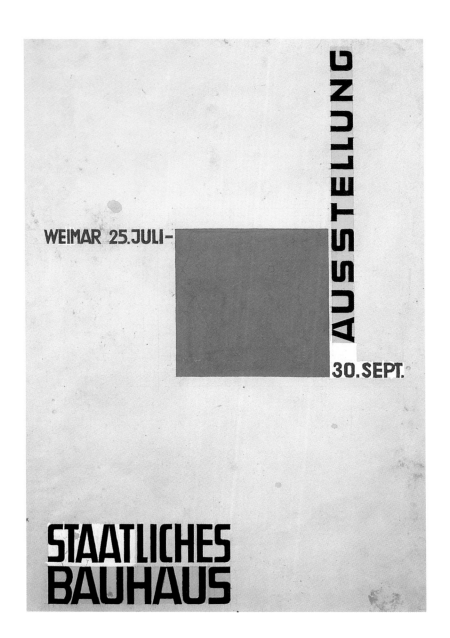

Plate 27
HERBERT BAYER
Staatliches Bauhaus Ausstellung
(Bauhaus exhibition)
Design for poster, Germany, 1923
Pencil, ink, gouache, 16 15/16 x 11 7/8

Plate 28
HERBERT BAYER
Ausstellung (Exhibition)
Design for Bauhaus exhibition sign
Germany, 1923
Pencil, ink, gouache, 12 x 3 3/4

Plate 29
HERBERT BAYER
Mural design for Bauhaus stairwell
Germany, 1923
Gouache, pencil, cut paper, 22 7/8 x 10 3/8

Plate 28

Plate 29

Plate 30

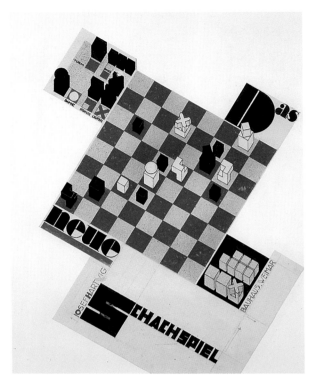

Plate 31

Plate 32

Plate 30
JOOST SCHMIDT
Schach (Chess)
Postcard, Germany, 1924
Lithograph, 4 11/16 x 5 7/8

Plate 31
JOOST SCHMIDT
Das Neue Schachspiel (The new chess game)
Design for poster, Germany, 1923
Ink, pencil, 15 3/4 x 16 3/16

Plate 32
LASZLO MOHOLY-NAGY
Fototek 1
Book, Germany, 1930
Letterpress, 9 13/16 x 6 13/16

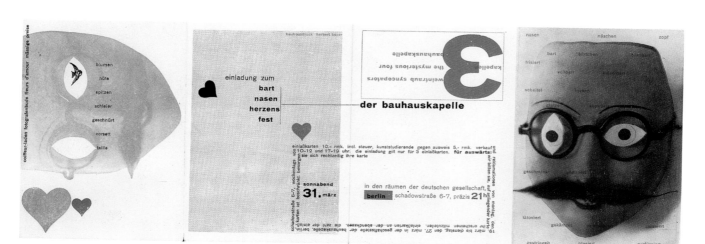

Plate 33

Plate 33
HERBERT BAYER
Bart-Nasen-Herzensfest
(Beard-Nose-Heart Festival)
Invitation, Germany, 1928
Letterpress, 5 13/16 x 16 5/8

Plate 34
OSKAR SCHLEMMER
Das Triadische Ballet (The triad ballet)
Poster, Germany, 1921
Lithograph, 32 1/2 x 22 1/8

Plate 34

Figure 3.1
ALEKSANDR MIKHAILOVICH RODCHENKO
Kakao (Cocoa)
Design for poster, USSR, c. 1923–24
Pencil, gouache, 33 1/8 x 23 1/2

SELLING AN IDEA

MODERNISM AND CONSUMER CULTURE

DARRA GOLDSTEIN

IN 1913 IN PARIS a young Marcel Duchamp was questioning the very meaning of art and whether the value of a work resides in its production and reception. "Can one make works which are not works of 'art'?" he mused in a note he later placed inside *The Green Box*. Duchamp began to play with mundane objects from daily life, transforming them into arguably artistic creations. His *Bicycle Wheel*—no more than the front wheel of a bicycle mounted upside down in the center of a white kitchen stool—became his first "readymade," albeit avant la lettre.[1] Duchamp's focus on the object challenged the most fundamental ideas about perception, leading to a new dynamic between artist and audience, as the traditionally passive viewer was coaxed—at times bullied— into active engagement. This essay explores the early modernist urge to involve the audience and the means by which artists sought to provoke new ways of seeing.

Artists of the avant-garde contended that what constitutes art is a matter of perception, that even the most ordinary objects can become extraordinary when seen through the artist's eye. No matter the medium, modernist art challenged the receiver to participate in creating art. It was no longer sufficient to feed a self-contained work of art to the public for passive absorption; instead, modernist artists sought to engage their viewers (or readers or listeners), to enter into a dialogue with them and thereby distill new meaning. In the first decades of the twentieth century, the idea of audience response was still new and exciting, and artistic challenges to a complacent public reverberated throughout Europe and the United States as myriad progressive groups competed to discover novel forms of expression.

While Duchamp was creating his uncommon objects in Paris, sixteen hundred miles away in Moscow a young painter and poet named Vladimir Maiakovskii was writing startlingly original verses for which he could not find a publisher. So with a group of fellow Futurists, Maiakovskii decided to tour the Russian provinces to promote this new, unconventional art. The outlandishly dressed poets left little but indignation and confusion in their wake.

1. Although *Bicycle Wheel* was produced in 1913, Duchamp did not actually use the term "readymade" until 1915.

Revolution, the social impetus of consumerism was highly pronounced: in buying goods, consumers could help not only the new socialist state but also the progress toward worldwide revolution. During the early Soviet period, every object, from the morning newspaper to the porridge bowl, from the day's dress or shirt to the ubiquitous tram advertisements and sidewalk bill-boards, was designed to create a new awareness of the changing society. In this way the consumer's choices actually came to be constructed by others, whether in the realm of fashion, commerce, or politics.[3] Although in Western Europe consumer needs were more individualized and self-indulgent by comparison, a new approach to graphic art evolved there, too.

In the 1920s, this modern look was realized in flattened images and typefaces devoid of ornamentation. A machine-age aesthetic informed much commercial design, with trademarks and logos now drawn in a sleeker and more geometric manner to reflect an increasingly mechanical, as opposed to organic, world. Enthralled with clean images and visionary ideals, modernist artists translated their excitement into works so full of energy as to seem electrically charged. (E. McKnight Kauffer represents this energy literally in a poster for the London Underground [see fig. 3.21], in which a zigzag charge emanates from the worker's hand.) The artists entered into a partnership with their audience, using art as a means to provoke new perceptions. Although the seeds of crass manipulation were present even in the heyday of modernism, the best works were informed by such passion and belief that they came across as fresh and vital. In many cases, their perceptual challenges still involve the viewer today. Gustav Klutsis's design for a rostrum (see fig. 3.7), for instance, appears first as a beautiful construction in its own right and only secondarily as the propagandistic tool it was intended to be.

Artists believed that they could help change the world by associating a given commodity with progress, personal independence, or an uncluttered aesthetic quite antithetical to the musty drawing rooms and social strictures of paternalistic European society. For artist and consumer alike, fashion came to be equated with freedom, or at least the pretense of it. But as modernism declined, lesser artists used the same graphic styles over and over again, in the process contradicting the very precept of novelty that had originally character-

3. For more on consumer culture, see Alan Tomlinson, "Introduction: Consumer Culture and the Aura of the Commodity," in Tomlinson, ed., *Consumption, Identity, and Style: Marketing, Meanings, and the Packaging of Pleasure* (London: Routledge, 1990), 1–38.

ized modernism. Having lost the passion that once imbued them, images became stale and institutionalized; now they were used not to evoke new responses but to ensure prescribed ones. The motive to sell and sell again to the same public unbalanced the partnership between artist and consumer, whose participation—rather than contributing to a broadened perceptual awareness—was soon limited to being led from purchase to purchase by vanity and hope. In this way participation, so key to the modernist aesthetic, eventually devolved into rank manipulation.

THE ESSENTIAL OBJECT

Happily, however, works from the Berman collection return us to the source of the modernist ideal, enabling us to reconsider early twentieth-century graphic design at a time when it was vibrant and experimental. In particular, images depicting objects reveal a good deal about the type of explorations that engaged the avant-garde. The object often looms large in these works, shown as necessary to the well-being of either the consumer or society at large—in other words, as essential. The object is also frequently portrayed in its most elemental form, as if reduction of form were part of a larger investigation of its intrinsic nature; and in this second regard, too, it appears as essential. The interplay between the function of the object and the way it is meant to be perceived is especially apparent in Otis Shepard's poster for Wrigley's Spearmint Gum (fig. 3.2). In its simple portrayal of the Wrigley's pack with the word "gum" beneath it, drawn to look three-dimensional, the poster appears to be straightforward. However, the edges of the poster truncate the pack, making the gum loom larger than life. Even more provocative is Otis's brilliant small touch of the red wrapper band beginning to unwind. The viewer unwittingly participates in this unwrapping, subliminally tasting the refreshing spearmint and no doubt agreeing with Wrigley's slogan that this is "the perfect gum."

In addition to satisfying the commercial and governmental demands of the clients who commissioned them, these portrayals follow from the early Cubist examinations of form and the Constructivist inquiries into the inherent properties of different materials. The exploration of a thing's essential nature had, in fact, been a concern of the avant-garde for many years. As early as 1912, for instance, a group of Russian Futurist painters and poets issued

Figure 3.2
OTIS SHEPARD
Wrigley's Spearmint Gum
Poster, USA, 1930s
Lithograph, 39 3/4 x 26 3/8

"A Slap in the Face of Public Taste," a manifesto printed on coarse paper and covered with sackcloth. Its closing message messianically proclaims "the New Coming Beauty of the Self-sufficient (self-centered) Word."[4] In poetry, the word was not to be used simply as a means to an end; on the contrary, it has intrinsic value and significance. By analogy, in the visual arts the object is not merely a decorative element, part of a larger artistic whole; rather, it contains meaning in and of itself. This foregrounding of the thing or object was one of the motivations behind the journal *Veshch.Objet.Gegenstand,* published in Berlin during 1922 by El Lissitzky and Ilya Ehrenburg.[5]

A number of works from the Berman collection demonstrate how in avant-garde graphics the initial Cubist fragmentation of the object gave way to its solidification until the object itself appeared tangible, no longer merely a reflection of external reality but a thing in itself. For the Russian Constructivist Aleksandr Rodchenko, the object was tangible enough to seem an actual collaborator in his work. In a letter of 1925 to his wife from Paris, Rodchenko wrote that "our things in our hands must also be equals, comrades, and not these black and dismal slaves, as they are here."[6] His attitude toward the thing or object was fully in sync with Constructivist ideology; in the same year the theorist Boris Arvatov wrote of the object "as an active 'co-worker' in the construction of socialist life."[7] Furthermore, in an era of contradictions and uncertainty, people clamored for something tangible to hold on to. One of the first things that struck the critic Walter Benjamin on a visit to Moscow in 1926 was "that everywhere, even in advertisements, the people characteristically demand that some tangible action be represented."[8] The challenge for the avant-garde artist was to depict the object concretely without, however, making the depiction predictable or traditional. New art called for a new sensibility, which Rodchenko perfected in his commercial designs of the 1920s. These designs represent visual communication at its best: clear, thick lettering makes the message unambiguous, while large sweeps of pure color and sharply defined geometric forms add energy.[9] Rodchenko found the use of the essential object especially effective in advertising. Conversely, advertising allowed him to make the aesthetic point that the thing is crucial, boldly present in its pure form, its essence unobscured by any decorative urge.

4. For an English translation of the manifesto, see Vladimir Markov, *Russian Futurism: A History* (Berkeley: University of California Press, 1968), 45–46. The Russian original has been reprinted in Vladimir Markov, *Manifesty i programmy russkikh futuristov* (Manifestos and programs of the Russian Futurists) (Munich: Wilhelm Fink Verlag, 1967), 50–51.

5. Only three issues appeared. For more on the journal, see *The First Russian Show: A Commemoration of the Van Diemen Exhibition, Berlin 1922* (London: Annely Juda Fine Art, 1983), 73–79, and John E. Bowlt and Béatrice Hernad, *Aus vollem Halse: Russische Buchillustration und Typographie, 1900–1930* (Munich: Prestel-Verlag, 1993), 152–53.

6. Letter of 4 May 1925, in A. M. Rodchenko, *Stat'i, vospominaniia, avtobiograficheskie zapiski, pis'ma* (Articles, memoirs, autobiographical notes, letters) (Moscow: Sovetskii khudozhnik, 1982), 95; first published in *Novyi Lef* 2 (1927).

7. Boris Arvatov, "Byt i kul'tura veshchi" (Everyday life and the culture of the thing), in *Al'manakh Proletkul'ta* (Almanac of proletarian culture) (Moscow, 1925), 79; cited in Christina Kiaer, "Rodchenko in Paris," *October* 75 (Winter 1996): 4.

8. Walter Benjamin, *Moscow Diary*, entry for 13 December, published in *October* 35 (Winter 1985): 20.

9. Lissitzky articulates the importance of typography and the use of lettering to give form to ideas in his "Topography of Typography," *Merz* (Hannover) 4 (July 1923), in Sophie Lissitzky-Küppers, ed., *El Lissitzky: Life, Letters, Texts* (London: Thames and Hudson, 1967).

Beginning in 1923, and continuing for two years, Rodchenko worked with Maiakovskii on an advertising campaign for Mosselprom, the state-run Moscow Food Stores. They called their firm *reklam-konstruktor*, or "Ad-Constructor," and together they designed a number of posters, working out of a house in the center of Moscow on a historic trading street. As Constructivists, they engineered their designs, with Maiakovskii providing witty, rhyming captions for Rodchenko's striking graphics, which relied on bold letters, unadorned geometric forms, and such agitational symbols as exclamation points. Their collaborative work produced a highly successful series of posters, packages, and signs in a radically new style of advertising that reflected—even as it helped to create—the Soviet Union's progressive new way of life. The slogan *net nigde krome kak v Mossel'prome* ("Nowhere else but at the Moscow Food Stores") became as familiar to Russian consumers as jingles like "You'll wonder where the yellow went / when you brush your teeth with Pepsodent" did to a later generation of Americans. This slogan literally towered over Moscow on the facade of Mosselprom headquarters, where it was painted at every other floor level, alternating with the names of products available at the stores.[10]

Under the New Economic Policy (NEP), which Lenin instituted in 1921 in response to the economic devastations of the Revolution and Civil War, limited private enterprise was allowed.[11] But the NEP also meant that the state-run stores, previously fully subsidized, now had to operate at a profit. Rodchenko's and Maiakovskii's work for Mosselprom was complicated by the lack of identifying brand names or trademarks on the products; all fell under the purview of the government, whose only logo was a highly traditional medallion with a young woman in the center, apparently signifying a good harvest and abundance. Unable to identify a product with a catchy brand name or logo, they were left with the task of making their advertisements eye-catching enough to compete with the more attractively packaged products proliferating from private concerns. In fact, the problems facing Rodchenko and Maiakovskii went far deeper than visual appeal. In the new socialist society, education—"enlightenment" in Soviet terminology—necessarily took precedence over aesthetics. As the German critic Frederick Ku put it succinctly in

10. For a photograph of the Mosselprom headquarters and a variety of Mosselprom ads, see S. O. Khan-Magomedov, *Rodchenko: The Complete Work* (Cambridge, Mass.: MIT Press, 1987), 143, 151–53, 156, 159.

11. The NEP remained in place until 1928, when Stalin instituted the first Five-Year Plan and all private enterprise was once again abolished.

Figure 3.3
ALEKSANDR MIKHAILOVICH
RODCHENKO
Stolovoe maslo (Vegetable oil)
Poster, USSR, 1923
Lithograph, 26 11/16 x 19 1/2

the journal *Press and Revolution:* "In order to sell soap in the West, a merchant has only to say that his soap is cheaper and better than the rest. In the USSR, the problem is more complex: first, you have to convince Ivan that soap, in general, is useful and that it serves health and cleanliness and that this cleanliness is something desirable."[12]

Rodchenko and Maiakovskii thus designed the Mosselprom posters to agitate on the most basic level, using rousing punctuation, bold colors, and exuberant language to urge consumers to frequent the Moscow Food Stores, even as they provocatively comment on the act of perception. Their work is marked by a striking combination of ingenuousness about the power of advertising in consumer culture and absolute canniness in terms of technique. Figure 2.18 shows Rodchenko's poster design for vegetable oil. A bottle filled with amber liquid stands solidly in the center of the poster within a targetlike circle. Buy this oil, the poster seems to say, and you'll hit the bull's-eye; you'll win the prize and be rewarded with the best oil that money can buy. The circle overlies a background of strong red and white stripes, with Maiakovskii's informative text balancing the four corners of the composition. The most important information—the product and where to find it—appears in the two black boxes in the upper left- and lower right-hand corners. The white lettering stands out against the dark background, giving it the appearance of a photographic negative. The predominant use of red, white, and black not only speaks to a Russian audience on an emotional level (these colors had become symbolic of the Revolution's black night, white snows, and red blood), they also make the yellow oil in the bottles conspicuous, like liquid gold. The hortatory statements "Twice as cheap as butter!" and "More nutritious than other fats!" are made even more emphatic by the elongated exclamation points that follow them. Finally, the central image of the bottle is reinforced by its label, which is an exact copy of the poster on which it is advertised. In a second vegetable oil poster (fig. 3.3), the background is identical to that in the design illustrated in figure 2.18, but within the central circle stand three bottles of oil. Here Rodchenko shows the consumer the different container sizes available but, more important, implies wide availability and abundance in the triad of bottles. In both designs, however, the viewer's eye is drawn to the central cir-

12. See "Sovremennyi plakat" (The contemporary poster), in *Pechat' i revoliutsiia* 8 (1926): 58.

Figure 3.4
WILLEM HENDRIK GISPEN
Giso Lampen
Poster, Netherlands, 1936
Lithograph, 39 1/4 x 27 3/8

Figure 3.5
FRANCIS BERNARD
Gaz
Poster, France, 1928
Lithograph, 63 x 47 1/4

cle, and here Rodchenko plays with the idea of seeing, his circles mirroring the shape of an eye or camera lens focused quite clearly on a chosen object in its field of vision.

Russia was not the only country where the object appeared as the central focus of design. In his poster for Giso lamp manufacturers, the Dutch artist Willem Gispen provides highly realistic likenesses of the stylish lamps (fig. 3.4). Appropriate to his message, Gispen articulates the idea of light, showing reflections in the lamps' surfaces and modulating the lettering of the word *lampen* from white to black, as if part of a photographic process. The sense of light captured through photography is enhanced by the images of the lamps themselves, which appear to be photographed but are actually painted in wash and stippling. The broad red band behind the lamps not only sets them off forcefully but averts any threat of monotony from the otherwise muted palette. As in most of the commercial posters represented in this exhibition, the lettering is bold and unadorned. Here the name of the manufacturer is prominently splayed across the top of the poster, providing ballast, as it were, for the pendulous lamp hanging down and balancing the verticality of the composition. Or, in a slightly different reading, the prominence of the name emphasizes the manufacturer, in the process effectively objectifying the company name along with the lamps.

As other designs from the Berman collection show, it is also possible to portray the essential nature of an object in a less representational manner. Two posters that promote the same product—natural gas—illustrate how modern graphics can make a commodity tangible even without a realistic rendering. Gas is obviously an ephemeral substance that cannot accurately be drawn. How, then, can it be advertised effectively? In his 1928 poster *Gaz* (fig. 3.5) the French artist Francis Bernard manages to render gas nearly concretely. We see the brass cock that regulates its flow, appearing solid and bright against the black background that seems to dissipate into nothingness. The large letters spelling "GAZ" embody the essence of gas with their luminous yet hazy colors. Though the letters are plain, their edges are blurred, with a fuzziness that creates a scintillating effect. Without portraying the commodity, Bernard nevertheless objectifies its essence. The efficacy of gas is underlined (literally) by the text at the bottom, which informs the viewer that gas cooks, heats, and cools.

Another advertisement for natural gas by the German artist Walter Dexel (fig. 3.6) provides similar information: here gas is touted for cooking, baking, heating, and lighting. One in a series of advertising lamps (*Reklamelampen*) that Dexel designed for the city of Jena's municipal gasworks, it is executed in typically spare style. At first glance the impact of the design would seem to rely on the strong typography, but in fact Dexel provides a highly reductivist image of gas. The three-quarter circle of yellow appears brilliant against the black background; once illuminated as an advertising lamp against the dark night, as Dexel intended, its intensity would be even greater. Coupled with the small red rule at the left center of the design, it represents the colors of flames and heat. Suddenly the yellow disc is not just a circle truncated by an informative message but a round burner, the very image of a searing flame of gas, a circle of fire. Dexel's design reduces gas to its most elemental functions of light and heat, heightening its essence in the process.

Each of these posters does more than simply convey the basic message that a certain brand of lamps is best or that gas is preferable to other fuels. Both objectify the essence of the product advertised even as they challenge viewers to regard it in a fresh way that accentuates its intrinsic properties.

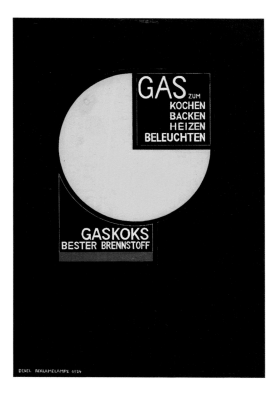

Figure 3.6
WALTER DEXEL
Gas zum kochen, backen, heizen, beleuchten
(Gas for cooking, baking, heating, and lighting)
Design for illuminated sign, Germany, 1924
Ink, gouache, pencil, pasted paper, hand lettering, 19 3/4 x 13 3/8

IMAGE AND IDEOLOGY

Figure 3.7
GUSTAV GUSTAVOVICH KLUTSIS
Ekran (Screen)
Design for propaganda stand, USSR, 1922
Linocut, 9 1/16 x 4 7/16

The graphic design of the 1920s and 1930s was largely directed at the consumer, intended for mechanical reproduction and wide circulation (with the exception of works produced by the avant-garde for the avant-garde). How did these new graphics fit into the modern world? Many of the largest works were designed to give urban areas a more contemporary look. In most major cities, new construction could not keep pace with demand, so one way to counterbalance the ornate trim of the older buildings in urban centers was to superimpose streamlined billboards or painted modernist advertisements. Large-scale posters were not the only way to encourage a more modern look, however. By the mid-1920s, the theoretical investigations of the avant-garde had moved from the studio into the street, reflected in new styles of furniture, clothing, ceramics, and packaging. As new technologies allowed for mass production and consumption, modernist art—itself often imitating a machine aesthetic—found an ever wider audience. The new graphic designers drew on early experiments in painting, photography, and typography to produce images often startling in the flatness and spareness of their composition. In Germany, Walter Dexel pioneered the use of clocks and lampposts (*Leuchtsäulen*) as advertising props.[13] His inclination toward industrial design was especially fitting for the city of Jena, which was renowned for its pioneering work in the heat-tempered glass produced at the Jena glassworks. An interest in industrialization also furthered avant-garde design in the Soviet Union. There Gustav Klutsis designed a series of agitational stands that allowed for a variety of simultaneous activities from speeches to radio broadcasts to film projections and foreshadowed our current multimedia presentations by more than half a century.[14] Figure 3.7 shows one such propaganda stand, with steps leading up to a soapboxlike rostrum for the speaker over which looms a large projection screen (*ekran*).

In Frankfurt, Robert Michel applied his architectural training to the design of gas stations, building facades, and large advertising panels. Like Dexel, he was concerned with functional design, making certain that both artistic and societal needs would be met. Figure 3.8 shows his sketch for a building facade in Frankfurt advertising Persil laundry detergent (the company conducted a vigorous ad campaign in which Dexel also participated). The

13. For more on Dexel's work in advertising, see Gerd Fleischmann, ed., *Walter Dexel: Neue Reklame* (Düsseldorf: Edition Marzona, 1987).

14. Klutsis's agit-prop stands are reproduced in Hubertus Gassner and Roland Nachtigäller, ed., *Gustav Klucis: Retrospektive* (Stuttgart: Verlag Gerd Hatje, 1991), 110–25.

brand name announces itself prominently, the white letters bright against a red background. And although a picture of the detergent box is similarly set within a red quadrilateral, its importance recedes in relation to the bold letters that spell out "PERSIL." In Michel's design, we can see the influence of Russian Constructivism, largely effected by Lissitzky and the *First Russian Exhibition* held at Berlin's Van Diemen Gallery in 1922.[15] Michel's work is set apart from the Constructivists' early theoretical exercises, however, by its contextual placement on a building elevation. By showing the advertisement in the setting in which it is meant to be seen, Michel offers up a piece of social history, causing us to think beyond formal questions to societal ones, such as building usage and urban aesthetics. Because the design is drawn quite high up on the side of the building, it is probably intended for a building that faced a major square or plaza, where it could catch the attention of a large number of people.

By the 1920s, designing for mass consumption was no longer necessarily considered beneath an artist's talent; on the contrary, many artists welcomed mechanical reproduction because it meant even greater visibility and influence. As we have seen, public art could range from the political to the decorative to the unabashedly commercial. At times the intended goals overlapped, as in the case of the ROSTA windows produced for the Russian Telegraph Agency (ROSTA) between 1919 and 1922.[16] After years of civil unrest, Russian cities looked grim and desolate, with empty storefronts everywhere. Artists such as Maiakovskii, Ivan Maliutin, and Mikhail Cheremnykh stepped into the breach with their crudely stenciled and hand-colored posters based on the old Russian *lubok,* or broadside, which reported the late-breaking news of the day in picture and in verse. These posters not only provided the populace with political guidance, they also enlivened the cities, bringing color and humor to an otherwise dreary reality. Maiakovskii threw himself wholeheartedly into this agitational work, working for ROSTA day and night and by his own account (likely exaggerated) completing approximately three thousand posters and six thousand captions.[17] By the end of the ROSTA period, "Art into Life" had become the definitive rallying cry in the Soviet Union, as the Constructivists denounced easel art in favor of other forms of artistic

Figure 3.8
ROBERT MICHEL
Persil, für alle Wäsche
(Persil, for all your laundry)
Design for billboard, Germany, 1926
Colored ink, ink, pencil, 20 1/2 x 17 1/4

15. Michel's wife, Ella Bergmann-Michel, is cited among those "artists influenced by the First Russian Exhibition, Berlin 1922." See *First Russian Exhibition*, 153. Thus we can assume that Michel himself had either direct or indirect contact with contemporary Russian art.

16. Technically, ROSTA ceased producing posters in January 1921, when Glavpolitprosvet, the political enlightenment branch of the People's Commissariat of Enlightenment, took over. Stephen White provides a thorough look at the ROSTA windows in chapter 4 of his *Bolshevik Poster* (New Haven and London: Yale University Press, 1988).

17. Vladimir Maiakovskii, "Ia sam" (I myself), in *Polnoe sobranie sochinenii* (Collected works), vol. 1 (Moscow: GIKhL, 1955), 26. Stephen White, drawing on other sources, places the number closer to six hundred. *Bolshevik Poster*, 67.

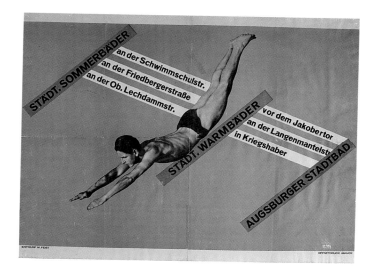

Figure 3.9
WERNER DAVID FEIST
Städtische Bäder (Municipal pools)
Poster, Germany, 1928
Offset lithograph, 23 9/16 x 31 5/16

expression, such as textile design, ceramics, theater, and film.[18] Because the Russian populace had little exposure to the consumer concepts that were already rather well developed in the West, early Soviet artists had unprecedented opportunity to mold and define public taste (mass participation in the arts was not only encouraged but expected, as a necessary component of enlightenment).[19] And this the artists did with a heady spirit of genuine belief in their enterprise. The vision they offered up was one of utopian material abundance untainted by capitalism. In fact, the mass production of goods and the effort to distribute them widely represents a kind of democratization, even in socialist Russia; for the first time, goods were available to everyone, not just the monied classes. And the same held true for art: where the commissioned painting was single, personal, and elite, the poster was multiple, social, and egalitarian.

Thus, even when a poster or package design was commercially inspired, it was often simultaneously ideological. In works from the Berman collection consumer images frequently contribute to the ideological sphere, selling a way of life quite distinct from the commodity itself. The design as carrier of a social message thus gained a significant new dimension. One German example is Werner David Feist's poster for the Augsburg municipal pools (fig. 3.9), which lists the pools open for summertime swimming. Yet its subtext tells far more than the printed material reveals. In Weimar Germany, as in Soviet Russia, physical fitness became a national cult, a means of displaying patriotism. Feist's well-muscled diver (actually, the artist himself) has his arms extended as if to greet the future, a gesture emphasized by the dynamic red rules running parallel to the diver.[20] Feist's composition implies

18. Unfortunately, the ostensible freedom to apply their talents to radically different fields evolved into a mandate to do so, which ultimately became a constraint. For more on how the Russian avant-garde was responsible for its demise, see Boris Groys, *The Total Art of Stalinism: Avant-Garde, Aesthetic Dictatorship, and Beyond* (Princeton, N.J.: Princeton University Press, 1992).

19. For an introduction to 1920s consumer culture in Russia, see Mikhail Anikst and Elena Chernevich, *Soviet Commercial Design of the Twenties* (New York: Abbeville, 1987).

20. Feist's technique adds humor here: he had himself photographed lying down outstretched and then manipulated the photograph to make his body appear to be in motion (see fig. 2.34).

Figure 3.10
VILMOS HUSZAR
Miss Blanche Virginia Cigarettes
Poster, 1926
Lithograph, 11 3/4 x 7 1/2

that physical agility and boldness (diving headlong into something) contribute not only to one's personal well-being but to the national well-being as well.

Although the success or failure of such designs as ideological tools is often difficult to gauge, their very ubiquity through mass production serves as an effective form of inculcation. The best designs, however, result from an awareness of consumer psychology, which may differ from culture to culture but is essentially universal in its most basic belief that by purchasing a given item, the consumer will simultaneously come to possess a whole array of other things, including increased status, "coolness," and social mobility.[21] Buying and smoking Miss Blanche Virginia cigarettes, as portrayed by Vilmos Huszár (fig. 3.10), guarantees sophistication. It also suggests independence from social strictures and even sexual liberation. Drawn in the signature de Stijl colors of red, blue, and yellow, the woman smoking is reduced to disembodied parts as her face merges with the background of the poster. Only her features, hat, and sleek shirt give the face definition, yet even in their minimalness, they are highly expressive, her lips convincingly erotic. The woman's hand is similarly abstracted yet vivid, with its cobalt blue glove and finger provocatively crooked. The elongated mass of blue draws the eye upward to the cigarette, its hot red tip mirroring the hot red lips. Miss Blanche stirs and beckons us, her name elegant in a cursive script that contrasts with the blocky sans serif lettering of "Virginia Cigarettes." If we buy the eponymous cigarettes, she implies, we can share her style—or even be her.

Though less alluring than Huszár's Miss Blanche, the anonymous design for Russia's Hammer Cigarettes (fig. 3.11) is equally stirring, albeit politically rather than sensually. Here the letters that spell "MOLOT" ("hammer" in Russian) appear three-dimensional and are used as a representational element in the composition. The word *is* the hammer, and by buying this product the consumer will contribute to the urgent need for industrialization, to which the cogwheel in the lower right also attests.

In Soviet Russia, even products not generally associated with social causes were politicized. You could pop a sweet into your mouth while pondering the bridge depicted on its wrapper in the "Our Industry" series designed by Rodchenko in 1924 (fig. 3.12). The graceful floral designs, cherubs, and

Figure 3.11
DESIGNER UNKNOWN
MOLOT, Hammer Cigarettes
Package, USSR
Lithograph, 8 3/8 x 5 1/8

21. Tomlinson, *Consumption, Identity, and Style*, 24.

"chocolate-box girls" of yesteryear have disappeared; and instead of soft lavenders, yellows, and greens we find the stark red, white, and black so closely associated with the Revolution and the new Soviet state. Flourishes and curlicues have been replaced with Constructivist rules and black-and-white drawings that resemble documentary photographs; exhortation, instruction, seriousness, and salience supplant the urge to prettify. The fact is that Russian society needed rebuilding, so even a modern candy wrapper became an agitational tool, urging the consumer to action in rhyme: "Don't stand by the river till you're old and gray / Far better to sling a bridge across the river." Should you crave cookies instead of candy, the Ad-Constructors are ready. Their package label for "Red Aviator" cookies (fig. 3.13) depicts an airplane with whirling propeller; the text bluntly states that "everywhere we advance the idea [of Soviet superiority in aviation] / Even in the case of sweets." Because the airplane signifies freedom and flight, in his design Rodchenko cleverly uses its futuristic appeal to sell sweets, even as he sweetens the machine by associating it with cookies.

Indeed, in the Soviet Union no forum was too small, no product too trivial to serve as a means to political or social engagement through art. In *Kakao* (see fig. 3.1), cocoa becomes a pretext for patriotism as Rodchenko and Maiakovskii presuppose a lively give-and-take with the purchaser. "Comrades, don't argue!" Maiakovskii's text cries, mimicking the oral traditions of street hawkers.[22] Believe me, it implies, I know what's best for you. Rodchenko's graphics similarly sway the consumer, challenging him or her to perceive a trivial product anew: cocoa not merely as comfort but as an important societal tool. The can of cocoa stands at the center of the composition, its old-fash-

Figure 3.13
ALEKSANDR MIKHAILOVICH RODCHENKO
Pechen'e 'Krasnyi aviator'
("Red Aviator" cookies)
Wrapper, USSR, 1923–24
Lithograph, 10 1/8 x 11 1/16

Figures 3.12
ALEKSANDR MIKHAILOVICH
RODCHENKO AND VLADIMIR
VLADIMIROVICH MAIAKOVSKII
Karamel' 'Nasha industriia'
("Our Industry" candy)
Two wrappers, USSR, 1924
Letterpress, 3 1/4 x 3 each

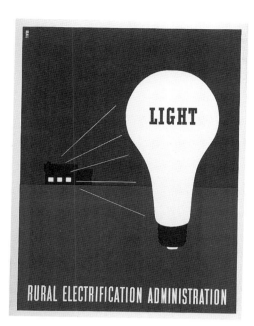

Figure 3.14
LESTER BEALL
Light
Poster, USA, 1937
Silkscreen, 39 7/8 x 30 1/8

ioned, ornamental label and round packaging seemingly at odds with the rigidly angular, truncated triangle in which it sits. Two bright blue arrows pick up the curves of the can to direct the viewer's eye to the product. Unlike commercial appeals of the past, however, this message is not exclusively personal. The advertisement claims that strength lies in cocoa, which not only tastes good but also makes you strong, and being strong is the duty of every loyal Soviet citizen, the path toward the betterment of society. In this way the prosaic objects of daily life become invested with deeper meaning while social abstractions achieve concrete form for an unsophisticated audience.

In his autobiographical sketch Maiakovskii wrote that his advertising jingles constituted "poetry of the highest caliber."[23] Though he tended to exaggeration, it is harder to dismiss the assessment of the noted Formalist critic Yurii Tynianov, who wrote in regard to Maiakovskii's work for Mosselprom that "any regrets over the fact that poets are 'wasting' their talent are mistaken; where we think they are wasting it, they are actually gaining something new."[24] In Maiakovskii's case, this meant freedom from the constraints of traditional verse-making and an opportunity for social effectiveness. Rodchenko's and Maiakovskii's hallmark commercial designs represent the Constructivist belief in the inseparability of art and everyday life, in the social utility of art.

Although social and economic exigencies were less urgent outside of the Soviet Union, they were bad enough, and posters by European and American artists reveal a similar preoccupation with the object and its larger meaning for society. Lester Beall's *Light* (fig. 3.14) from 1937 is one of a series of works he completed for the U.S. Rural Electrification Administration. As intangible as the natural gas promoted by Bernard and Dexel, electricity is similarly objectified in Beall's poster into a lightbulb. Yet the artist implies that light in and of itself is not sufficient; it gains meaning only through its connection to the home, to humankind. The house in the background shows lighted windows that bespeak both security and domesticity, thereby promising not only a brighter life but also a more comfortable and protected one, an image particularly appealing during this era of widespread deprivation and dislocation. And, as in many early Soviet posters, the dominant colors are

22. Maiakovskii brilliantly explores the issues of consumption and desire in act 1 of his 1928 play *The Bedbug*, for which Rodchenko designed the stage sets and costumes. He humorously reproduces the vivid language of street hawkers, as NEP-men peddle their various wares, from fish to brassieres. For the people seeking to buy these goods, each purchase represents either a forward step up the social scale or a retreat to the poverty of the past. For an English translation, see Vladimir Mayakovsky, *The Bedbug and Selected Poetry*, ed. Patricia Blake and trans. Max Hayward and George Reavey (Bloomington: Indiana University Press, 1975). For more on the history of Russian advertising, see *Torgovaia reklama i upakovka v Rossii XIX–XX vv* (Advertising and packaging in Russia in the nineteenth and twentieth centuries) (Moscow: State Historical Museum, 1993).

23. Maiakovskii, *Polnoe sobranie sochinenii*, 1:27.
24. Iurii Tynianov, "Promezhutok" (Interlude), in *Arkhaisty i novatory* (Archaists and innovators) (Leningrad, 1927). Reprinted in *Slavische Propyläen*, vol. 31 (Munich: Wilhelm Fink Verlag, 1967), 556.

Figure 3.15
ATTRIBUTED TO WILLI BAUMEISTER
Die Wohnung (The dwelling)
Poster, Germany, 1927
Lithograph, 45 1/16 x 32 1/8

Figure 3.16
LADISLAV SUTNAR
Výstava harmonického domova
(Exhibition of the harmonious home)
Poster, Czechoslovakia, 1930
Lithograph, 37 1/2 x 23 15/16

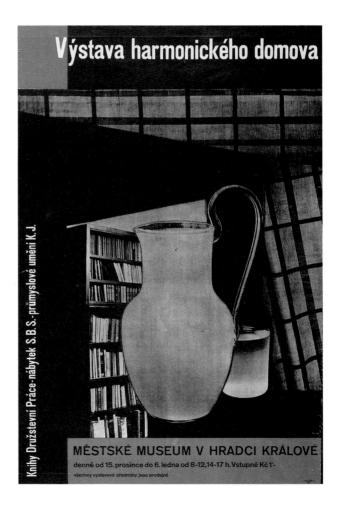

intended to evoke patriotic identification. Beall's poster ostensibly promotes electrification for the private comforts it will bring; its underlying purpose, however, is to domesticate electrification, to sell the idea of industrialization. Just as Rodchenko promoted industry through sweets, Beall promotes electrification through association with hearth and home. All of these works show how in the hands of talented artists abstract, coolly scientific concepts can achieve personal meaning by association with the commonplace and wholesome; it is all a matter of perception.

The issue of domesticity was of special ideological concern. Two posters in the Berman collection offer interesting interpretations of the proper image of home. Willi Baumeister designed a poster entitled *Die Wohnung* (The dwelling) for the German Werkbund's 1927 exhibition (fig. 3.15). The central photographic image depicts a cluttered and plush bourgeois interior over which a massive red "X" is superimposed, effectively crossing it out. The "X" is drawn free-form, extending as if angrily beyond the edges of the photograph. This sort of simple "X," usually large and usually drawn by hand (implying the artist's personal challenge to the status quo), became a leitmotiv of sorts in posters from Germany, Russia, England, and the United States. The "X" declares a radically new perspective, an eradication of the past, and in this regard it came to signify the twentieth-century change in the world order. The text poses the simple question: "How do you live?" Baumeister's crossed-out drawing room is a microcosm of a world canceled by revolutionary ideas, the crudely drawn red "X" a graphic demonstration of their power to eliminate the past in almost one stroke.

Baumeister's rejection of interior clutter set the tone for the Werkbund exhibition, which advocated a minimalist style far removed from the overstuffed bourgeois style. The new look was streamlined and modern, with objects chosen and appreciated for their clean lines. An exhibition poster by the Czech artist Ladislav Sutnar depicts just such a modernized interior, one that has not lost its domestic appeal, however. The *Exhibition of the Harmonious Home* (fig. 3.16) features the comforting objects of everyday use: books lining the shelves, a few comfortably askew; a caddy; and most prominent, a water pitcher with a graceful, arching handle. The regular grid of the windowpane-like curtains echoes the smooth lines of the pitcher and caddy. The simplicity and purity of this interior (not to mention the purity of essence implicit in the water held by the pitcher) seem to promise a simple and pure life, free from the bourgeois trappings of the past.

Figure 3.19
FRANCIS BERNARD
Arts ménagers (Domestic arts)
Poster, France, 1933
Lithograph, 61 3/4 x 46 1/16

Figure 3.18
VLADIMIR O. ROSKIN
GET (GET—State Electric Trust)
Design for poster, USSR, 1925–26
Gouache, ink, pencil, 8 1/2 x 11 3/16

HUMANS AND MACHINES

Figure 3.17
THEO VAN DOESBURG
Mécano No. Bleu, Blauw, Blau, Blue, 1922
Journal, Netherlands, 1922
Letterpress, 6 1/2 x 5 1/8

If an "X" recurs in certain graphic works of the modern period, regardless of their countries of origin, so, too, do certain other motifs, such as concentric circles, infinitely repeating images, cogwheels and other machine parts, and the hand. Of these, all but the hand are clearly mechanistic and hardly surprising for an era when each advance in technology held boundless promise as the key to a bold future. Much of the success of these images had to do with the avant-garde fascination with the machine as both an agent of change and an aesthetic object in its own right. From the use of new technologies that allowed for innovations in typography to using machine imagery as a metaphor for progressive thought, modernist artists explored the manifold relationship between humans and machines. And as they sought to connect mechanical operations such as repetition and speed with the physical act of seeing, their investigations comprised issues of perception and cognition.

In some cases, artists introduced mechanistic figures as simple symbolic gestures, as in Theo van Doesburg's logo for his *Mécano* publications—a table-saw blade—which he reproduced on both his Dada and De Stijl works (fig. 3.17). In the Soviet Union, predictably, machine imagery was used more literally, as in Vladimir Roskin's poster design for the State Electric Trust (fig. 3.18), in which the faithfully reproduced generators with their spinning belts in the background are the obvious source of the electricity being advertised.

Elsewhere, people and machines are intricately intertwined. Francis Bernard's poster of 1933 for an exhibition of domestic arts in Paris (fig. 3.19) depicts a housewife or housekeeper with broom in hand, surely a traditional interpretation of domestic duties. But this female figure has no features, making her somewhat less than fully human, and this impression is reinforced by the cogwheel that takes the place of her internal organs. Obviously, mechanization affects the domestic sphere as well, and this woman-cum-robot looms large over the realistic photomontage figures in the foreground, who gaze up at her in awe.[25] Despite their photographic realism, these people seem to be caught in a cloud, enhazed, while the larger-than-life mechanical figure appears solid by comparison.

25. At the time of this poster, the idea of the robot had only been current for little over a decade. The word was coined in 1921 by the Czech playwright Karel Capek in *R.U.R.* and entered the English language in 1923 with the play's translation.

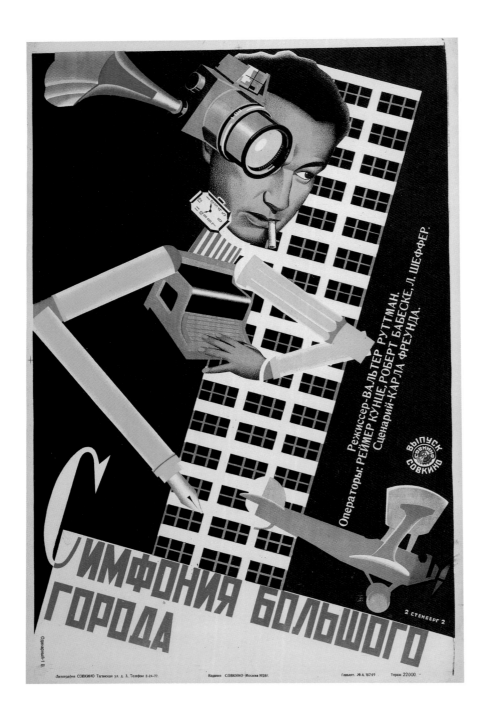

Figure 3.20
VLADIMIR AVGUSTOVICH STENBERG AND
GEORGII AVGUSTOVICH STENBERG
Simfoniia bol'shogo goroda
(Symphony of a great city)
Poster, USSR, 1928
Lithograph, 42 1/2 x 27 3/4

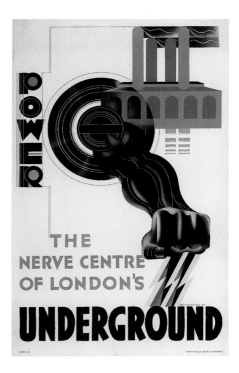

Figure 3.21
EDWARD MCKNIGHT KAUFFER
Power: The Nerve Centre of London's
Underground
Poster, England, 1930
Lithograph, 39 13/16 x 24 3/4

The Stenberg brothers, Georgii and Vladimir, also plied the boundaries of the human and the mechanical. Their poster for the Russian release of Walther Ruttman's film *Berlin, Symphony of a Great City* (fig. 3.20) makes use of a photomontage done in 1926 by the Bauhaus student Otto Umbehr, which shows a man's face and hand.[26] But that is as far as the human element goes. One of the man's eyes is replaced by a large camera lens, his ear by a horn speaker. What would appear to be a shirt collar actually blends with the facade of the building behind it, which curves up slightly beneath the man's chin, extending into the mechanized face of a watch. The man's body is a typewriter, and his arms resemble mechanical pencils, with one arm ending not in a hand but in the nib of a pen. The filmmaker and his camera are one, this poster declares, and the documentary could not have been produced had the two not worked in tandem.[27] The small yet discerning human eye and the larger but more opaque camera eye are accorded equal importance. This photomontage is a wonderfully overt statement of the relation between the mechanical and the human, where the camera serves as a prosthesis for the otherwise not fully adequate human eye.

A third poster, by the expatriate American artist Edward McKnight Kauffer, similarly shows the important melding of the human and the mechanical. In one of the series of posters he designed for the London Underground (fig. 3.21), the extraordinary power of the factory and its turbines is transmitted not by sheer force of electricity but by the muscular arm and hand of the worker. The slogan, "Power: The Nerve Centre of London's Underground," is realized in the fine blue veins that run through the worker's arm and into the spinning steel of the turbine, which simultaneously represents the wheels of the subway trains with the Underground logo in the center. As the Stenberg brothers did in their poster, Kauffer visually portrays the symbiosis of humans and machines, touting the machine for its extraordinary powers yet keeping alive its connection to humankind. In this way technology remains within a comprehensible domain, as the fear of the mechanical is assuaged by the nearly palpable excitement of machine dreams.

26. Umbehr's photomontage was conceived as a portrait of the Austrian reporter Egon Erwin Kirsch, but the Stenbergs used it for their own purposes. For more on Umbehr, see Anna Rowland, *Bauhaus Source Book* (New York: Van Nostrand Reinhold, 1990), 144.

27. This idea is similarly visualized in Dziga Vertov's 1926 film *Man with a Movie Camera,* for which the Stenberg brothers also designed a poster (fig. 3.29).

Figure 3.23
EL LISSITZKY
(LAZAR' MARKOVICH LISITSKII)
Pelican Drawing Ink
Advertisement, 1925
Lithograph, 12 3/4 x 17 3/8

Other posters focus more on the human element than on the mechanical, and in this type of work a hand is often prominent. The importance of human agency comes across forcefully, demonstrating that without a guiding intellect, mechanics alone cannot work efficaciously. We see this in Lissitzky's famous photogram self-portrait, *The Constructor,* in which his hand, holding a compass, overlies his face (fig 3.22). The hand is partially transparent, however, and allows the artist's eye to show through. This hand with compass reappears in the same posture in an advertisement that Lissitzky designed a year later for Pelican Drawing Ink (fig. 3.23), part of a series commissioned by the Pelikan office supply company. Here the essential object, the ink, is represented both visually and semantically, but Lissitzky's rendering emphasizes that the ink is useless without a hand to employ it. Ever sensitive to commercial concerns, Lissitzky further defines the hand by extending it from a highly elegant suit complete with cufflinks; that the hand itself is not the calloused palm of a worker but the smooth palm of a professional artist or engineer reinforces the point that the artist, too, is an active participant in production.[28]

A different disembodied hand appears in a later poster by Jean Carlu urging Americans to join in the effort toward increased factory output on the eve of the United States's entrance into World War II (fig. 3.24). As in Lissitzky's poster, the hand has an obvious presence and power, but here the heavy glove and wrench leave no doubt that it belongs to a worker. Where Lissitzky's advertisement appears graceful and refined, Carlu's expresses intensity and urgency; Lissitzky's hand holds the compass lightly, while

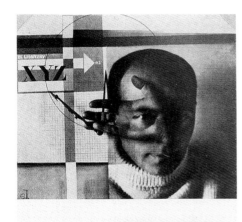

Figure 3.22
JAN TSCHICHOLD
(photomontage by EL LISSITZKY
[LAZAR' MARKOVICH LISITSKII])
Foto-Auge: The Constructor
Prospectus, Germany, 1929
Letterpress, 5 3/8 x 4

28. For more on Lissitzky's and Klutsis's use of the hand, see Margarita Tupitsyn, "From the Politics of Montage to the Montage of Politics: Soviet Practice 1919 Through 1937," in Matthew Teitelbaum, ed., *Montage and Modern Life: 1919–1942* (Cambridge, Mass.: MIT Press, and Boston: Institute of Contemporary Art, 1992), 99–103.

Figure 3.25
CASSANDRE
Thomson
Poster, France, 1931
Lithograph, 46 15/16 x 31 1/2

Carlu's menacingly grips the weaponlike wrench. The first "o" in the word "Production" has become a nut with bolt, and in the poster's diagonals and the wrench's angle we sense tremendous energy and incipient movement.

A hand also figures in Cassandre's poster for Thomson electric products (fig. 3.25), where the cord and plug exist in relation to the hand that plugs them in. Electricity alone cannot bring us into the future, the poster seems to say; people are necessary, too. Cassandre's hand gives literal representation to the French *main-d'oeuvre,* which is modified by the seemingly oxymoronic *electro-domestique.* Yet without the conjunction of the technical and the manual, we will be unable to master the universe that is implied by the stars hovering over each of the five fingertips. The human element remains indispensable despite the technological advances of the early twentieth century, and Cassandre's design reassures us of our importance even as he humanizes the machine and promotes it as our necessary partner for a bright, prosperous, and graphically uncluttered future.

Figure 3.24
JEAN-GEORGES-LEON CARLU
Production
Poster, USA, 1941
Lithograph, 29 7/8 x 40 1/8

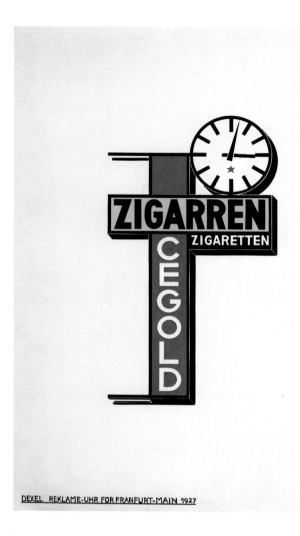

Figure 3.26
WALTER DEXEL
Zigarren, Zigaretten (Cigars, cigarettes)
Design for advertising clock, Germany, 1927
Ink, gouache, pencil, 14 1/2 x 10 5/8

Figure 3.27
PAUL SCHUITEMA
Superior Dutch Ham
Poster, Netherlands, c. 1925
Lithograph, 19 3/4 x 19 7/8

THE UTOPIAN IDEAL

Many of the most striking graphic designs from the period between the two world wars evince the artists' attempts to fuse art with life, to show that it is not distinct from reality, existing somewhere above or beyond it, but that it *is* reality. If in the Soviet Union the goal was to create an artistic and proletarian culture where artists were not caught up in abstractions but were instead firmly rooted in the actualities of the new socialist state, then elsewhere the utopian ideal was less clearly defined. However, no matter where the artists of the avant-garde worked, they were all engaged in the search for new expression. As the Berman collection so vividly shows, fresh expression did not always involve the representation of an image. Often typography was the primary element in a design, as in Dexel's prominent lettering for Cegold cigars and cigarettes (fig. 3.26). Conceived as an advertising clock for the city of Frankfurt, the metal supports on the upper and lower left were meant to affix the clock to a building. The base of the clock has been reduced to cubic, architectural shapes that are otherwise unadorned. The black-and-white lettering of the brand name and products, set against blocks of bold color, draws attention to the type and the information it conveys. The clean lines of Dexel's modern typeface, along with the words themselves, are designed to make the consumer identify with the product advertised: have a clean smoke with Cegold cigars or cigarettes, and you, too, will be up-to-the-minute (as the clockface subliminally suggests). Even in the absence of any literal image, passersby can instantly take in not only the hour but also the product message.

The attention value of colors is especially apparent in Paul Schuitema's poster for the Superior Dutch Ham canned by the van Berkel company (fig. 3.27). Reproduced in the characteristic De Stijl colors of red, yellow, and blue, the design relies on color, geometrics, and lettering for its effect rather than resorting to any image representing the product. The words "superior" and "luxury" immediately tell the viewer that this ham is a quality product, and the fat, almost juicy letters emphasize its succulence. Equally effective is the prominent red circle, which suggests a cutaway view of a whole ham with a slice shaved from its bottom. Through its simple design, the poster denotes ampleness and plenty.

Figure 3.29
VLADIMIR AVGUSTOVICH STENBERG
AND GEORGII AVGUSTOVICH STENBERG
Chelovek s kinoapparatom
(Man with a movie camera)
Poster, USSR, 1926
Lithograph, 43 1/2 x 28

Figure 3.28
NATAL'IA SERGEEVNA PINUS-BUKHAROVA
Trudiashchiesia zhenshchiny—v riady . . . !
(Women workers—Into the ranks . . . !)
Poster, USSR
Lithograph, 38 5/8 x 28

Graphic artists elsewhere used cinematic conventions to express a utopian ideal of abundance. Following filmmakers, graphic designers made striking use of montage, close-up shots, split screens, and repeating images. The use of repetition, in particular, proved advantageous for both societal and commercial purposes in that it fixes an image in the viewer's mind. Repetition promises the infinite through never-ceasing rhythms or endless supplies. Consider, for instance, Natal'ia Pinus-Bukharova's *Women Workers—Into the Ranks of Active Participants in the Industrial and Social Life of the Country!* probably from the early 1930s (fig. 3.28). Except for the patriotic woman worker's obligatory red scarf, the poster is done in washed-out shades of gray, white, and straw, yet the woman's nearly beatific expression as she gazes off into a radiant future belies any ostensible dullness. Her hand holds a thread that comes off the last bobbin, and the bobbins themselves are repeated in endless rows. Those in the foreground are truncated by the picture frame, suggesting their continuation; those in the background recede into a vanishing point. Although the woman's posture seems frozen, the dynamic axis of the bobbin holders suggests vigorous forward motion. And against the backdrop of happy children playing in a schoolyard, the endless bobbins juxtaposed with the woman also suggest extraordinary fecundity. The message is that whether in the factory or at home, the woman worker bears especial responsibility for the productivity of the nation, variety and individuality being the price of exceptional productiveness in the conveyor-belt age.

In other works, a sense of infinite motion is expressed more thrillingly. The Stenberg brothers played with concentric circles to suggest vertiginous movement into a rapidly expanding (or, at times, contracting) universe. Their classic film poster for Dziga Vertov's *Man with a Movie Camera* (fig. 3.29) shows a woman's head, arms, and legs caught in a spiral of information about the film. The spiral mimics the lens aperture of a movie camera with its shifting iris diaphragm. The woman and spiral are set against the backdrop of a modern city, each skyscraper soaring into black infinity. She appears animated, caught up in an exhilarating ride into the vortex of the universe. The poster objectifies a tumultuous state of perpetual motion, in which each subsequent whirl causes a shift in perspective, a vision of something new.

Figure 3.31

Concentric circles, or fragments of them, also appear in Cassandre's 1935 poster *Nicolas* (fig. 3.30), which advertises a wine merchant's wares. Here the circular lines operate in combination with diagonal rules to give a sense of swirling motion, suggesting, perhaps, an inebriated state. Amid this eddy of circles and stripes stands a stable, upright figure whose shadow casts a purple haze across the bright background. This figure stands half in shadow, as if emerging from a dream. In his hands he holds the bottles of wine that are being advertised; but like the background, they radiate out in circles from his hands and seem to be caught in a spinning motion. That this poster has a dreamlike quality is certainly not utopian in the social sense of many Soviet posters, but it does evoke a feeling of liberation and freefloatingness akin to a state of utopia.

The Stenberg brothers' *Man with a Movie Camera* conveys the optimistic spirit of Soviet Russia in the mid-1920s before the repressive shift in political (and artistic) climate. It is telling that a later film poster attributed to them represents spiraling motion more ambiguously. In *The Last Flight* (fig. 3.31), two trapeze artists perform against a backdrop of concentric circles that

Figure 3.30
CASSANDRE
Nicolas
Poster, France, 1935
Lithograph, 94 1/2 x 126

end—or begin—with a solid, blazing circle of color, the circular pattern echoing the tiers of seats that surround the central ring in a circus. In swinging high above the arena on their trapezes, the artists are freed from the confines of daily existence, and the ever widening circles give the impression of freedom in flight. Yet given the title of the film (and considering the expression on the left-hand artist's face), it is possible to read this design differently, more apocalyptically, with the artists about to tumble headlong into the vortex represented by the flame-colored central circle. They seem bound for unknown territory, whether into the infinite beyond or into a bottomless abyss; and their plunge appears inexorable. Because *The Last Flight* tells the story of a circus troupe stranded by the disruptions of the Revolution, an obvious political message lies not far from the surface. But the Stenberg brothers add layers of meaning. The four black circles outlined in white are reminiscent of eyes, and in a cue from the world of film, the large, golden circle appears as an iris of a camera lens, bringing it into sharp focus. The "eyes" also resemble celestial bodies, either sunspots or full lunar eclipses, lending the artists' last flight (and the poster) a sense of cosmic importance, true to the cataclysmic nature of the era.

The Stenberg brothers show an unusual awareness about where the passionate flight of revolution would lead, and indeed, by the 1930s the heady flight of modernism was similarly spiraling into a fall. In the Soviet Union, the avant-garde found itself increasingly (and, finally, fatally) constricted. Maiakovskii committed suicide in 1930; within less than a decade, Georgii Stenberg had been killed in a suspicious accident and Klutsis had been executed for political incorrectness. Though modernism did not end abruptly in the West, political pressures were placed on a number of artists, including Oskar Schlemmer, who died in Germany in extreme isolation and penury after years of governmental harassment.

What we see in the Berman collection is therefore all the more precious: modernism in its full flush of exuberance. Through unabashed promotion, the artists sought to sell the public something hitherto beyond its reach—whether a commodity, an ideology, or a better way of life. No longer

ARTFUL PERSUASION

was mere material comfort or ease the standard but rather progressiveness coupled with a certain savoir vivre. Modernist artists engineered new perceptions of even the most mundane objects, causing the viewer, as consumer, to participate in the making of this new life, to support it through informed purchases and an evolving sense of style. What had hitherto been perceived as nonessential—the visibility and style of consumable objects—now seemed a cultural imperative. As a sleek, streamlined look became synonymous with modernity, up-to-date consumers changed their taste. The public embrace of this new look completed the artistic process, and in this way a newly reductive and angular aesthetic took hold in advertising and packaging, in furniture, clothing, and building design.

Such practices as the use of the object as a design focus, the manipulation of letters to convey ideas and colors to evoke emotions, the predominance of abstracted realism, and the artist's direct communication to a broad public and not just a private patron continue to influence our consumer environment and contribute to our collective sense of self. Even when trite and hackneyed, the modernist consumer ideal still anchors our identity as "with-it" sophisticates. Not only did the artists of the avant-garde play an important role in shaping public taste, through their artful persuasion they redefined modern life.

This redefinition was part of the larger utopian experience of the early twentieth century, when technology promised material abundance and a carefree future. Although the human potential to change the world had long been the stuff of futurist fantasy, what had been merely prophecy was now reality as technology transformed life daily. As heralds of the new age, the graphic artists of the era celebrated the technology that enabled the mass reproduction of their work and the general amelioration of life. At the same time, they did not neglect the importance of human agency. Ultimately, their best works demonstrate the unity between image and idea, between production and reception—the unwavering connection between art and life.

DESIGN AND COMMERCE

Plate 35
ALEKSANDR MIKHAILOVICH RODCHENKO
SMOTRI (Look)
Design for signboard, USSR, c. 1924
Gouache on cut board, 17 1/2 x 18 5/8
(irregular)

Plate 36

Plate 36
ALEKSANDR MIKHAILOVICH RODCHENKO
Pechen'e 'Zebra' ("Zebra" cookies)
Wrapper, USSR, 1924
Lithograph, 13 7/8 x 5 11/16

Plate 37
EL LISSITZKY
(LAZAR' MARKOVICH LISITSKII)
Pelikan—Siegellack (Pelikan Sealing Wax)
Packages, c. 1925
Two lithographs, 3 1/2 x 8 3/8 x 1 1/2
and 4 x 9 5/8 x 1 1/16

Plate 37

Plate 38

Plate 39

Plate 38
VILMOS HUSZAR
Miss Blanche Virginia Cigarettes
Halftone photograph of display cart, 1920s
Letterpress, 5 13/16 x 9

Plate 39
VILMOS HUSZAR
Miss Blanche Virginia Cigarettes
Display object, 1926
Lithograph, 9 1/4 x 6 5/8 x 3

Plate 40
THEO VAN DOESBURG
Prima Goudsche Kaas (Fine Gouda cheese)
Label, Netherlands, 1919
Lithograph, 7 3/8 diameter

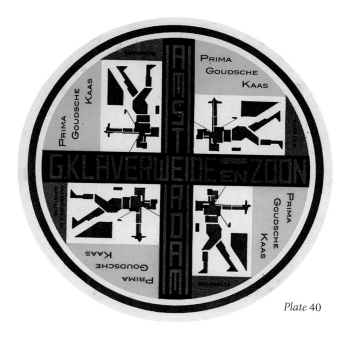

Plate 40

Plate 41

Plate 42

Plate 41
PAUL SCHUITEMA
Centrale Bond 30.000 Transportarbeiders
(Central Union 30,000 transport workers)
Poster, Netherland, 1930
Lithograph, 47 3/4 x 31 1/2

Plate 42
PIET ZWART
Papier: Isolatie (Paper: Insulation)
Advertising sheet, Netherlands, 1925
Letterpress, 11 11/16 x 8 5/16

Plate 43
PIET ZWART
N. C. W. Cable
Catalogue, Netherlands, c. 1928
Letterpress, 12 x 8 3/8

Plate 43

Plate 44

Plate 44
OTTO BAUMBERGER
PKZ
Poster, Switzerland, 1923
Lithograph, 50 1/4 x 35 1/2

Plate 45
JEAN-GEORGES-LEON CARLU
Disques Odéon
Poster, USA, 1929
Lithograph, 99 x 52

Plate 46
EDWARD MCKNIGHT KAUFFER
Vigil, the Pure Silk
Poster, England, 1919
Lithograph, 31 5/8 x 23 1/8

Plate 45

Plate 46

WIRKUNG DER TRANSPARENTE VOM BAHNHOF GESEHEN,

H. BAYER

Plate 47
HERBERT BAYER
Glasmaler Kraus (Glass painter Kraus)
Design for illuminated roof sign
Germany, 1923
Pencil, ink, gouache, pasted paper, 11 1/4 x 8 3/8

Plate 48
HERBERT BAYER
Ventzky Ackergeräte
(Ventzky Agricultural Machinery)
Design for exhibition stand, Germany, 1928
Pencil, gouache, paste, halftone photograph
19 5/8 x 26 13/16

Plate 49
HEINZ LOEW
Design for exhibition, Germany, 1929
Gouache, halftone photographs,
rotogravure, pencil, 21 1/2 x 18

Plate 51

Plate 50

Plate 50

CASSANDRE

Restaurez-vous au wagon-bar
(Refresh yourself at the wagon bar)
Poster, France, 1932
Lithograph, 39 1/2 x 24 1/2

Plate 51

CASSANDRE

L'Atlantique
Poster, France, 1931
Lithograph, 39 3/4 x 25

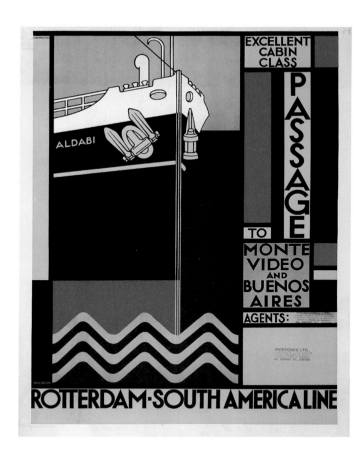

Plate 52

WILLEM HENDRIK GISPEN
Rotterdam–South America Line
Poster, Netherlands, 1927
Lithograph, 33 11/16 x 25 1/4

Plate 53

LEO MARFURT
Flying Scotsman
Poster, Great Britain, 1937
Lithograph, 40 x 50 1/8

Plate 52

Plate 53

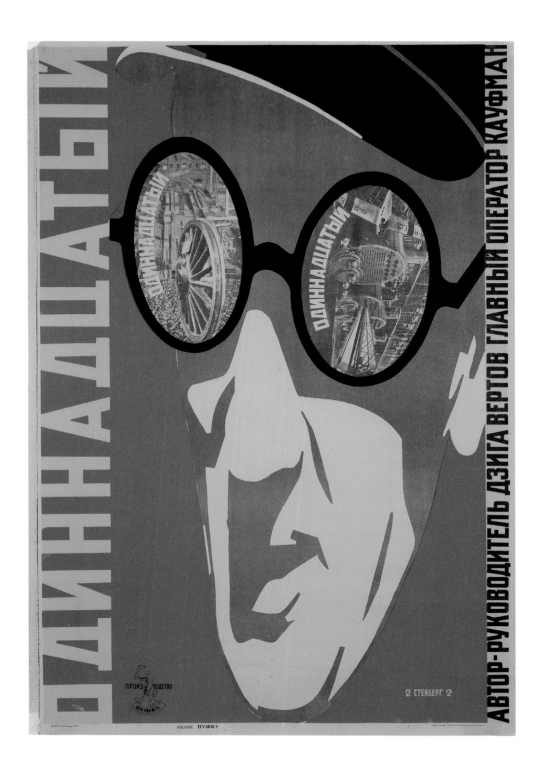

Plate 54
VLADIMIR AVGUSTOVICH STENBERG
AND GEORGII AVGUSTOVICH STENBERG
Odinnadtsatyi (The eleventh)
Poster, USSR, 1928
Lithograph, 37 7/8 x 26 3/4

Plate 55

Plate 56

Plate 55
C. O. MÜLLER
Elisabeth Bergner in Donna Juana
Poster, Germany, 1920s
Letterpress, 47 5/8 x 34 5/8

Plate 56
JAN TSCHICHOLD
Die Frau ohne Namen, Zweiter Teil
(The woman without a name, part two)
Poster, Germany
Lithograph, 48 3/4 x 34

DESIGN AND
SOCIAL CHANGE

Plate 57

Plate 57
EL LISSITZKY
(LAZAR' MARKOVICH LISITSKII)
Russische Ausstellung (Russian exhibition)
Poster, Switzerland, 1929
Rotogravure, 49 3/4 x 35 5/8

Plate 58
LESTER BEALL
Rural Electrification Administration
Poster, USA, c. 1937
Silkscreen, lithograph, 40 x 30

Plate 58

Plate 59

Plate 60

Plate 59

GUSTAV GUSTAVOVICH KLUTSIS
Elektrifikatsiia vsei strany
(Electrification of the entire country)
Design for poster, USSR, 1920
Ink, gouache, gelatin silver prints,
colored paper, pencil, printed letters, paste
18 1/8 x 10 3/4

Plate 60

VLADIMIR VASIL'EVICH LEBEDEV
Soiuz derevni i goroda, rabochie i krest'iane
(The union of country and city,
workers and peasants)
Drawing, USSR, c. 1920
Ink, gouache, 10 1/2 x 8 5/16

Plate 61

B. POPOV AND I. VILKOVIR
Luchshie udarniki (The best shockworkers)
Design for factory wall, USSR, 1931
Gouache, pencil, cut paper, halftone
photographs, paste, hand lettering
9 1/4 x 33 9/16

Plate 62
VASILII NIKOLAEVICH ELKIN
Production
Design for poster, USSR
Halftone photographs, printed letters,
pencil, cut paper, paste, 22 x 16 1/2

Plate 63
VALENTINA NIKIFOROVNA KULAGINA
Stroim (We are building)
Design for poster, USSR, 1929
Watercolor, gouache, sandpaper,
halftone photographs, cut paper,
paste, 22 5/8 x 14 1/4

Plate 63

Plate 61

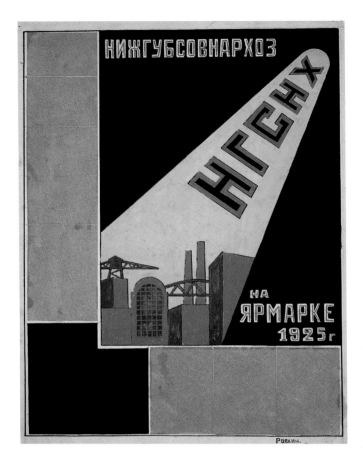

Plate 64

Plate 64
VLADIMIR O. ROSKIN
NGSNKh
(Commissariat of the National Economy)
Design for poster, USSR, 1925
Gouache, pencil, ink, hand lettering
13 1/2 x 10

Plate 65
ALEKSANDR MIKHAILOVICH RODCHENKO
AND VLADIMIR VLADIMIROVICH
MAIAKOVSKII
Daite solntse noch'iu (Give me sun at night)
Design for poster, USSR, 1923
Gouache, ink, pencil, gelatin silver print
4 3/8 x 11 3/16

Plate 65

Plate 67

Plate 68

Plate 66

Plate 66
MAX BURCHARTZ
AND JOHANNIS CANIS
Bochumer Verein (Bochum Union)
Catalogue, Germany, 1929
Lithograph, 11 7/8 x 8 1/2

Plate 67
MAX BURCHARTZ
Rotes Quadrat (Red square)
Collage, Germany
Gouache, halftone photograph,
printed logo, 20 3/8 x 13 7/8

Plate 68
ALEKSANDR MIKHAILOVICH
RODCHENKO
LEF No. 3
Design for magazine cover, USSR, 1924
Halftone photograph, printed letters,
cut paper letters, hand lettering, pencil,
gouache, colored paper, paste
9 1/8 x 6 1/8

Plate 69
MIKHAIL IOSIFOVICH
RAZULEVICH
Sovetskaia vlast' plius elektrifikatsiia
(Soviet power plus electrification)
Vintage photomontage, USSR
Photograph, 6 9/16 x 23

Plate 70
GUSTAV GUSTAVOVICH KLUTSIS
Pod'niat proizvoditel'nost' truda
(Raise the productivity of labor)
Design for poster, USSR, 1933
Ink, pencil, gouache, gelatin silver prints,
hand lettering, handwriting, paste, 9 3/8 x 12

Plate 71
EL LISSITZKY
(LAZAR' MARKOVICH LISITSKII)
Pressa Köln 1928
Book, Germany, 1928
Rotogravure, 8 3/8 x 12 (c. 80 inches
wide fully extended)

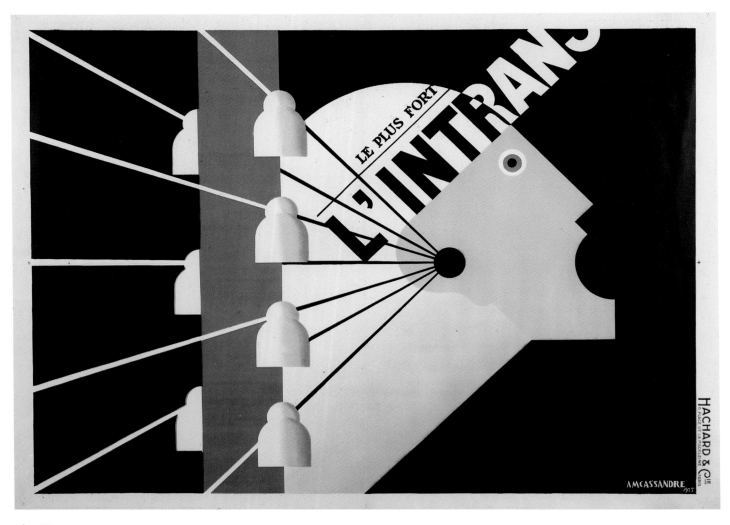

Plate 72

Plate 72
CASSANDRE
L'Intransigéant
Poster, France, 1925
Lithograph, 35 3/8 x 63

Plate 73
MAN RAY
Keeps London Going
Poster, England, 1932
Lithograph, 39 11/16 x 24 1/2

Plate 73

Plate 74
LESTER BEALL
Cross Out Slums
Poster, USA, 1930s
Lithograph, 39 3/4 x 29 7/16

Plates 75–78
LESTER BEALL
Radio, Wash Day, Running Water, Light
Four posters, USA, 1937
Silkscreen, approximately 40 x 30 each

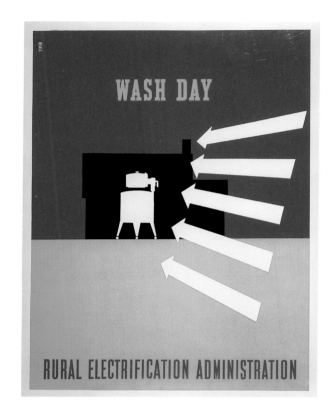

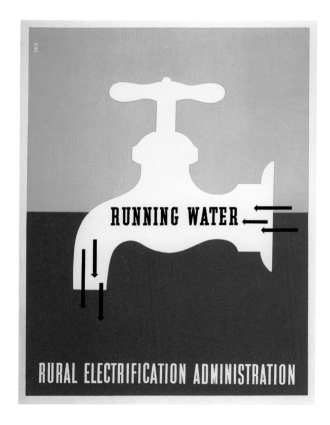

Plate 79
LESTER BEALL
It's Fine for Us
Poster, USA, 1930s
Silkscreen, lithograph, 40 x 29 7/8

Plate 80
DESIGNER UNKNOWN
V pokhod za chistotu
(Get on the march for cleanliness)
Poster, USSR
Lithograph, 26 5/8 x 20 9/16

Plate 81

MARIANNE BRANDT

Nos soeurs d'Amérique (Our American sisters)
Collage, Germany
Halftone photographs, printed letters,
hand lettering, paste, 19 9/16 x 12 5/8

Plate 82

MARIANNE BRANDT

Les sports—le sport
Collage, Germany, 1928
Halftone photographs, printed letters, paste
19 x 12 1/4

Plate 83
GUSTAV GUSTAVOVICH KLUTSIS
Spartakiada Moscow 1928
Design for poster, USSR, 1928
Halftone photographs, gelatin
silver prints, colored paper, paste
23 3/4 x 27 1/2

Plates 84–87
SOLOMON BENEDIKTOVICH
TELINGATER
10 Posters of Exercise and Sports
Four designs for posters, USSR
Halftone photographs, rotogravure
photographs, gouache, colored
paper, paste, hand lettering
Dimensions vary, c. 12 x 10 each

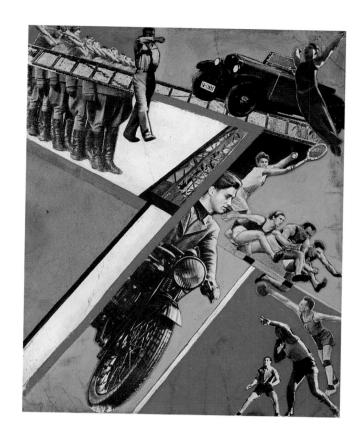

DESIGN AND
POLITICS

Plate 88

Plate 88
VASILII NIKOLAEVICH ELKIN
Da zdravstvuet krasnaia armiia—
vooruzhennyi otriad proletarskoi revoliutsii!
(Long live the Red Army—the armed
detachment of the proletarian revolution!)
Design for poster, USSR, c. 1933
Vintage photomontage with gouache
11 11/16 x 8 5/16

Plate 89
VASILII NIKOLAEVICH ELKIN
Da zdravstvuet krasnaia armiia—
vooruzhennyi otriad proletarskoi revoliutsii!
(Long live the Red Army—the armed
detachment of the proletarian revolution!)
Poster, USSR, 1932
Lithograph, 51 3/8 x 33 7/8

ДА ЗДРАВСТВУЕТ КРАСНАЯ АРМИЯ—
ВООРУЖЕННЫЙ ОТРЯД ПРОЛЕТАРСКОЙ РЕВОЛЮЦИИ!

Plate 89

Plate 90

Plate 91

Plate 92

Plate 90
GUSTAV GUSTAVOVICH KLUTSIS
Real'nost' nashei programmy
(The reality of our program)
Poster, USSR, 1931
Lithograph, 56 3/8 x 40 3/4

Plate 91
GUSTAV GUSTAVOVICH KLUTSIS
Real'nost' nashei programmy
(The reality of our program)
Design for poster, USSR, 1931
Ink, pencil, gelatin silver prints
10 x 14

Plate 92
GUSTAV GUSTAVOVICH KLUTSIS
Real'nost' nashei programmy
(The reality of our program)
Design for poster, USSR, 1931
Photographs, ink, gouache, paste,
photomechanically reproduced letters
9 1/2 x 6 1/2

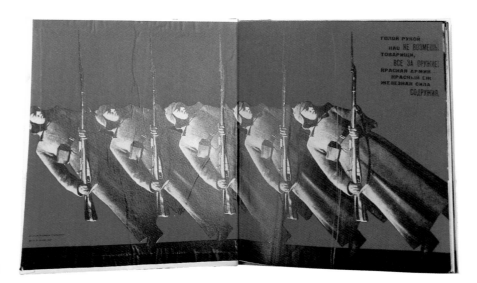

Plate 93

Plate 94

Plate 93
VARVARA FEDOROVNA STEPANOVA
Goloi rukoi nas NE VOZMESH'
(You won't take us with your bare hand)
Book, USSR, c. 1932
Letterpress, 9 9/16 x 17 1/4

Plate 94
VARVARA FEDOROVNA STEPANOVA
(Photograph by IGNATOVITCH)
KREPI chem mozhesh' oboronu!
(Strengthen defense with whatever you can!)
Design for poster, USSR
Photograph pasted on red paper
9 15/16 x 6 7/8

Plate 95
MIKHAIL IOSIFOVICH RAZULEVICH
Shest' uslovii pobedy (Six conditions of victory)
Design for book cover, USSR, 1932
Rotogravure photographs, gouache, cut
paper, paste, 14 3/4 x 11 5/8

Plate 95

Plate 96

Plate 97

Plate 96
JOHN HEARTFIELD
Upton Sinclair: Petroleum
Book jacket, Germany, 1927
Letterpress, 7 7/16 x 18 3/8

Plate 97
JOHN HEARTFIELD
Das letzte Stück Brot
(The last piece of bread)
Poster, Germany, 1932
Lithograph, 37 3/4 x 28 1/2

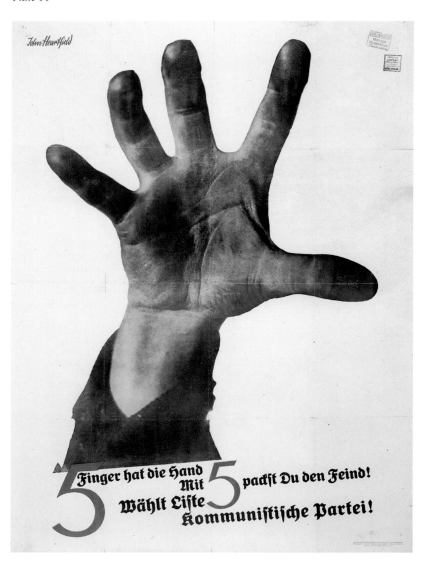

Plate 98

Plate 99

Plate 98

JOHN HEARTFIELD
Hurra! Der Panzerkreuzer ist da!
(Hurray! The warship has arrived!)
Design for magazine cover, Germany, 1927
Vintage photomontage, retouched
8 1/4 x 6 1/8

Plate 99

JOHN HEARTFIELD
5 Finger hat die Hand (Five fingers has the hand)
Poster, Germany, 1928
Lithograph, 39 1/2 x 29 1/8

Plate 100

Plate 101

Plate 100
CHIAREL
Duce a noi (Il Duce for us)
Poster, Italy, 1930s
Lithograph, 12 5/16 x 37

Plate 101
JO VOSKUIL (photograph by CAS OORTHUYS)
De olympiade onder dictatuur
(The Olympics under dictatorship)
Poster, Netherlands, 1936
Rotogravure, letterpress, 22 5/8 x 16 1/4

Plate 102

Plate 102
CESAR DOMELA
Des armes pour l'Espagne antifasciste
(Arms for antifascist Spain)
Poster, France, 1930s
Lithograph, 47 1/8 x 31 7/8

Plate 103
EDWARD MCKNIGHT KAUFFER
Yugoslav People Led by Tito
Poster, USA, 1940s
Lithograph, 24 3/4 x 19 1/4

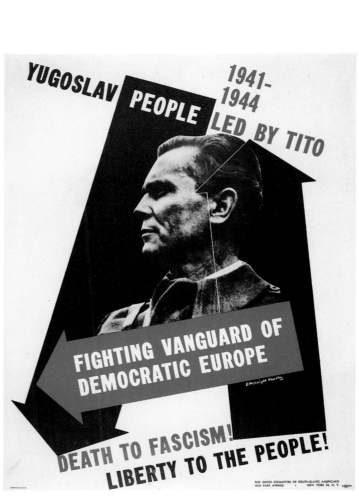

Plate 103

Plate 104

Plate 105

Plate 104
DESIGNER UNKNOWN
Equal Rights for Negroes !Everywhere!
Poster, USA, 1932
Lithograph and letterpress
29 9/16 x 19 1/4

Plate 105
DESIGNER UNKNOWN
Demand Unemployment Insurance Relief.
Vote Communist.
Poster, USA, 1932
Letterpress, 22 x 17

Plate 106
CHARLES TOUCEY COINER
NRA. We Do Our Part.
Poster, USA, 1934
Silkscreen, 28 1/4 x 21

Plate 106

Plate 107
LESTER BEALL
It Mustn't Happen Here
Design for poster, USA, 1930s
Gouache, gelatin silver prints,
pencil, cut paper, 27 1/2 x 19 1/2

ARTISTS' BIOGRAPHIES

ISABEL TAUBE, JENNIFER RAAB, IAN BERRY

NATAN ISAEVICH AL'TMAN
Born in Vinnitsa, Russia, 1889
Died in Leningrad, 1970

Best known for his theater designs and his agitprop decorations for Palace Square, Petrograd (1918), Al'tman experimented with Cubist, Futurist, and Suprematist styles throughout his career. From 1901 to 1907 he studied at the Odessa School of Art, and following his initial artistic training, he exhibited with the *First Izdebskii International Salon* in 1909–10 and with the Society of South Russian Artists in 1910. During this period, he belonged to the group Apartment no. 5 with Vladimir Tatlin, Lev Bruni, and other Russian avant-garde artists, which met in Bruni's apartment for discussions about art. Beginning in 1910 he studied for two years in Paris at the Free Russian Academy of Marie Vassilieff and exhibited at the *Salon* in 1911. On his return to Russia, Al'tman displayed his work with the *World of Art* group in 1913 and 1915–16 and at several avant-garde exhibitions, including the *Union of Youth* (1913–14), *0.10 The Last Futurist Exhibition of Paintings* (1915), and the *Knave of Diamonds* group shows (1916 and 1917).

During the late 1910s and early 1920s, his influence on the Russian art world spread due to his teaching and participation in the founding of a number of art associations in Petrograd. From 1915 to 1917 he instructed at the private school of Mikhail Bernshtein in Petrograd, and from 1918 to 1921 he taught at the SVOMAS (the State Free Art Workshops) in Petrograd. In conjunction with Vladimir Maiakovskii, Vsevolod Meyerhold, and Sergei Tretyakov, among others, Al'tman established the Freedom to Art Association in Petrograd in 1917. In January 1919, he founded the Komfut (Communist Futurism) group with Osip Brik, Maiakovskii, and others. At the same time, he was involved with IZO Narkompros (the Department of Fine Art of the Commissariat of Enlightenment) and contributed to its journal *Iskusstovo kommuny* (Art of the commune) from 1918 to 1919.

Al'tman's work included street decorations, theater designs, paintings, sculpture, book illustrations, and film posters. He exhibited both in Russia and at international venues and served as a commissioner for the *First Exhibition of Russian Art* in Berlin in 1922. He held a one-person show in Leningrad in 1926, and he won gold medals at the 1925 *Exposition international des arts décoratifs et industriels modernes* and at the 1937 *International Exposition*, both in Paris. He lived and worked in Paris from 1928 to 1935 and returned in 1936 to Leningrad, where he designed theater sets and illustrated and designed books. I. T.

JOHANNES BAADER
Born in Stuttgart, Germany, 1876
Died in Bavaria, 1955

German Dada troublemaker Johannes Baader was one of the oldest members of the group that included Raoul Hausmann, Hannah Höch, and Richard Huelsenbeck. The self-appointed Oberdada sometimes went by the name "secret President of the League of Superdadaist Intertelluric Nations" and was a chief instigator of the disorder that frequently occurred at Dada events. In 1918 he commandeered the pulpit in the Berlin Cathedral and sermonized on the exploits of the Dada movement, and he often disrupted meetings and speeches, notably one at the National Assembly. A frequent performer at Dada functions, his contribution was to not appear occasionally when scripted, leaving chaos and confusion in his absence. He published *Green Cadaver*, a supplement to a nonexistent newspaper, and in it proclaimed Dada as a means to world revolution. Sometimes thought to be mad, Baader wrote a book that consisted of letters to Kaiser Wilhelm and Jesus Christ. He created his most famous work, *Plastic-Dada-Dio-Drama,* in 1920. The large architectural sculpture, made of collected rubbish, was a response to Vladimir Tatlin's *Monument to the Third International*. Baader is best known not for his art but for his many provocations that secured attention for Dada within the European media. I. B.

GIACOMO BALLA
Born in Turin, Italy, 1871
Died in Rome, 1958

Balla attended the Albertina Academy in Turin from 1886 to 1889 and studied photography soon after. He settled in Rome in 1895, working for the next five years as an illustrator and as a private teacher to Umberto Boccioni, Gino Severini, and others. In 1900 he traveled to Paris; there he was exposed to Impressionism and Neo-Impressionism, which influenced his style on his return to Italy. His early paintings depicted personal drama through a careful examination of reality, and by 1910 he had become an established artist. His work reflected his deep interest in capturing the quality of light and motion, which he later represented in the abstract. Balla signed the first *Manifesto of Futurist Painters* in 1910, beginning his critical involvement with the movement he helped to found.

During his Futurist years, Balla explored scientific theories of light diffusion onto the canvas. The movement was also concerned with the artistic rendering of speed, which Balla achieved through the use of abstract rhythms and contrasting colors. He signed the other Futurist manifestos until 1931, when he left the group and began to paint more conventionally. Balla was also involved in innovative theater, designing stage sets that enlisted all the visual arts by unifying music, lights, and action on the stage with functional stage design—one that might include revolving panels and mobile floors to create a sense of continuous action. In addition, whenever possible the artist acted on the stage; Balla also designed fabrics and furniture, worked on graphics for advertising, and experimented with "concrete" poetry. J. R.

OTTO BAUMBERGER
Born in Zurich, 1889
Died in Zurich, 1961

Baumberger is best known for his fundamental role in the establishment of a Swiss school of graphic design at the beginning of this century and for his 1923 poster designs for Burger-Kehl, Zurich's renowned men's clothier. His most famous poster features a large-scale depiction of a coat whose "PKZ" label also serves as the poster's text. Baumberger spent most of his life in Zurich, with brief periods of schooling in Munich, Paris, and London. In Zurich, he apprenticed with a lithographer, and in 1911 he began to create advertising and poster designs. In 1914 he became affiliated with the Wolfensberger printing firm, which actively promoted the Swiss poster and allowed artists to supervise the printing themselves. As early as 1918 Baumberger attempted to make his advertising images as objective and straightforward as possible. After World War I, he was actively involved in set design, and by 1920 he was working for Max Reinhardt's Deutsches Theater in Berlin and for the Stadtheater and Schauspielhaus in Zurich. I. T.

WILLI BAUMEISTER
Born in Stuttgart, Germany, 1889
Died in Stuttgart, Germany, 1955

Baumeister worked as a painter's apprentice from 1905 to 1907 before attending the Kunstakademie in Stuttgart, where he was deeply influenced by Adolf Hölzel. His paintings were exhibited in Zurich in 1912 and appeared the next year in the *First German Autumn Salon* in Berlin. He collaborated with his friend Oskar Schlemmer, among others, on a wall frieze for the 1914 Cologne Werkbund exhibition, and would return to this medium after the war. Before World War I, Baumeister traveled to Paris, where he was most notably influenced by Paul Cézanne, developing a style that fused Cubism and Constructivism. During the war he served as a soldier in the Balkans and Caucacus Mountains before resettling in Stuttgart to work as a typesetter, stage designer, and architectural perspective artist. In 1924 he came into contact with Fernand Léger, whose work profoundly influenced his own.

In 1928 Baumeister was given a professorship at the Frankfurt School of Art, and his career was boosted when he became a member of the groups Cercle et Carré in 1930 and

Abstraction-Création in 1933. His paintings moved from more abstract compositions to configurations having "primitive"—often African—symbolism. With the rise of fascism in Germany, however, his art was deemed "degenerate" by Hitler's government, and he was dismissed from his post in Frankfurt and banned from exhibiting. Unlike most artists thus condemned, Baumeister remained in his homeland during World War II, spending much of his time experimenting in a paint factory in Wuppertal. He was reinstated as a professor after the war ended and resumed painting. His later work explored his metaphysical and scientific views through abstract, colorful, geometric shapes, which were especially popular in the 1950s. J. R.

HERBERT BAYER
Born in the Haag, Austria, 1900
Died in Santa Barbara, California, 1985

Throughout his long career, Bayer played a significant role in the development of typography and advertising design. A member of the first generation of Bauhaus students, he perpetuated the school's aim to integrate all aspects of artistic creativity into the modern industrial world. After serving in the Austrian army during World War I from 1917 to 1918, he apprenticed with architects in Linz and Darmstadt before entering the Bauhaus in 1921. He was a student there until 1923, studying mural painting with Vassily Kandinsky and experimenting with typography, creating the Universal alphabet, which consisted only of lowercase letters. This alphabet, along with Bayer's sans-serif type and his economical style of design, became the hallmark of many Bauhaus publications. After spending some years at the Monte Verità colony—a retreat for artists and philosophers in Ascona, Italian Switzerland—he returned in 1925 to the Bauhaus, which had moved from Weimar to Dessau, and taught advertising, layout, and typography until 1928. He was a leader in the development of new trends in these areas; he reacted against the decorative compositions of earlier periods and promoted well-ordered and economically rendered images and forms of type.

In 1928 he left the Bauhaus to become a commercial artist, and for the next ten years, he based his business in Berlin. Bayer worked as art manager for *Vogue* from 1929 to 1930 and as director of the Dorland advertising agency. In 1938 he emigrated to the United States, where he remained for the rest of his life, working as a painter, sculptor, and designer. From 1938 to 1948 he lived and worked in New York. He later moved to Colorado and served as a design consultant for the development of the town of Aspen (1946–76), for the Container Corporation of America (1945–56), and for the Atlantic Richfield Company (1966). He also worked with photography and in the field of environmental design. Bayer had a profound influence on two generations of graphic designers. I. T.

LESTER BEALL
Born in Kansas City, 1903
Died in New York City, 1969

After receiving a degree in art history from the University of Chicago, Beall started a freelance graphic design firm in 1926. He had a rather conservative style until he became interested in avant-garde European typography. In the early 1930s, Fred Hauk, an art director at the agency Batten, Barton, Durstine and Osborne, who had studied with Hans Hoffman, introduced Beall to Bauhaus design. In 1935 he moved his practice to New York, where he pursued a variety of advertising projects from package design to corporate identity programs to posters. For each client, Beall strove to develop an original and practical design by carefully researching the company, its staff, its facilities, and its products. Several of his corporate logos, including the one he created for International Paper, are still in use today. In 1937 he became the first American graphic designer to have a solo show at the Museum of Modern Art. During the 1930s and 1940s, Beall designed his most famous posters for the U.S. Rural Electrification Administration. The posters revealed the artist's distinctly American version of European modernism. In 1952 he opened an office at Dumbarton Farm in Connecticut, closing his New York office in 1955. Throughout his life Beall worked as both an artist and a designer, best known for his clear, functional designs and his claim that there is really no distinction between art and design.   I. T. and J. R.

HENRYK BERLEWI
Born in Warsaw, 1894
Died in Paris, 1967

Berlewi attended the School of Art in Warsaw from 1904 to 1909 before moving to Antwerp and then to Paris, where he attended the Ecole des Beaux-Arts from 1910 to 1912. Influenced by Futurism and the Russian avant-garde, he helped originate Polish Constructivism. After living in Berlin in 1922–23, he returned to Warsaw, where he joined the Constructivist group Blok. The year 1924 brought new beginnings, public recognition, and professional development for Berlewi. He exhibited his work in a solo show at the Warsaw branch of the Austro-Daimler automobile company, an exhibition that literally united art and technology. He published the booklet *Mechano Faktura* (Mechanotexture), and he established an advertising company called Reklama-Mechano. His paintings from this period consist of geometric shapes and flat colors applied as though intended for mechanical reproduction. His advertising designs combine geometric forms with expressive typography. In 1927 his career took a dramatic shift—he began to paint portraits in response to the new classicism that was sweeping Europe. After 1928 Berlewi

spent the rest of his life in Paris, where he established the *Archives de l'art abstrait de l'avant-garde international* in 1960. His late works invoke many of the principles and formal qualities of Op Art.   I. T.

FRANCIS BERNARD
Born in Marseilles, France, 1900 (living as of 1995)

Bernard, a French designer and poster artist, attended the Ecole Supérieure de Commerce in Marseilles and the Ecole Nationale des Beaux-Arts in Paris. In 1930 he began working as a book illustrator and soon broadened his repertoire to include posters, cartoons, and advertising displays. In 1945 he became head of publicity for the Radiodiffusion-Télévision Française. Later he was appointed art director of the Salon des Arts Mènagers and became a member of the Union des Artistes Modernes. Bernard exhibited in the Alliance Graphique Internationale shows and in 1957 was awarded a Diploma of Honor at the Milan Triennale.   J. R.

MARIANNE BRANDT
Born in Chemnitz, Germany, 1893
Died in Kirchberg, Germany, 1983

Although Brandt is most famous for her metalwork, particularly her lamps, she also made poster designs and collages. From 1911 to 1914 she studied painting and sculpture at the Kunstakademie in Weimar. In 1919 she went to Paris to study for a year. Around 1923 she began studying at the Bauhaus, and after completing the required foundation course, she followed László Moholy-Nagy's advice and joined the metal workshop. Her work corresponds to the developments at the Bauhaus, from its craft orientation during the Weimar years (1919–25) to its interest in technology and industrial design throughout the Dessau period (1925–33). Her lamps were mass-produced, and their great success helped earn the Bauhaus a leading role in industrial design. After Moholy-Nagy left the Bauhaus, Brandt became head of the metal workshop from 1928 until 1929, when she left the school and worked briefly for Walter Gropius's studio in Berlin. For several years, she was a designer at the metal factory of Ruppelwerk in Gotha/Thuringia before eventually retreating to her birthplace, Chemnitz, in 1932 to become an independent designer. In 1949 she began teaching at the Hochschule für Bildende Künste in Dresden, and from 1951 to 1954 she instructed at the Institut für Angewandte Kunst (Institute for Applied Art) in Berlin.   I. T.

MAX BURCHARTZ
Born in Elberfeld, Germany, 1887
Died in Essen, Germany, 1961

Burchartz, a graphic and industrial designer, actively confronted the problems of advertising and graphic design throughout his career; he is best known for his inclusion of photography in his printed work. He studied in Düsseldorf, Munich, and Berlin between 1906 and 1908 and visited Paris in 1910. Following World War I, he lived in Hannover, where he met Kurt Schwitters and El Lissitzky, and in Weimar, where he encountered Theo van Doesburg, Paul Klee, and Wassily Kandinsky. These contacts were critical to his artistic development. In the 1920s, he founded the advertising agency Werbebau in Bochum and wrote pamphlets to disseminate his ideas about modern advertising. In 1926 he went to Essen to work for the staff of the Folkswangschule and taught photography, commercial art, typography, and advertising design. The rise of fascism led to his dismissal in 1933, but he returned in 1949. In the interim, he had his own industrial design business in Essen. In his later years, he published several writings elaborating on his ideas from the 1920s.
    I. T.

JEAN-GEORGES-LEON CARLU
Born in Bonnières-sur-Seine, France, 1900
(living as of 1995)

Carlu is known for his dramatic, direct posters employing geometrical forms and minimal text. He grew up in a family of architects and began his training in architecture. In 1918, however, after an accident in which he lost his right arm, he turned his focus to graphic design. From 1918 to 1923 he, like A. M. Cassandre, integrated the Cubist style into his designs. He favored an emphasis on the formal aspects of the poster, including line, color, and composition, rather than on the representation or illustration itself. By the time Paris was invaded in 1940, Carlu was safely living and working in the United States. In 1941 he created the first U.S. defense poster for the Office of War Information. Between 1945 and 1953 he produced designs for several American firms and organized a French educational and commercial exhibition in the United States. He returned in 1953 to France, where he designed posters until his retirement in 1974.
    I. T.

CASSANDRE (ADOLPHE JEAN-MARIE MOURON)
Born in Kharhiv, Ukraine, 1901
Died in Paris, 1968

Adolphe Jean-Marie Mouron adopted the name Cassandre soon after he began designing posters in the early 1920s. Born in the Ukraine to French parents, he moved to Paris in 1918, where he studied painting briefly at the Ecole des Beaux-Arts, then entered Lucien Simon's studio, and completed his training at the Académie de la Grande Chaumière and at the Académie Julian. After obtaining a strong background in painting, he turned to poster design in 1922–23, signing his images "A.M.Cassandre." His style, with its rigid geometric forms, restrained use of color, and dynamic lines, recalls some of the compositional elements of Cubist and Purist painting movements that dominated the Paris art scene of this period.

In the late 1920s and 1930s, at the height of his success, Cassandre helped to promote graphic design and received numerous commissions from French and foreign firms. His book *Revue de l'union de l'affiche* (1926), drew connections between modern design and ancient and medieval equivalents. With Charles Loupot and Maurice Moyrand, he founded the Alliance Graphique in 1930. He also ran his own art school in 1934–35. During this time, he began to design typefaces, including the advertising display face Bifur (1927), the sans-serif display face Acier (1930), and the all-purpose typeface Peignot (1937). The Museum of Modern Art organized an exhibition of his work in 1936. During the winters of 1936–37 and 1937–38, he remained in New York, working for *Harper's Bazaar*. Following his return to Paris in 1938, Cassandre focused on painting. Beginning in the 1940s, he became preoccupied with stage designs and continued to create typefaces, including one for Olivetti in 1958. By the 1960s, his artistic production had dwindled, though he did produce the well-known logo for Yves Saint Laurent and several paintings in this decade. He committed suicide in 1968. I. T.

CHIAREL
Active in Italy
No further information available

CHARLES TOUCEY COINER
Born in Santa Barbara, California, 1898
Died in Mechanicsville, Pennsylvania, 1989

Following his studies in commercial art at the Chicago Academy of Fine Arts, Coiner worked as a designer for six years in the Chicago office of the advertising agency Erwin and Wasey. He then moved to Philadelphia to join the art department at N. W. Ayer, one of America's most prominent advertising agencies. At this time, N. W. Ayer promoted a progressive and modern style that corresponded with Coiner's own ideas. Coiner began by creating advertisements for such luxury goods as automobiles, jewelry, and pianos; during the Depression, he designed a widely used symbol, the "Blue Eagle," for the National Recovery Administration (NRA). During World War II, although he had numerous advertising accounts at N. W. Ayer, he again accepted projects for the government such as the design of symbols for the Citizens's Defense Corps (CDC), which would have directed ambulance drivers, rescue squads, and others in the event of war on American soil. In 1964, after serving as art director for thirty-five years, Coiner retired from N. W. Ayer to pursue his interests in nature and painting. In addition to developing a distinct modern design style, Coiner was instrumental in bringing European artists, including Cassandre, to the United States, as well as encouraging such American designers as Lester Beall. I. T.

JEAN CROTTI
Born in Bulle, Switzerland, 1878
Died in Paris, 1958
Born in Switzerland, Crotti moved to Paris in 1901, where he remained for most of his life. He studied painting at the Académie Julian, and his early work reflects the influence first of Impressionism, then of Fauvism and Art Nouveau. Beginning about 1910 he entered a Cubist phase. From 1914 to 1916 he lived in New York, where he met fellow European exiles Francis Picabia and Marcel Duchamp. In the fall of 1915, while sharing a studio with Duchamp, Crotti became actively involved in the New York Dada movement. As a result of his interactions with Duchamp and other members of the New York avant-garde, Crotti changed his working methods and style, incorporating words and typography into his paintings and reliefs. After returning to Paris in 1916, he divorced his first wife, Yvonne, and in 1919 married Suzanne Duchamp, Marcel's sister. Together, they established an artistic enterprise of their own creation, Tabu, an extension of Dada. In the 1930s, following various experiments with kaleidoscopes and color light projections, Crotti developed a technique for creating pictures out of colored glass, called Gemmaux, which he patented in 1939. His late paintings consist of visionary images dealing with themes of birth, death, and the galaxies. I. T.

FORTUNATO DEPERO
Born in Fondo, Italy, 1892
Died in Rovereto, Italy, 1960
An Austrian born in Italy, Depero participated in the second wave of Futurism after World War I. Little is known about his early training. In 1910 he went to Turin to serve as an apprentice decorator at the *Esposizione Internazionale*. After spending a year as a marble-worker, he decided to become a painter. In 1913 he

published a collection of poetry, prose, and illustrations and moved to Rome, where he met Filippo Tommaso Marinetti at Giuseppe Spovieri's Galleria Permanente Futurista, where Depero exhibited with the Futurists in the spring of 1914. The following year Depero and Balla co-signed the manifesto *Ricostruzione futurista dell'universo* (March 1915) just before Depero's departure for the front. Both artists advocated animating the world with dynamic sculptural forms constructed from diverse materials.

After his discharge from the army because of poor health, Depero returned to art-making, experimenting with new media and techniques. Like many Futurists, he also worked in the theater, creating stage sets and costumes for Igor Stravinsky's *Le chant du rossignol* and other productions. Depero created marionettes for the *Balli plastici*, performed in Rome in 1918. He established the Casa d'Arte Depero in 1919, also called the Casa d'Arte Futurista, where he and his wife, Rosetta Depero, designed and produced household items, tapestries, and advertising posters. During the 1920s, he created covers for *Vogue* and *Emporium* and managed publicity for the Campari company. From 1928 to 1930 he visited France and the United States. In the 1930s, he served as an art critic and continued to produce decorative commissions and exhibition designs. The Galleria Museo Depero, which houses much of his work, opened to the public in 1959. I. T.

WALTER DEXEL
Born in Munich, 1890
Died in 1973
Dexel began his studies in art history at the Universities of Munich and Jena. In 1916 he graduated with a doctorate from Jena and became the director of Jena's Art Union, remaining there until 1928. During this period, he organized many exhibitions for German Expressionist groups, including shows of Wassily Kandinsky, Oskar Schlemmer, and Paul Klee for Der Sturm Gallery and for the Bauhaus. He also exhibited his own work at Der Sturm in 1918, 1920, and 1925 and was represented in major international exhibitions in Paris and Moscow. In 1927 Dexel organized *New Advertising*, one of the first exhibitions to survey the trends and developments in early twentieth-century commercial design. Dexel was a Constructivist painter, though especially interested in typography and commercial art. In addition to his contacts at the Bauhaus between 1921 and 1923, Dexel developed a close friendship with Theo van Doesburg, one of the founders of De Stijl. In 1925 Adolf Meyer and Ernst May invited Dexel to Frankfurt to work as an advertising consultant, and, beginning in 1928 he taught commercial art at the School of Arts and Crafts in Magdeburg. He remained there until he was discharged for being "decadent" in 1935. In 1937 his paintings were included in the *Entartete Kunst* (Degenerate art) exhibition in

Munich. From 1936 to 1942, he was on the faculty at the State College of Art Education in Berlin-Schöneberg. Thereafter, until 1955, he worked on building up the *Formsammlung der Stadt Braunschweig*. Following a 1961 retrospective of Der Sturm at the National Gallery in Berlin, Dexel's work was rediscovered and shown in numerous solo exhibitions. I. T.

THEO VAN DOESBURG (CHRISTIAN EMIL MARIE KÜPPER)
Born in Utrecht, the Netherlands, 1883
Died in Davos, Switzerland, 1931

Champion of Neoplasticism, Doesburg began his artistic career making copies of masterworks by Rembrandt, Jan Vermeer, and Frans Hals. After military service in 1914–15, he met painter Piet Mondrian and architect J. J. P. Oud, with whom he discussed his plans to create a magazine called *De Stijl*. During these years he also continued to write reviews and articles, and in 1917 *De Stijl* was founded with Piet Mondrian, Bart van der Leck, and others. The magazine provided a platform for writers, artists, and architects to contribute to a "new art" that would represent the modern age with blocks of primary colors and an emphasis on horizontal and vertical line. An outspoken proponent of the De Stijl philosophy, Doesburg published his first book *The New Movement in Painting* in 1917, while his artwork grew to incorporate designs for stained glass windows, tile floors, and other interior schemes.

While at the Weimar Bauhaus in the mid-1920s, Doesburg published another book, *Fundamentals of the New Art*, created architectural designs, and continued his Dada work in an offshoot of *De Stijl*, the journal *Mécano*. He also published Dadaist poems and "anti-philosophy" under the pseudonyms I. K. Bonset and Aldo Camini, and designed the interior of the Café Aubette in Strasbourg with Hans Arp and Sophie Taeuber-Arp. In 1930, he published the only issue of the magazine *Art concret*. Van Doesburg died suddenly in 1931, and the last issue of *De Stijl*, dedicated to him, appeared one year later. I. B.

CESAR DOMELA (-NIEUWENHUIS)
Born in Amsterdam, 1900

Domela was a self-taught artist who began his career painting landscapes and still lifes in the style of Synthetic Cubism. While traveling to Jena, Bern, and Berlin, he encountered Constructivist artists, and in 1923 he exhibited with the November-gruppe in Berlin. After moving to Paris, he became friends with Theo van Doesburg and Piet Mondrian and joined De Stijl. In 1927 he moved to Berlin and pursued advertising commissions for such clients as AEG and Ruths-Speicher. He also made posters and did printing work for anarchist publications. He experimented with typography and photomontage techniques, which eventually led to his exploration of three-dimensional art forms. In 1931 he organized the first large international exhibition of photomontage for the Staatliche Kunstbibliothek. In 1933 Domela fled Berlin with his family and moved to Paris, where he established a silkscreen studio. He continued to develop the relief technique that he had begun in Berlin, using hard materials like crocodile leather and rosewood in conjunction with painting. Beginning in 1937, together with Sophie Taeuber-Arp, Hans Arp, and George L. K. Morris, he established the magazine of abstract art *Plastique*. After the war he continued to refine the construction of his reliefs and designed several for architectural settings. I. T.

VASILII NIKOLAEVICH ELKIN
Born in 1897
Active in Russia
No further information available

WERNER DAVID FEIST
Born in Augsburg, Germany, 1909

Feist trained at the Bauhaus in Dessau from 1927 to 1930, taking the *Vorkurs*—a "preliminary" course—with Josef Albers. He also took classes with Paul Klee and Wassily Kandinsky in painting, with Walter Peterhans in photography, collaborated with Oskar Schlemmer on his theater projects, and studied advertising with Joost Schmidt. After completing his training he moved to Prague, where he found employment as a commercial artist. From 1933 to 1939, he was an independent graphic designer and commercial photographer with such clients as Twentieth Century Fox and AB Film. He began to experiment with color photography at this time. In March 1939, following the German seizure of Czechoslovakia, he fled to Poland and then to Great Britain. During World War II, he served in Britain's Military Intelligence. Many of his family members were sent to concentration camps, and much of his early work was destroyed. After the war, he assumed the position of studio leader and art director at the London publishing firm Creative Journals, working on a variety of publications. In 1951 he moved to Canada, where he continued to work as an art director for several advertising agencies and as a lecturer in art at various colleges. He resides in Côte-St.-Luc, Montreal. I. T.

WILLEM HENDRIK GISPEN
Born in Amsterdam, 1890
Died in The Hague, 1981

An industrial designer, Gispen is known primarily for his sleek Bauhaus-influenced lamp designs. Also an accomplished graphic artist and furniture designer, Gispen began his education in architecture at the Academy of Fine Arts in Rotterdam, where he was a student from 1913 to 1915. During time spent in England he was exposed to the Arts and Crafts Movement, and he soon established a design studio in Rotterdam. His store Het Gulden Vlies opened in 1916, and three years later he founded Gispen's Industrieele Ondernemingen, also in Rotterdam. In 1920 he met architect J. J. P. Oud and became involved with the theories of De Stijl and the Bauhaus. I. B.

GEORGE GROSZ
Born in Berlin, 1893
Died in Berlin, 1959

Grosz, born Georg Grosz, anglicized his name during the German campaign against Britain in 1916. He was a painter, illustrator, and draftsman who made caricatures and images with overt political messages. He grew up in the provincial town of Stolp (now Slupsk, Poland), where he attended the Oberrealschule, from which he was dismissed for unruly behavior. From 1909–11, he studied at the Akademie der Künste in Dresden. In 1912 he moved to Berlin and trained with Emil Orlik at the Kunstgewerbeschule, and the following year he went to the Académie Colarossi in Paris. His early artistic training was grounded in the academic tradition, but after the war, which profoundly affected him, he began to experiment and to instill his works with political significance. He invested his art with a pessimistic worldview, creating a biting critique of German society.

In 1915 Grosz met John Heartfield and his brother, Wieland. The following year, he shared a studio with John and contributed to Wieland's left-wing literary-political journal *Neue Jugend*. In 1918, along with the two brothers and Richard Huelsenbeck, he was a founding member of the Berlin Dada group. He developed the technique of photomontage and exhibited his works with other Dada artists. In 1920, with Heartfield, Raoul Hausmann, Hannah Höch, and Otto Dix, he participated in the Dada-Messe. He also contributed to the Dada publication *Der Blutige Ernst*. During the mid- to late 1920s, Grosz created his most famous works—paintings and prints that viciously attacked those in power, including rich industrialists and members of the military and judicial elite. In 1933 he emigrated to the United States, where he taught at the Art Students League until 1955. In 1959 he returned to West Berlin, where he died shortly after his arrival. I. T.

RAOUL HAUSMANN
Born in Vienna, 1886
Died in Limoges, France, 1971

Hausmann, a central figure in the Berlin Dada movement, spent his career experimenting with various media in search of a new language of forms and signs to express the modern age. He was steeped in the academic artistic tradition by his first teacher, his father Victor Hausmann (1859–1920). In 1900 his family moved to Berlin, where he met Johannes Baader, an artist-architect who later became active in Berlin Dada. By the early 1910s Hausmann was blending an Expressionist manner with the styles of such artists as Fernand Léger, Alexander Archipenko, Robert Delaunay, and Sonia Delaunay, whose work he saw exhibited at Herwarth Walden's Der Sturm Gallery. In 1915 he met Hans Richter and Hannah Höch, who became his close companion until 1922, when he divorced his first wife and within a year married Hedwig (Heta) Mankiewitz. In addition to producing paintings during this period, he also wrote theoretical and satirical pieces for *Der Sturm, Die Aktion,* and *Die freie Strasse* among other publications.

By 1917 he was acquainted with Richard Huelsenbeck, George Grosz, John Heartfield, and Wieland Herzfelde, who formed the core of the Berlin Dada group from 1918 to 1922. Hausmann now abandoned oil painting and woodcuts in favor of new visual and auditory art forms. His work included "poster-poems" and "optophonetic" poetry that consisted of random sequences of letters as phonetic sounds, assemblages, and photocollages. He participated in Dada events and exhibitions, including the *Dada-Messe,* an important exhibition in 1920 that challenged art movements, politics, and German militarism. In the late 1920s, Hausmann gave up photomontage and turned to drawing, photography, and stream-of-consciousness fiction. He wrote numerous articles about photography for *A bis Z, Camera,* and other periodicals. After Hitler's accession to power, Hausmann fled with his family to the island of Ibiza, where he documented indigenous architecture. Following the war, he lived in Paris, Zurich, and Prague before settling in Limoges, France, where he took up painting again for the first time since the 1920s. Beginning in the 1950s, he turned to writing autobiographical books. I. T.

JOHN HEARTFIELD
Born in Berlin, 1891
Died in Berlin, 1968

Heartfield is known for his innovative use of photomontage as a political tool. Born Helmut Herzfeld in Berlin, he anglicized his name in 1916 in an antinationalist response to a campaign against the British. He grew up in Switzerland and then lived in several Austrian foster homes. After a traumatic childhood that included the persecution of his father for his political beliefs and his parents' subsequent abandonment of their children, he and his brother, Wieland, settled in Wiesbaden, Germany, in 1905. There he became an apprentice to a bookseller and later an assistant in a painter's studio. His formal artistic training began in 1907 at the Munich Königliche Kunstgewerbeschule, where he specialized in poster design. He completed his studies at the Kunstgewerbeschule in Berlin, where he moved with his brother in 1913. In Berlin, the Heartfields began to make contact with avant-garde circles. In 1914 Heartfield was conscripted into military service but was released from active duty after claiming to have had a nervous breakdown. He then worked as the director of the Military Educational Film Service.

After the war, Heartfield destroyed his early work and decided that his art should have a social message and should focus on social realities. Beginning in 1916 he shared a studio with George Grosz, and along with Wieland (who changed his last name to Herzfelde), Richard Huelsenbeck, and others, they established the Berlin Dada group in 1918. That same year, Heartfield became a member of the Communist Party, for which he produced posters and literature until 1933. He created designs and photomontages for its periodicals, including *Der Knüppel* (1923–27) and *Rote Fahne,* whose front cover often contained a photomontage. He also designed book jackets, books, theater sets, banners, and agitprop decorations, and he created photomontages for the magazine *Arbeiter Illustrierte Zeitung (AIZ)*. From 1927 until his exile in London in 1938, he worked regularly for *AIZ*. In keeping with his Dadaist and activist view of his art, Heartfield was insistent that his photomontages not be seen as sacred, one-of-a-kind works but rather that they serve as effective political propaganda aimed at a broad public audience. First aimed against the Weimar Republic and later against the Nazi regime, Heartfield's Communist works incorporated pictures from books, magazines, photographic agencies, and newspapers. After fleeing to London in 1938 he took a position at the publishing house of Drummond. In 1950 he returned to East Germany, where he focused on creating stage designs. I. T. and J. R.

HANNAH HOCH
Born in Gotha, Germany, 1889
Died in Berlin, 1978

Hannah Höch, born Johanne Höch, was the only woman regularly associated with the Berlin Dada group. After moving to Berlin in 1912 she enrolled in the Städtischen Kunstgewerbe und Handwerksschule, the decorative arts school in the Charlottenberg section of the city, but her studies were interrupted by World War I. Following the war, she attended the Lehranstalt des Kunstgewerbemuseums in Berlin, where she studied under Emil Orlik until 1920. During that time she supported herself by working at the Berlin newspaper and magazine publishing house Ullstein Verlag. In 1915 she met Raoul Hausmann, and they joined the Berlin Dada group in 1918. Höch and Hausmann both experimented with painting, collage, and photomontage and participated in the exhibitions, demonstrations, and multimedia events organized by the Dada artists. Her best-known photomontage is titled *Cut with the Dada Kitchen Knife Through the Last Era of the Weimar Beer-Belly Culture* (1919–20). In 1922, after a tempestuous and destructive relationship, Höch left Hausmann and, in turn, the Berlin Dada group, though she still collaborated with Dada artists Kurt Schwitters and Jean Arp on several projects from 1922 to 1925. In 1939, in response to the Nazi rise to power, she retreated from the art world and moved to a small suburb of Berlin. She continued to work there, producing several pieces that comment on the situation in Germany under Nazi rule. I. T.

VILMOS HUSZAR
Born in Budapest, 1884
Died in Hierden, the Netherlands, 1960

Huszár trained at the Academy of Applied Arts in Budapest from 1901 to 1903 before attending the academy in Munich in 1904. After returning to Hungary, he briefly belonged to the artists' colonies of Tecsö and Nagybánya and in 1906 moved to The Hague, where he became a portrait painter for the local aristocracy. In 1916 Huszár met Theo van Doesburg, who admired the artist's work in stained glass. The following year, together with Doesburg and others, Huszár became one of the founding members of the magazine *De Stijl*, designing the cover of the first issue and contributing several articles. His association with *De Stijl* ended in 1923, when he returned to figurative painting. Throughout the 1910s and 1920s, he worked as a typographer and collaborated with the architects P. Klaarhamer and Piet Zwart on interior designs. By the mid-1920s, he had become friendly with Kurt Schwitters, El Lissitzky, and numerous Hungarian avant-garde artists and lived in Paris for short periods. During World War II, he settled in Harderwijk in the Netherlands in an attempt to escape Nazi persecution. I. T.

MARCEL JANCO
Born in Bucharest, Romania, 1895
Died in Ein Hod, Israel, 1986

After aligning himself with the Romanian avant-garde through an association with the journal *Symbolul*, Marcel Janco enrolled as an architecture student at the Zurich Polytechnic. There he made the acquaintance of Hans Arp and Tristan Tzara, and became immersed in the nightlife scene that would become the Cabaret Voltaire. With Tzara, Arp, Hugo Ball, and Emmy Hennings, he helped create the Zurich Dada movement, which held many soirees at the infamous café. Janco involved himself with the decorations, posters, and costumes for the nightly events and exhibited his sculptural reliefs and plaster on burlap paintings on the café walls. He also collaborated on many Dada publications, including the 1916 *Dada Collection,* in which his woodcuts were reproduced. Janco was a founding member of the group Das neue Leben (The new life), and Radical Artists, both with Arp, Alberto Giacometti, Sophie Taeuber, and others. After a break with Tzara in 1921 he left for Paris, where he expressed disapproval of the growing Surrealist movement. He continued to regularly show his work in Romania and became the founder and editor of the avant-garde magazine *Contimporanul*. In 1942 Janco fled to Tel Aviv and began exhibiting his work at the Tel Aviv Museum. He represented Israel at the Venice Biennale of 1952, and in 1953 he established the artist's colony Ein Hod, where he lived until his death.   I. B.

VASILII VASIL'EVICH KAMENSKII
Born in Borovskoe, Russia, 1864
Died in Moscow, 1961

Kamenskii moved to St. Petersburg in 1906 to study agriculture but soon began writing poetry and editing the journal *Vesna*. He was introduced to Futurism after meeting David Burlyuk in 1909. Kamenskii co-wrote his first book, *A Trap for Judges,* in 1910. The book, a joint anthology on painted paper to which Kamenskii contributed Primitivist poems, was the first product of Russian Futurism. After a brief, unsuccessful attempt at stunt-piloting, he returned in 1913 to organize a Futurist tour of Russia, which promoted the movement through evenings of poetry and lectures on Futurist art. Kamenskii also founded the Poets' Café in Moscow in 1917 and ASIS (Association of Socialist Art), a publishing venture that printed the *Futurist Gazette*.

He was part of the Flying Federation of Futurists—a group of Futurist poets who advocated the independence of art from the state and who promoted a new style of teaching through Free Art Studios. The group participated in "street demonstrations," during which they distributed copies of the *Futurist Gazette* and read aloud, attempting to engage their audience on multiple levels.

Kamenskii developed "ferro-concrete" poetry—a new type of poetry that doubled as visual art by using both the graphic and symbolic meaning of words.   J. R.

E(DWARD LELAND) MCKNIGHT KAUFFER
Born in Great Falls, Montana, 1890
Died in New York, 1954

Kauffer, an American-born artist and painter who spent much of his life in England, adopted the name of his patron, Professor Joseph McKnight (1865–1942), early on in his career (1912). From 1910 to 1912 he studied painting at the Mark Hopkins Institute in San Francisco and followed that with a six-month stint at the Art Institute of Chicago. While in Chicago, he attended the famous Armory Show, which influenced his decision to study in Europe. Between 1913 and 1914 he attended the Académie Moderne in Paris; he moved to London in 1914 with the start of World War I. Beginning in 1915 Kauffer received numerous commissions from the London Underground, and throughout the next twenty-five years, he produced his best-known posters for this company. His designs, characterized by their simplicity and legibility, convey their message clearly and boldly. His early work displayed the influence of Cubism and the English movement Vorticism, an offshoot of Cubism and Futurism. In 1920 he helped to found Group X, which consisted of several artists devoted to reestablishing Vorticism. At the height of his success in the 1930s, Kauffer created book jacket designs, illustrations, and theater and ballet costumes and sets. His "Tube" posters appeared throughout the Underground, making the innovations of modern painting accessible to a diverse audience. In 1937 he had a solo show at the Museum of Modern Art. In 1940 he returned permanently to the United States, designing posters for war relief agencies, the United Nations, and American Airlines.   I. T.

GUSTAV GUSTAVOVICH KLUTSIS
Born near Riga, Latvia, 1895
Died in Siberia, 1944

Klutsis often synthesized Suprematist and Constructivist elements in his photomontages, theater sets, kiosk and poster designs, paintings, and sculpture. He studied at the teacher's seminary at Volmar and the Art School of Riga before moving to Petrograd in 1915 to attend the school managed by the Society for the Encouragement of the Arts. At this time, he also served as scene painter at the Okhtensky Workers' Theater. Klutsis participated in both the February and October Revolutions. As a member of the Ninth Regiment of Latvian Rifles, he fought against anti-Bolshevik forces in 1917 and defended the Kremlin during the Civil War a year later. Following the Revolution, he remained in Moscow and continued his artistic training at the second SVO-

MAS (the State Free Art Workshops), where he studied with Konstantin Korovin, Kazimir Malevich, and Antoine Pevsner, who took over Malevich's studio in the summer of 1919. At this studio, Klutsis met his future wife, Valentina Kulagina.

Throughout the 1920s, he was actively involved in the Moscow avant-garde movement. He participated in exhibitions with members of Malevich's Suprematist UNOVIS group (Affirmers of the New Art) in Vitebsk (1920) and in Moscow (1921). He joined the Communist Party in 1921 and with Sergei Sen'kin established a studio within the organization to promote concepts developed by UNOVIS. In 1922 he applied his ideas to utilitarian designs for agitational stands for the celebration of the fifth anniversary of the Revolution and the Fourth Congress of the Comintern. He also exhibited internationally at the *First Russian Art Exhibition* in Berlin that year, and in 1923 he joined INKhUK (the Institute of Artistic Culture).

His participation in VKhUTEMAS (the Higher State Artistic and Technical Workshops) continued throughout the 1920s. With Sen'kin, he founded the Masterskaia revoliutsii (Workshop of the Revolution) within VKhUTEMAS in 1924 in order to subvert the notion of artistic genius and focus the artist's attention on revolutionary and political aims. In addition, he taught color theory in the wood and metalworking division from 1924 to 1930. During this period, he showed his work at such international venues as the *Pressa* exhibition in Cologne (1928), *Film and Foto* in Stuttgart (1929), and *Photomontage* in Berlin (1931) and assisted with the organization of the Russian section of the *Exposition international des arts décoratifs et industriels modernes* in Paris.

Klutsis contributed to the Constructivist journal *Lef* from 1923 to 1925, was a founding member of the *Oktiabr'* group, showing at its first and only exhibition in 1930, and served as vice-president of the Association of Revolutionary Poster Artists from 1929 to 1932. After his arrest and imprisonment in 1938 during the Stalinist purges, he was sent to a labor camp, where he died in 1944. I. T.

VLADIMIR IVANOVICH KOZLINSKII
Born in Kronstadt, Russia, 1897
Died in Moscow, 1967
Kozlinskii, a printmaker and theater designer, spent most of his career in St. Petersburg. He began his artistic training in 1907 at the Society for the Encouragement of the Arts. He also studied at the Zvanteseva School and received private instruction from D. N. Kardovskii. By 1911 he was already under the tutelage of the printmaker Vasilii Mate in St. Petersburg. Following the Revolution in 1918 he created agitprop decorations for the revolutionary festivals in Petrograd and became the head of the engraving studio at SVOMAS (the State Free Art Workshops). In 1920,

Kozlinskii joined ROSTA (the Russian Telegraph Agency) and with Vladimir Lebedev and Lev Brodaty directed its Petrograd branch. He designed numerous posters during this period. Kozlinskii's work, representing the Impressionist tendency in Russian art, appeared in both national and international shows. In 1922 he exhibited with the Union of New Tendencies in Art in Petrograd and at the *First Russian Art Exhibition* in Berlin. In 1925 he participated in the *Third Exhibition of Paintings by Artists from Kaluga and Moscow* and in the *Seventh Exhibition of L'Araignée* (The spider) in Paris. In 1928 his work appeared at the Moscow exhibition that commemorated the tenth anniversary of the Revolution. I. T.

VALENTINA NIKIFOROVNA KULAGINA
Born in 1902
Died in 1987
Kulagina designed Constructivist posters and books and exhibited at several major shows in Russia and in Europe. In 1919 she joined the studios of Antoine Pevsner and Vladimir Favorsky at the SVOMAS (the State Free Art Workshops) in Moscow, where she met her future husband, the artist Gustav Klutsis. During 1920–21 she studied with Klutsis at the VKhUTEMAS (the Higher State Artistic and Technical Workshops). Her first photomontages and Constructivist typography were displayed in 1925. In 1928 she assisted in the organization of the Soviet section of the *Pressa* exhibition in Cologne, and that same year she became a member of the *Oktiabr'* group and exhibited at their 1930 show in Moscow. Beginning in the late 1920s Kulagina, sometimes with Klutsis, designed and produced posters in association with Izogiz (the State Publishing House for Art). She showed her work at the *Photomontage* exhibition in Berlin (1931) and at the exhibition *Posters in the Service of the Five-Year Plan* (1932). She continued to produce posters and display her art at numerous exhibitions in Russia and throughout Europe until her husband's arrest during the Stalinist purges. At this time, Kulagina retreated from public life. I. T.

VLADIMIR VASIL'EVICH LEBEDEV
Born in St. Petersburg, 1891
Died in Leningrad, 1967
Known for his political and socially critical works, Lebedev was actively involved in the Petrograd/Leningrad art world and incorporated Cubist, Futurist, and Suprematist elements into his paintings, posters, and prints. In 1909, he studied drawing with Aleksandr Titov in St. Petersburg, and in 1910 he studied with the battle painter Frants Rubo. From 1912 to 1916 he trained at the Academy of Fine Arts. During this period, he befriended Vladimir Tatlin, and in 1915 he was one of the founding members, with Tatlin, Lev bruni and other avant-garde artists, of the group

Apartment no. 5, which met in Bruni's apartment. In 1915 he married the sculptor Sarra Lebedeva. He participated in the Revolution and made *lubok* prints with themes reflecting the upheaval. He also created agitprop decorations for the Politseisky Bridge in Petrograd.

From 1918 to 1921, he taught at the SVOMAS (the State Free Art Workshops) in Petrograd and produced designs for the State Porcelain Factory in 1918–19. Following Meyerhold's call for an art of propaganda, Lebedev became actively involved, along with Vladimir Kozlinsky, in the Petrograd branch of ROSTA (the Russian Telegraph Agency). His political posters of the 1920s resembled paper cutouts in their sharpness and economy of design. He worked with Maiakovskii on posters for ROSTA windows in 1920–21 and belonged to UNOVIS (Affirmers of the New Art), whose members embraced Suprematism.

Lebedev was represented in most of the major art shows of the 1920s, both in Russia and in Europe, including the *First Russian Art Exhibition* in Berlin (1922), the *Paris International Exhibition* (1925), and the Moscow exhibition that marked the tenth anniversary of the Revolution (1927). He also had a solo show in Leningrad in 1928. During World War II, he returned to designing propaganda posters, this time depicting antifascist subjects. I. T.

BART ANTHONY VAN DER LECK
Born in Utrecht, Netherlands, 1876
Died in Blaricum, Netherlands, 1958

Raised in poverty, Leck left school at age fourteen to work at various stained glass studios in Utrecht. After eight years of training, which formed his aesthetic taste for outlined blocks of color and developed his interest in the connection between technology and art, he was awarded a scholarship to study at the National School for the Applied Arts in Amsterdam. From 1900 to 1904 he studied painting under August Allebe, and his traditional figure studies and landscapes methodically began shifting toward abstraction. During this time he also continued a close friendship and occasional collaboration with fellow artisan Piet Klaarhamer and began a series of contracts with influential art critic Hendrik P. Bremmer. In 1914 he began a long relationship with the Kröller-Müller family that included stained glass commissions, architectural and interior design, and graphic work. Two years later he met Piet Mondrian and Theo van Doesburg, and in 1917 he became one of the originators of the magazine *De Stijl*. During these years Leck also began to paint his purely abstract *Compositions* and published several manifestolike articles in *De Stijl*, among them "The Place of Modern Painting in Architecture" (1917) and "On Painting and Building" (1918). He left *De Stijl* in 1920 and thereafter maintained a focused, solitary life that includ-

ed several exhibitions and many designs for textiles, ceramics, and furniture. The largest collection of his work is found in the Kröller-Müller State Museum in Otterlo, the Netherlands. I. B.

ANDRE LHOTE
Born in Bordeaux, France, 1885
Died in Paris, 1962

Lhote was trained in decorative sculpture in Bordeaux and spent ten years as a commercial woodcarver before moving to Paris in 1906. Without formal training, he became a full-time painter, his works deeply influenced by African sculpture as well as by Paul Gauguin's paintings. He soon began to exhibit in the salons. In 1910 Lhote had his first solo exhibition to critical acclaim, establishing his place in the Parisian art world. In 1912 Lhote became a member of La Section d'Or, a group that included Francis Picabia, Robert Delaunay, Marcel Duchamp, and Fernand Léger. By this time Lhote had come into contact with the Cubists and adopted some of their stylistic techniques in his work, although he continued to depict everyday objects and scenes. In addition to his painting, Lhote regularly contributed criticism and articles to *La nouvelle revue française* and wrote a number of books on art from 1923 to 1950. Beginning in 1918 he taught painting at the Académie Notre-Dame des Champs, and then at his own art academy, the Académie Montparnasse, which he founded in Paris in 1922. He founded a South American branch of the school in Rio de Janeiro in 1952. J. R.

EL LISSITZKY (LAZAR' MARKOVICH LISITSKII)
Born in Pochinok, near Smolensk, Russia, 1890
Died in Moscow, 1941

Lissitzky was a prominent figure in the Jewish cultural renaissance, an intermediary between the Eastern and Western art worlds, and an advocate of Suprematism and Constructivism. He was instrumental in the shift from two-dimensional to three-dimensional Suprematism and worked in a diverse number of media and areas, including architecture, exhibition design, typography, photography, and painting.

He began his artistic training at thirteen in 1903 under the tutelage of Yehuda Pen, who was also Marc Chagall's instructor. After completing secondary school, he was denied admission to the St. Petersburg Academy, probably because of quotas for Jewish students. He spent 1909 to 1914 in Germany, studying architecture at the Technische Hochschule in Darmstadt. After returning to Russia in 1914 he worked briefly in the studio of Osip Zadkine, whom he had met in Paris, and from about 1915 to 1917 he studied at the Riga Polytechnical Institute. Upon receiving his diploma in architecture and engineering, he worked for several architectural firms and participated in exhibitions sponsored by such organizations as the World of Art group. About this time he began to create designs and illustrations for Jewish books. He helped to establish the Society for the Encouragement of Jewish Art and the *Exhibition of Paintings and Sculpture by Jewish Artists* in 1918 and the Yiddish publishing house Kultur Lige in 1919.

In May 1919 Chagall invited Lissitzky to teach graphics and architecture at the Vitebsk Art School. Shortly after his arrival, Kasimir Malevich joined the faculty. Lissitzky soon embraced Malevich's Suprematist style and became a member of his UNO-VIS group (Affirmers of the New Art). In 1919–20, Lissitzky extended Suprematism to his concept of the PROUN (Project for the Affirmation of the New), abstract art comprised of spatial elements, architectonic forms, and geometric shapes. During this period, Lissitzky also used Suprematist designs for revolutionary festival decorations and posters, including his most famous work, *Beat the Whites with the Red Wedge* (1919). He joined the Moscow INKhUK (Institute of Artistic Culture) in 1920.

In 1921 he moved from Vitebsk to Moscow to teach painting and architecture at VKhUTEMAS (the Higher State Artistic and Technical Workshops). By the end of 1921 he began his travels between Russia and Europe. In 1921 shortly after his arrival in Berlin, in conjunction with the Russian writer I'lia Erenberg, he established the journal *Veshch.Objet.Gegenstand* (Object) as a means for Western Europeans to learn about Russian art and literature and for the Russians to learn about Western artistic developments. Lissitzky helped organize and design the *First Exhibition of Russian Art,* in which he also participated, in Berlin in 1922.

In Europe Lissitzky made contacts with a variety of avant-garde artists, including members of Dada, De Stijl, and the Bauhaus. He participated in international exhibitions and contributed to avant-garde journals, working with Mies van der Rohe on the magazine *G,* publishing articles in *De Stijl,* and designing covers for the British review *Broom.* In 1924, after moving to Switzerland to recover from tuberculosis, he worked on numerous projects and began to experiment with photography. He assisted Kurt Schwitters with an issue of his magazine *Merz,* edited *Die Kunstismen* with Hans Arp, took part with Mart Stam and others on the journal *ABC,* produced advertisement designs for the Pelikan Ink Company in Hannover, and translated articles by Malevich into German.

He returned to Moscow in 1925, remaining in Russia for the rest of his life. From 1925 to 1930 he taught again at the Moscow VKhUTEMAS in the wood and metalwork division, and allied himself with ASNOVA (the Association of New Architects), a group that opposed the extreme utilitarianism of the Constructivists. In the late 1920s, he designed the Soviet sections at international expositions. During the 1930s, he began to experiment with photomontage, photography, photograms, and collage, and in the later 1930s he designed layouts for such magazines as *USSR in Construction.* His last works, done in the late 1930s and early 1940s, were antifascist posters. I. T.

HEINZ LOEW
Born in Leipzig, Germany, 1903
Died in London, 1981

After graduating from the foundation course at the Bauhaus in Dessau, Loew collaborated with Oskar Schlemmer on the Bauhaus stage project from 1926 to 1927. In 1927 he established the plastic workshop at the Bauhaus with Joost Schmidt. Before founding *Studio Z* in Berlin in 1930, Loew organized exhibitions and worked on advertising design in Magdeburg, Leipzig, and Berlin. His own work—photographs that used contrasting scales and lighting—was particularly successful in Germany during the late 1920s. In 1936 Loew emigrated to London and there continued his photographic career. J. R.

VLADIMIR VLADIMIROVICH MAIAKOVSKII
Born in Bagdadi, Georgian Republic, 1893
Died in Moscow, 1930

Although he is primarily known as a poet and playwright, Maiakovskii was actively involved in the Russian and European art scene and collaborated with several artists, including Aleksandr Rodchenko, Varvara Stepanova, and Alexei Levin, on poster designs. Two years after his family moved to Moscow, Maiakovskii, aged fifteen, joined the Bolshevik Party and began his artistic training at the Stroganov School of Applied Arts, where he remained from 1908 to 1909. He continued his studies under Stanislav Zhukovsky in 1909 and P. I. Lelin in 1910–11 before enrolling at Moscow College in 1911, where he met the poet-painter David Burlyuk and joined his Cubo-Futurist group Hylaea. Maiakovskii and Burlyuk became seminal figures in promoting the Futurist movement in Russia.

After the Revolution, Maiakovskii dedicated his artistic efforts to the cause of the new Soviet state. He was one of the first members of the avant-garde to collaborate with the Bolsheviks, and he started to work for IZO Narkompros (the Department of Fine Art of the Commissariat of Enlightenment) in 1918. That same year, his play *Mystery-Bouffe,* an allegory about the Revolution, was produced by Vsevolod Meyerhold at the Communal Theater of Musical Drama. By 1914 Maiakovskii was creating poster designs, and from 1919 to 1922 he created window posters for ROSTA (the Russian Telegraph Agency) for which he provided both texts and images. Beginning in 1923 Maiakovskii and Rodchenko collaborated to create advertisements for state-produced goods.

In January 1919 he helped to establish Komfut (Communist

Futurism), an organization in Petrograd that included the theorists Boris Kushner and Osip Brik and the painters Natan Al'tman and David Shterenberg. He was one of the founders of *Lef* magazine, which joined literary and political thinkers with avant-garde artists and writers.

Maiakovskii participated in the international art scene and was well known outside Russia. He traveled several times to Paris, first in 1922 and again in 1924 and 1929. There he encountered numerous French avant-garde artists, such as Pablo Picasso, Robert Delaunay, Georges Braque, and Fernand Léger, as well as fellow Russian artist Il'ia Zdanevich. He was included in the *Paris International Exhibition* in 1925, and that same year visited Cuba, Mexico, and the United States. During this trip, he established ties with Diego Rivera in Mexico and saw Burlyuk in the United States for the first time since 1918. Until his suicide in 1930, Maiakovskii continued to work as a poet and writer, his publications frequently illustrated by such avant-garde Russian artists as Lissitzky and Rodchenko.   I. T.

LEO MARFURT
Born in Aarau, Switzerland, 1894
Died in Antwerp, Belgium, 1977
Marfurt studied at the Aarau School of Arts and Crafts before going to Basel to assist the Belgian artist Jules de Praetere in his advertising workshop. In 1921 Marfurt followed Praetere to Belgium and established an agency in Brussels. While directing his agency, Les Créations Publicitaires, from 1927 to 1957, Marfurt also taught at the Plantin Institute of Typographic Studies in Antwerp. He is best known as a designer and poster artist.   J. R.

FILIPPO TOMMASO MARINETTI
Born in Alexandria, Egypt, 1876
Died in Bellagio, Italy, 1944
Marinetti began studying at the Sorbonne in 1893 and proceeded to get his doctorate in jurisprudence in Genoa in 1899. While studying in Paris, Marinetti began to associate with the literary avant-garde and with the "naturiste" reaction against Symbolism. Upon completing his law degree, he moved to Milan and founded the literary journal *Poesia* in 1905. The journal, to which Marinetti regularly contributed his own poems, anticipated the central beliefs of Futurism—that artistic freedom and innovation should be allowed to flourish and that modernity should prevail over the ideas and traditions of the past. Marinetti officially introduced Futurism in a 1909 manifesto in *Le Figaro*.

Until the 1930s, Marinetti carried the banner of Futurism from London to Moscow, organizing and participating in exhibitions and theatrical performances with relentless energy and zeal,

making both strong friendships and hostile enemies. Even after the dissolution of the first phase of Futurism in 1916, Marinetti organized a second group of followers around him, though the movement was significantly weakened. During this time, Marinetti, a strong Italian nationalist, was arrested with Fascist leader Benito Mussolini in a prowar demonstration. Soon after, he fought for Italy in World War I. Between the wars Marinetti continued to direct the Futurist movement while writing poetry about speed, warfare, and technology. He volunteered to serve on the Russian front in 1942 but quickly had to return home because of illness. Marinetti died soon after becoming the archivist for the former Academia d'Italia in Bellagio.   J. R.

ROBERT MICHEL
Born in Vockenhausen, Germany, 1897
Died in Titisee-Neustadt, Germany, 1983
Michel, an architect, typographer, and painter, began his artistic training at the Kunstakademie in Weimar while on leave from the army during World War I. Along with his future wife, Ella Bergmann, he protested the antiquated instruction at the school and was dismissed in 1918. He chose to remain in Weimar to work as an independent artist and designer. During this period he was closely associated with the former students of the Van de Velde workshops and such other artists as Johannes Molzahn and Karl Peter Röhl. Together they saw the founding of the Bauhaus in Weimar in 1919. Walter Gropius, who had visited their studios before the Bauhaus opened, established a rapport with them and often exhibited their works at Bauhaus receptions. From 1917 to 1921, Michel documented the history of the Dada revolution in collage. He also collaborated with Bergmann on a film and participated in the project *Die Neue Stadt* (The new city) with members of Das Neue Frankfurt group. In the late 1920s he was represented at both the Art Council 1928 in New York and the Société Anonyme exhibition, which traveled throughout the United States. As a result of this show, he developed friendships with Kurt Schwitters and Adolf Meyer. Michel belonged to the avant-garde group Circle of New Advertising Designers, and until 1933 was a member of the Association of German Architects.   I. T.

LASZLO MOHOLY-NAGY
Born in Bacsborsod, Hungary, 1895
Died in Chicago, 1946
A Hungarian law student and World War I veteran, Moholy-Nagy moved to Berlin in 1920 to start a career in art. Through his involvement with the Hungarian art review *MA*, he met many members of the avant-garde, including Dadaists Hannah Höch, Raoul Hausmann, and Hans Richter and the Constructivist El Lissitzky. His first solo show, at Der Sturm Gallery in 1922,

included abstract constructions in metal that reflected the influence of his then studio-mate Kurt Schwitters. In 1923 he was asked by Walter Gropius to join the faculty of the Weimar Bauhaus, which relocated to Dessau in 1925. After Johannes Itten's departure, Moholy was made leader of the faculty, and his work became increasingly dedicated to technological concerns, with photography and film his usual media. After leaving the Bauhaus in 1928 he worked at a commercial design firm until 1935, when he moved to London to continue work at a second company. He made several experimental films and the multimedia work *Light Prop* during this period, and continued to collaborate on other directors' films and work on his photography. He moved to Chicago in 1937 to become the director of the short-lived New Bauhaus. Moholy founded his School of Design in Chicago in 1939. His last book, *Vision in Motion*, was published one year after his death in 1947. I. B.

FARKAS MOLNAR
Born in Pécs, Hungary, 1897
Died in Budapest, 1945

Molnàr was schooled in Budapest at the Fine Arts College and at the Hungarian Palatine Joseph Technical University but left for Germany before receiving his degree. From 1921 until 1925 he studied at the Bauhaus in Weimar, producing a portfolio of lithographs and a house design that was featured in the 1923 Bauhaus exhibition. Molnàr worked in the office of Walter Gropius, who deeply influenced his work, before returning to Budapest in 1925. After completing his degree in 1928, Molnàr was appointed the Hungarian delegate to the new organization Congrès Internationaux d'Architecture Moderne (CIAM). Established by modernist architects primarily as a venue for discussion, CIAM ultimately solidified the modernist movement in architecture by providing it with a central committee, a manifesto, and statutes from which to work. Molnàr was a delegate for ten years and in 1937 was also made secretary of the short-lived CIAM-Ost. However, this exclusively Eastern European offshoot disbanded when World War II broke out. Remaining in Hungary until his death, Molnàr concentrated on designing villas and residential blocks in Budapest. One such villa received first prize at the 1933 *Esposizione Triennale* in Milan. His final work, the Hungarian Holy Land Church, begun in 1940, remained unfinished at his death. J. R.

FRANCIS PICABIA
Born in Paris, 1879
Died in Villejuit, France, 1953

Picabia entered the Ecole des Arts Décoratifs in 1895 but two years later ran away to Switzerland with an older woman. Back in Paris in 1899 he began exhibiting Impressionist-style work regularly at the Salon des Artistes Français and soon after at galleries across Europe. In 1908 he met his future wife, Gabrielle Buffet, a music student, who introduced him to the theory of "correspondence." Picabia applied this Symbolist-driven notion to his painting by relating color and form to mental and emotional experiences. A restless spirit, Picabia continued to search for further modes of self-expression, borrowing elements of Fauvism and Cubism as his work moved toward complete abstraction.

Traveling to New York in 1913 for the opening of the Armory Show, Picabia met Alfred Stieglitz and established an important connection with the American art world. Two years later he exhibited at Stieglitz's 291 Gallery. In 1915 Picabia produced his first mechanomorphic drawings, using mechanical diagrams to represent human subjects, and in 1917 he began to publish *391*, a Dada review that included poetry, graphics, and articles. Tristan Tzara, the leader of the Zurich Dada movement, invited Picabia to join him, and for a year Picabia contributed to Tzara's Dada review; both then returned to Paris to strengthen the movement there. With the first Dada event—the Premier Vendredi de Littérature— and Picabia's subsequent Manifesto Cannibale Dada, the Parisian Dada group successfully outraged the public.

By 1921 the group began to fall apart. Picabia disassociated himself from the movement, feeling that it inhibited individual expression. In his final issues of *391*, published in 1924, Picabia attacked the newly emerging Surrealist movement and proposed an alternate in the form of Instantaneism. However, by 1926 Picabia had agreed to be part of the Galerie Surréaliste, along with Giorgio De Chirico, Man Ray, Marcel Duchamp, Joan Miró, and Pablo Picasso, although he still resisted formally classifying his work as Surrealist. In 1936 he signed the Manifesto of Dimension, which promoted the search for four-dimensional space and presented a united front of avant-garde artists against Hitler's attacks on "degenerate" art. Picabia continued to experiment and innovate in his paintings throughout his later life, creating distorted "monster" pictures, multilayered drawings, collages, and "dot" paintings in which points of solid color stand out from a highly textured but monochromatic background. J. R.

NATAL'IA SERGEEVNA PINUS-BUKHAROVA
Born in Kursk province, Russia, 1902 (1901?)
Died in Moscow, 1980s
Pinus completed VKhUTEIN (the Higher State Artistic and Technical Institute) in Moscow in 1930. She studied with Gustav Klutsis and became a member of the *Oktiabr'* group, which was founded by Klutsis and several other avant-garde artists. Pinus exhibited with the group in Gorky Park in Moscow in 1931 but left the organization in response to extensive criticism that autumn along with Klutsis, Valentina Kulagina, and Sergei Sen'kin. As a result, Pinus requested membership in RAPKh (the Russian Association of Proletarian Artists). She remained thereafter in Moscow, working as a painter and exhibiting widely. I. T.

LIUBOV' SERGEEVNA POPOVA
Born in Ivanovskoe, near Moscow, 1889
Died in Moscow, 1924
Popova worked in several styles throughout her career, moving from Russian Cubo-Futurism to Suprematism to Constructivism. Born into a wealthy family, she had several private instructors and traveled extensively throughout Russia and Europe. After moving to Moscow in 1906 she studied with Stanislav Zhukovsky and later enrolled in the school run by Konstantin Yuon. In 1912 Popova went to Paris, where she studied under Jean Metzinger and Le Fauconnier, learning about Cubism firsthand while also coming into contact with Futurist ideas. Back in Moscow the following year, she worked in Tatlin's studio with Aleksandr Vesnin and Aleksei Morgunov, among others, and presented her Cubo-Futurist work at several important Futurist exhibitions: the *Knave of Diamonds* (1914 and 1916), *Tramway V* (1915), and *0.10 The Last Futurist Exhibition of Paintings* (1916). Popova married the art historian Boris von Edding in March 1918. From 1918 to 1920 she taught at SVOMAS (the State Free Art Workshops), which later became VKhUTEMAS (the Higher State Artistic and Technical Workshops).

In 1920 she participated in the debates about art at the Moscow INKhUK (the Institute of Artistic Culture) and in 1921 allied herself with the Constructivists when they criticized Wassily Kandinsky's psychologically oriented art. Her conversion to Constructivism was complete when she became one of the five artists to participate in the 5 x 5 = 25 exhibition. Her five works hung alongside pieces by Aleksandra Exter, Aleksandr Rodchenko, Varvara Stepanova, and Aleksandr Vesnin. In 1922 Popova renounced easel painting and turned her art toward more public and utilitarian ends. She began to experiment in a variety of areas, including graphic, theater, and textile design. Her most famous works from this period are her designs and costumes for Vsevolod Meyerhold's production of Fernand Crommelynck's *The Magnanimous Cuckold*. From 1923 until her untimely death in 1924 from scarlet fever, she worked on the magazine *Lef*, made graphics for a variety of publications, and collaborated with Stepanova on textile designs for mass production at the First State Textile Print Factory. I. T.

MAN RAY (EMANUEL RABINOVITCH)
Born in Philadelphia, 1890
Died in Paris, 1976
The son of Eastern European immigrants, Ray studied painting at the Ferrer Center in New York while working as an advertising agent and an engineering draftsman. He became interested in photography and European avant-garde art in 1915 after becoming acquainted with Alfred Stieglitz. That year he had his first solo exhibition, and soon he began to experiment with Synthetic Cubism. Ray met Marcel Duchamp and the two, with Francis Picabia, founded the New York Dada movement two years later. In 1921 Ray went to Paris, where he joined first the Parisian Dada group and later the Surrealists. During the 1920s Ray worked on films, and in the 1930s he published several albums of photographs accompanied by essays and poems by André Breton, Duchamp, and Tristan Tzara. He invented new photographic techniques that augmented his abstract and surreal compositions and pushed the limits of the medium. Among his innovations were the pivotal "rayograph" technique, light photographs taken without the use of a camera; the "aerograph" method of painting, using a spray gun to mimic photographic effects; and "solarization," or edge reversal. Man Ray left France for America during the Nazi occupation and settled in Hollywood until his return to Paris in 1950. J. R.

MIKHAIL IOSIFOVICH RAZULEVICH
Born in Niuksanishcha, Russia, 1904
Died in Russia, c. 1970s–1980s
Razulevich graduated from Leningrad's Academy of the Arts in 1927 and worked as a painter and book illustrator. Having survived the Stalin era, he continued to work well into the 1960s, when he published illustrations for a fine edition of *The Lay of Igor's Campaign*. D. G.

ALEKSANDR MIKHAILOVICH RODCHENKO
Born in St. Petersburg, 1891
Died in Moscow, 1956
After early training at the Kazan Art School, where he met his future wife, the artist Varvara Stepanova, Rodchenko moved to Moscow to study sculpture and architecture at the Stroganov School of Applied Arts in 1914. He quickly became discouraged with the school, and between 1915 and 1916 he allied himself with

Moscow's avant-garde artists, among them Vladimir Tatlin, Liubov' Popova, and Kasimir Malevich. Tatlin invited Rodchenko to exhibit at his May 1916 exhibition *The Store;* there Rodchenko presented his Cubist collages and the first of his experimental images with compass and ruler. In 1917 he helped to establish the Union of Painters. While serving as the secretary for the avant-garde section of this organization, he was given a solo exhibition. Also in 1917, Rodchenko and several other artists, including Tatlin and Georgii Yakulov, decorated the Café Pittoresque in Moscow. From 1918 to 1922 he was active in IZO Narkompros (the Department of Fine Art of the Commissariat of Enlightenment), where he acquired hundreds of contemporary works for the state. Beginning in 1918 he made three-dimensional abstract constructions, which appeared in the *Non-Objective Creation and Suprematism* exhibition in Moscow in 1919. Following the famous 5 x 5 = 25 exhibition of 1921, where he showed abstract paintings, he began to work in a variety of media, abandoning painting until the mid-1930s.

Rodchenko was instrumental in the early development of Russian Constructivism. He was a founding member of INKhUK (the Institute of Artistic Culture) in 1920, and along with Alexei Gan and Varvara Stepanova, he established the First Working Group of Constructivists within this organization in 1921. Until VKhUTEMAS (the Higher State Artistic and Technical Workshops) closed in 1930, he taught a course in construction and classes on the creation of objects in its metalwork division.

Beginning in 1923 Rodchenko delved into new media: photomontage, photography, graphic design, and set design for films and theatrical productions. He produced advertisements with the poet Vladimir Maiakovskii and made a series of photomontages to accompany Maiakovskii's poem "Pro Eto" (About This) in 1923. In 1925 he traveled to Paris to supervise the installation of his model worker's club at the *Exposition International des Arts Décoratifs et Industriels Modernes.* He created the sets for the second part of Maiakovskii's *The Bedbug* at the Meyerhold Theater in 1929. He was actively involved in the journal *Lef* (1923–25) and its sequel *Novyi Lef* (1927–28). Rodchenko not only did the layout and cover designs but submitted articles, photomontages, and photographs. During the 1930s, he collaborated with Stepanova, his wife, on numerous designs for publications, such as *USSR in Construction,* and pursued his interests in typography, graphic design, and photography while resuming his experiments in painting.   I. T.

VLADIMIR O. ROSKIN
Born 1896
Died 1929

Roskin began his artistic training in Moscow at the Stroganov School of Applied Arts from 1910 to 1913, and then studied under Fedor Rerberg (1913–14) and Il'ia Mashkov (1915–17). Following the Revolution, he designed posters for the Moscow branch of ROSTA (the Russian Telegraph Agency) and street decorations for the anniversary celebrations of the Revolution. In 1918–19 he was represented at the Moscow Fifth State Exhibition, *From Impressionism to Non-Objective Art,* and his name appeared on the list of artists whose work the Museum of Painterly Culture wanted to acquire. Beginning in 1924 until his death in 1929, he designed Soviet exhibitions abroad. He worked with El Lissitzky on the *International Press Exhibition* in Cologne in 1929 and received the Grand Prix posthumously at the 1936 *World Exhibition* in Paris for his display design.   I. T.

XANTI (ALEXANDER) SCHAWINSKY
Born in Basel, Switzerland, 1904
Died in Locarno, Switzerland, 1979

Schawinsky, a Bauhaus student and faculty member, was a painter and a designer of stage sets and posters. He studied music and art in Zurich, and from 1921 to 1923 he was an assistant in an architectural firm in Cologne. In 1924 he began his Bauhaus training and became involved in Bauhaus theatrical productions as a writer, designer, and dancer and as Oscar Schlemmer's assistant. His interest in theater continued after he left the Bauhaus. From 1926 to 1927 he designed stage scenery at the State Theater Zwichau in Saxonia before returning to the Bauhaus, now located in Dessau. There he taught stage design and pursued his interest in painting, exhibiting with the group Young Painters of the Bauhaus. He left the Bauhaus again in 1929 to become director of the graphic arts studios of the city of Magdeburg. In 1931, driven out by political persecution, he moved to Berlin to work as a freelance graphic artist and exhibition designer, and in 1933 he emigrated to Milan, where he worked as a graphic designer for such clients as Olivetti and Motta. During this period, he created photomontages using large images and small-scale typography. After accepting Josef Alber's invitation to teach at Black Mountain College in North Carolina, Schawinsky moved in 1936 to the United States and offered instruction in painting. While in the United States, he continued his stage experiments with students at the college. In 1938 he went to New York to design the North Carolina pavilion for the New York World's Fair and decided to settle there. He worked as a painter and designer until 1950, when he dedicated himself solely to painting.   I. T.

FRITZ SCHLEIFER
Born in Pfaffenhofen an der Ilm, Germany, 1903
Died in Hamburg, Germany, 1977

A German designer and architect, Schleifer studied painting and murals at the Bauhaus from 1922 to 1924 and architecture at the Technischen Hochschule in Munich between 1925 and 1927. He taught the foundation course at the Landeskunstschule in Hamburg from 1930 to 1933 and went on to become a freelance architect. During World War II Schleifer worked as both a site manager and a site engineer for the air force. After the war, he returned to Hamburg, where he taught architecture at the Landeskunstschule until 1958, when he left to work with his son, Jan Schleifer, at the Design Institute. Among his best-known graphic work is a poster for the 1923 Bauhaus exhibition in which he adapts the geometric profile designed by Oskar Schlemmer into a symbol of the Bauhaus. I. T.

OSKAR SCHLEMMER
Born in Stuttgart, Germany, 1888
Died in Baden-Baden, Germany, 1943

Schlemmer, a Bauhaus professor and a painter, sculptor, and stage set designer, studied art at the Kunstakademie in Stuttgart from 1906 to 1911. He then moved to Berlin for a year before returning to Stuttgart to work with Adolf Hölzel. Hölzel was a pioneer of abstract art with a close following of international students, including Willi Baumeister and the Swiss artists Otto Meyer-Amden and Johannes Itten, who later developed the foundation course at the Bauhaus and became one of Schlemmer's close friends. During World War I, Schlemmer volunteered as a medical orderly but was transferred into the infantry and wounded several times. After the war, he began to promote abstract art and developed a figurative variant of Constructivism. Along with Baumeister, he exhibited at such avant-garde galleries as Der Sturm gallery in Berlin and the Galerie Arnold in Dresden. In 1920 Walter Gropius gave both Schlemmer and Paul Klee teaching positions at the Bauhaus in Weimar. Schlemmer began as the master of the mural workshop and later became the master of the stone and wood workshop and the metal workshop. The murals he created for the Bauhaus were destroyed by the Nazis.

After the performance of his *Triadic Ballet* at the Bauhaus exhibition of 1923, Schlemmer was appointed director of the Bauhaus stage workshop and was instrumental in developing the Bauhaus theater. The *Triadic Ballet* consists of twelve scenes performed by one, two, or three dancers dressed in elaborate abstract geometric costumes designed by Schlemmer and executed by his brother, Carl Schlemmer. Schlemmer created posters to advertise this dance performance. His interest in poster design and typography later led to his role as an assistant in the typography work-

shop, established at the Dessau Bauhaus in 1925. His abstract concept of theater and dance caused controversy among his students, and Schlemmer eventually left the Bauhaus to assume a position at the Staatliche Akademie in Breslau. Throughout his career, Schlemmer remained interested in dance and theater, touring his dances throughout Germany in 1929 and designing stage sets for several operas by Igor Stravinsky in Berlin in 1930. After suffering the harassment of the Nazis and being reduced to poverty, he died of a heart attack in Baden-Baden while taking a cure there. I. T.

JOOST SCHMIDT
Born in Wuntsdorf, Hannover, Germany, 1893
Died in Nuremberg, Germany, 1948

Together with Herbert Bayer and László Moholy-Nagy, Schmidt was instrumental in shaping typography at the Bauhaus and shifting it away from Jugenstil and Expressionism toward a functionalist aesthetic. In 1911 his artistic training began at the Kunstakademie in Weimar and was interrupted in 1914, when he was recruited for war service. In 1919 he continued his study of art at the Bauhaus in Weimar. He focused primarily on sculpture and typography, and Walter Gropius appointed him head of the sculpture department and teacher of typography when the Bauhaus moved to Dessau in 1925. He later succeeded Bayer as the instructor of commercial typography. In 1933 the Nazis took away his studio, and in 1945 he was hired to teach architecture at the Hochschule für Bildende Kunst (High School for Arts) in Berlin. During that time, he also served as art director for the U.S. Exhibition Center in Berlin; he went to Nuremberg with this organization in 1948 and died there on 2 December. I. T.

PAUL SCHUITEMA
Born in Groningen, the Netherlands, 1897
Died in Wassenaar, the Netherlands, 1973

Trained in painting at the Academy of Art in Rotterdam from 1916 to 1920, Schuitema switched media to graphic design during the 1920s and began his career by designing advertising and promotional materials for the Berkel Manufacturing Company. His work, based in De Stijl philosophy and aesthetics is known for its reliance on the grid and the use of solid blocks of color as well as for bold lettering arranged in groups. Schuitema reduced his designs to enhance the poster's ability to communicate. He often used photography in his design work, and he made films from 1923 to 1954. He was a professor at the Royal Academy in The Hague for thirty-three years. I. B.

KURT SCHWITTERS
Born in Hannover, Germany, 1887
Died in Kendal, England, 1948

After attending Dresden Kunstakademie from 1909 to 1914 and performing a year of military service in 1917, Kurt Schwitters became involved with the influential Der Sturm Gallery in Berlin, where he met Hans Arp, Raoul Hausmann, and Hannah Höch. His first group of *Merz* pictures incorporated scraps of refuse as collage elements and was shown at the gallery in 1919. These intimate works focused on formal aspects of design but always maintained an expressionistic quality. At this time Schwitters began publishing his poems and prose, including his famous *Anna Blume* in 1919. In 1920 his works were shown in New York, and he began work on the elaborate *Merzbau* installation within his home, which occupied him for sixteen years. Denounced early on as an Expressionist, Schwitters was denied admission to the Dada group. Soon, however, Hausmann, Arp, and Höch demanded his inclusion, and in the early 1920s he gave many lectures promoting Dada. He attended the Constructivist Congress at Weimar in 1922, where he met Theo van Doesburg. In 1923 he began publishing *Merz* magazine, which continued until 1932, when he joined the Abstraction-Creation group in Paris. A graphic designer as well, in 1928 Schwitters founded the Circle of New Advertising Designers. To avoid Nazi persecution, he moved to Norway in 1937 and began work on the second *Merzbau*. After the German invasion of Norway, he escaped to England, where he spent seventeen months in an internment camp. An air raid in 1943 destroyed his Hannover *Merzbau* and he began work on a third such installation in 1947 in a barn in Elterwater, England, which was never completed. I. B.

ELENA VLADIMIROVNA SEMENOVA
Born in Moscow, 1898
Died 1986

Semenova, a poster and exhibition designer, finished secondary school in 1914, and after the Revolution studied art in Moscow in the Sculpture Faculty of the second SVOMAS (the State Free Art Workshops). In 1921, after three years, she left the Sculpture Faculty and transferred to the recently established architecture section of VKhUTEMAS (the State Higher and Artistic Technical Workshops) but remained there only until 1924 and never completed her degree. During the mid-1920s, her interests in architecture and Constructivism led to her participation in a number of subgroups within the Moscow INKhUK (Institute of Artistic Culture) and to the distinctive style in her architectural plans. She executed designs for several small-scale architectural structures, interiors, and display units, including her well-known Workers' Club designs. From the late 1920s to the early 1930s she focused primarily on graphic design. She made posters for the Blue Blouse Group and worked for journals, including Maiakovskii's *Lef* and *Novyi Lef*. Then, in 1927, along with Varvara Stepanova and E. Lavinskaya, she was asked to submit designs for the decoration of several squares in Moscow. At the same time, she made posters for the celebration of the tenth anniversary of the Revolution and worked with Lavinskaya on the design of window displays for the Dom Knigi GIZ-a (State Publishing House). After the 1930s, she devoted her time to exhibition and trade show design. I. T.

SENCO
Active in Italy
No further information available

OTIS SHEPARD
Active in the United States
No further information available

ARDENGO SOFFICI
Born in Rignano, Italy, 1879
Died in Forte dei Marmi, Italy, 1964

Soffici studied at the Academy in Florence before going to Paris in 1900, where he was influenced by Guillaume Apollinaire, Max Jacob, Pablo Picasso, Georges Braque, and Amedeo Modigliani, among others. Until his return to Italy in 1907, he wrote for Parisian avant-garde periodicals and exhibited his work with Robert Delaunay at Der Sturm Gallery in Berlin. He became the chief art critic for *La Voce*, where in 1911 he wrote the first discussion of Cubism to appear in Italy. This article provided a critical link between the new French and Italian art scenes. By 1913 Soffici had joined with the Italian Futurists, finding in the movement a synthesis of Impressionism and Cubism. However, his 1914 experiments with collage (Synthetic Cubism) mark his break from Futurism. Later, Soffici's art became more naturalistic as he took an increasingly antimodern stance. J. R.

VLADIMIR AVGUSTOVICH STENBERG
Born in Moscow, 1899
Died in Moscow, 1982
GEORGII AVGUSTOVICH STENBERG
Born in Moscow, 1900
Died in Moscow, 1933

The Stenberg brothers, instrumental in the founding and maturation of the Russian Constructivist movement, collaborated on most of their projects until Georgii's tragic death in a car accident in 1933. Encouraged early by their Swedish father, who was a painter, they decided to pursue a career in the arts. From 1912 to

1917 they studied at the Stroganov School of Applied Arts in Moscow, and after the Revolution they continued their training at the Moscow SVOMAS (the State Free Art Workshops). In 1918 they created agitprop decorations for May Day and the October Revolution anniversary celebration. The following year, they joined OBMOKhU (the Society of Young Artists) and presented their work at the group's annual exhibitions beginning in May 1919. These exhibitions consisted mostly of constructions from modern industrial materials, which were considered engineering experiments or assemblages rather than art objects.

In 1920 the Stenbergs joined INKhUK (the Institute of Artistic Culture), where they took part in its lectures and discussions in 1920 and 1921 and allied themselves with the First Working Group of Constructivists, established within INKhUK in 1921. It was not until 1922, however, that the term "Constructivists" was used to describe this group of artists. It first appeared in the title of the catalogue accompanying an exhibition of their spatial drawings and nonobjective constructions at the Poets' Café in Moscow. With Medunetsky, the brothers exhibited thirty-one works, including three-dimensional objects, which they deemed experiments in new types of buildings.

From 1922 to 1931 they created stage sets for Alexander Tairov's Kamernyi (Chamber) Theater in Moscow and for the Moscow Music Hall, and, in 1923 they toured Europe with the Tairov company. During this trip, they exhibited their work in Paris and visited Picasso in his studio, where they were disillusioned by his classical paintings. In 1925 they won a gold medal for their stage design at the *Exposition International des Arts Décoratifs et Industriels Modernes* in Paris.

Throughout the 1920s, the Stenberg brothers designed more than film posters, which they signed at first "2 Sten" and later "2 Stenberg 2." They also created architectural plans and did graphic design for such magazines as *Stroitel'stvo Moskvy* (Construction of Moscow), and from 1923 to 1925 they were associated with the magazine *Lef*. Beginning in 1928 they worked together on the Revolution celebration decorations for Red Square. They taught at the Institute for Architectural Construction from 1929 to 1932. The Stenbergs exhibited their work internationally at the *Film und Foto* exhibition in Stuttgart (1929) and in the *Photomontage* exhibition in Berlin (1931). They also helped arrange exhibitions of film posters in 1925 and 1927. After Georgii's death, Vladimir continued to create street decorations for the Revolution celebrations until 1948 and collaborated with his son on poster designs and other works. I. T.

VARVARA FEDOROVNA STEPANOVA
Born in Kovno (Kaunas), Lithuania, 1894
Died in Moscow, 1958

Stepanova was a major figure in the transition of Constructivism's early promotion of an autonomous artistic style to its later advocacy of utilitarian production. In 1910–11 she studied at the Kazan Art School; there she met Aleksandr Rodchenko, whom she later married. After moving to Moscow, she worked under the Impressionists Il'ia Mashkov and Konstantin Yuon and attended Stroganov School of Applied Arts from 1913 to 1914. Following the Revolution, Stepanova served as the deputy head of the literary-artistic section of IZO Narkompros (the Department of Fine Art of the Commissariat of Enlightenment). At this time, her painting revealed the influence of Cubism—most of her figures were shown in action and consisted of geometric planes and angles. During the late 1910s and early 1920s, she participated in many major national and international exhibitions. Along with Aleksandra Exter, Rodchenko, Liubov' Popova, and Aleksandr Vesnin, she was one of five Constructivist artists selected for the $5 \times 5 = 25$ show in Moscow in 1921.

From 1920 to 1923 she was an active member of the Moscow INKhUK (the Institute of Artistic Culture). Within INKhUK, she sided first with the Objective Analysis Group and then with the First Working Group of Constructivists, which she helped to establish. She taught art at the Krupskaya Academy of Social Education from 1920 to 1924 and textile design at VKhUTEMAS (the Higher State Artistic and Technical Workshops) from 1924 to 1925. In 1922 she designed the sets and costumes for Vsevolod Meyerhold's production of *The Death of Tarelkin* by Alexander Sukhovo-Kobylin and then began to focus on the design of magazines, books, and posters. She contributed to Maiakovskii's periodical *Lef* from 1923 to 1925 and to *Novyi Lef* in 1927–28; she also worked for the journals *Soviet Cinema, Literature and Art, Books and Revolution,* and *Class Struggle*. Stepanova collaborated with Rodchenko on photographic books, including *Fifteen Years of Soviet Cinema* and *The Moscow Metro,* and on the layout and typography for such publications as *USSR in Construction*. In 1945 she became art director for the magazine *Sovetskaia zhenshchina* (Soviet woman). I. T.

WLADYSLAW STRZEMINSKI
Born in Minsk, Russia, 1893
Died in Lodz, Poland, 1952

Strzeminski grew up in St. Petersburg and, after suffering a serious injury in World War I, studied at the Moscow SVOMAS (the State Free Art Workshops) from 1918 to 1919. Upon finishing his schooling, he worked for the Central Bureau of Exhibitions at IZO (the Department of Fine Art of the Commissariat of

Enlightenment) and then for the Moscow Council of Art and Art Industry. Strongly influenced by Vladimir Tatlin, Strzeminski's "material studies" were exhibited at the Museum of Artistic Culture in Moscow and Petrograd. In 1920 he married the Constructivist sculptor Katarzyna Kobro, and after moving to Vitebsk, both became followers of Kazimir Malevich's Suprematism and members of UNOVIS (Affirmers of the New Art). Strzeminski taught at the Free Art Workshops after moving to Smolensk and directed the poster-making branch of ROSTA (the Russian Telegraph Agency). In 1922 he went to Poland, where he directed the formation of the short-lived Constructivist group Blok. Rejecting the "Tatlinism" of his earlier art, Strzeminski experimented with a new form—Unism or Post-Suprematism—which fused Malevich's attention to form with Tatlin's attention to material. In Lodz, he and Katarzyna Kobro founded the School for Modern Typography in 1931. J. R.

LADISLAV SUTNAR
Born in Pilsen, Czechoslovakia, 1897
Died in New York, 1976

Sutnar received training at Prague's Academy of Applied Arts and Technical University, and in 1923 he became a professor at the State School for Graphic Arts. Following a visit to the Bauhaus, he became a strong advocate of its functional approach and ideals. Sutnar headed the State School for Graphic Arts until 1939, when he moved to the United States. After devoting himself to exhibition design, he won numerous awards, including gold medals for both his 1929 and 1936 designs for the Czechoslovakian pavilions at the World's Fair in Barcelona and in Paris. He decided to remain in New York after working there on the design for the 1939 Czechoslovakian pavilion. Later he was appointed art director of Sweet's Catalog Service. Stylistically, Sutnar was identified with Jan Tschichold's New Typography, which advocated the use of asymmetry, white space, heavy bars to delineate areas, and simple letterforms. In 1951 he established a design firm, and from 1959 to 1969 he was art director of *Theatre Arts* magazine. Sutnar's publications in English include *Catalog Design Progress* (with Knud Lonberg-Holm, 1950), *Package Design: The Force of Visual Selling* (1954), and *Visual Design in Action* (1961). From the 1960s until his death, Sutnar devoted himself almost exclusively to painting. J. R.

SOLOMON BENEDIKTOVICH TELINGATER
Born in Tiflis (Tbilisi), Georgian Republic, 1903
Died in Moscow, 1969

Best known for his photomontages, typography, and book designs, Telingater trained at the Art Studios in Baku, Azerbaijan, and at VKhUTEMAS (the Higher State Artistic and Technical Workshops). From 1921 to 1925, after returning to Baku, he worked for several journals and illustrated numerous books. He became a professional typographer in 1925, and from then until 1927 he worked for the review *Poligraficheskoe proizvodstvo* (Polygraphic production). In 1927 he helped to organize both the *All-Union Polygraphic Exhibition* in Moscow and *The Art of the Book* at Leipzig. By the late 1920s he had risen from printshop instructor to a figure of some renown. He collaborated with such artists as El Lissitzky on posters, making use of varied typographic and photomontage techniques. Along with Gustav Klutsis, he was a founding member of the *Oktiabr'* group, to which he belonged from 1928 to 1932. He worked for the Theater of the Red Army in Moscow in 1932 and experimented with photomontage and collage, using these media to demonstrate the success of the Five-Year Plan. His works from this period reflect Stalinist policies and aims. After the 1930s, he continued to design books and posters and to create photomontages and new typefaces. He also published several articles about typography. He was awarded a Gold Medal at both the 1937 *Exposition Universelle* in Paris and at the 1959 *International Exhibition of Book Design of Socialist Countries* in Leipzig. In 1963 he received the prestigious International Gutenberg Prize in Leipzig. I. T.

GEORG TRUMP
Born in Brettheim, Germany, 1896
Living as of 1984

Trump had begun studies at the Stuttgart State Academy of Arts and Crafts when World War I erupted, forcing him to delay his education until war's end. After graduating in 1923 he spent three years in Italy as a painter and ceramist. Next Trump headed the graphic art department of the Kunstgewerbeschule in Bielefeld. From 1929 to 1931 he taught typography in Munich and then at the Eastern Berlin College of Arts and Crafts. Returning to Munich in 1934, Trump became head of the School for Master Book Printers until 1953. Following his resignation, he began a freelance design practice and spent much of his time creating new typefaces. J. R.

JAN TSCHICHOLD
Born in Leipzig, Germany, 1902
Died in Locarno, Switzerland, 1974

Tschichold is best known for his involvement in New Typography, a movement he helped to found and promote. He was the son of a sign painter and type designer and inherited an interest in lettering from his father. From 1919 to 1922 he studied calligraphy at the Academy of Book Design in his hometown of Leipzig; after graduation, he became a freelance designer. The 1923 Weimar Bauhaus exhibition and Soviet Constructivism had a profound effect on his ideas, which he published in *Elementare Typographie* (1925) and in *Die neue Typographie* (1928). In these texts, he advanced a functionalist aesthetic, advocating an economy of design and expression, sans serif letterforms, and asymmetrical compositions. He was also one of the first modern designers to realize the value of photography in advertising. In 1926 Paul Renner invited Tschichold to teach typography and lettering at the Meisterschule für Deutschlands Buchdrucker (Munich School for Master Book Printers). In March 1933, accused by the Nazis of spreading radical ideas, Tschichold was arrested and dismissed from teaching. Shortly thereafter, he fled to Basel, Switzerland, where he worked as a book designer and published another manifesto on typography. During this period he abandoned New Typography because it reminded him of the rigid totalitarianism promoted by National Socialism, and he decided that serif typefaces were often more appropriate than sans serif. Having returned to a more classical typographic style, he moved to England in 1947 to work for Penguin Books. Two years later, he returned to Switzerland, where he continued to exert an international influence on typography through his writing and design. I. T.

TRISTAN TZARA
Born in Moineste, Romania, 1896
Died in Paris, 1963

As a young man. Tzara studied in Zurich, and it was there that he oversaw the birth of the Dada movement at the Cabaret Voltaire. He became the editor of the periodical *DADA* in 1917 and continued to explore sound poetry, nonsense poetry, and the poetry of chance with Hugo Ball, Richard Huelsenbeck, and Jean Arp in periodicals as well as in Dada performances. In the pivotal *Dada manifesto* of 1918, Tzara gave further power to the name of his movement and declared that the best system was no system at all. The *Manifesto,* calling for a "purge" in art, announced Tzara's quest to make Dada an international movement. He became involved in publications in Paris, New York, and Germany. His own work illustrated Dada's rebellion against tradition and support of spontaneity. In 1921 Tzara moved to Paris to strengthen the Dada movement there, but after disagreements with André Breton and Francis Picabia, he decided to disband the Dada movement and pursue his poetry. His poems focused on the nature of humanity and art, and his published collections from 1939 to 1959 were illustrated by Henri Matisse, André Mason, Joan Miró, and Pablo Picasso. Tzara married Greta Knutson, a Swedish artist from a wealthy family, in 1925, and they commissioned a house from the noted modernist Adolf Loos. In 1929 Tzara joined the Surrealists, contributing to that movement until 1935. J. R.

HENDRIK NICOLAAS WERKMAN
Born in Leens, the Netherlands, 1882
Died in Groningen, the Netherlands, 1945

Printmaking pioneer Hendrik Werkman began his life as a journalist and amateur photographer. He left the newspaper business in 1907 to become the foreman at Knoop printers in Wildervank and left a year later to found his own shop in Groningen. Werkman was associated with De Ploeg (The Plow) group in 1920, and with them exhibited Van Gogh–influenced landscapes and portraits. The first issue of his self-produced magazine, *The Next Call,* published in 1923, included typographical and other printmaking experiments as well as his own Dadaist poems and texts. Working in an attic studio, Werkman invented the printing process he called *hot printing,* which incorporated found materials as plate elements and consisted of the repeated addition of design elements, one by one, on the paper. Like the collages of Kurt Schwitters, these *druskels* were unique prints that soon included the use of rollers directly on the paper.

For the next decade, Werkman continued his experiments with stamping and stenciling, supporting himself by producing advertising leaflets and posters. His first exhibition was held in 1939 at Helen Spoor Gallery in Amsterdam, and in 1940 he began an association with the anti-Nazi magazine *De Blauwe Schuitt* (The blue barge). The underground magazine was produced by a group of Jewish dissident poets and writers, and Werkman printed all forty issues. Arrested by the German secret police in 1945, he was executed without trial after a month of incarceration. Many of his works were confiscated at the time of his arrest and were lost in a fire when Groningen was liberated three days after the artist's death. I. B.

HENDRICKUS THEODORUS WIJDEVELD
Born in The Hague, 1885
Died in Amsterdam, 1989

Wijdeveld began his career as an apprentice carpenter at age twelve and soon started work in the P. J. H. Cuypers architecture firm in Amsterdam. While working at J. Groll's office in England from 1905 to 1908, he attended evening classes at the Lambeth School of Art and was introduced to the works of John Ruskin and William Morris. After his return to Amsterdam in 1914, he set up shop as an architect and graphic designer and also designed furniture and toys. In 1918 Wijdeveld founded the journal *Wendingen,* and in its pages developed an influential text style that was known for its blocks of dense sans serif letters. His designs, known as the "Wijdeveld" or "Wendingen" style, were frequently copied within advertising and other journals, whereas his expressionistic utopian architecture style faltered in opposition to the cleaner lines of De Stijl. In the late 1920s he began concentrating on theater costume design and was one of the first in Europe to champion the work of the American architect Frank Lloyd Wright. I. B.

BEATRICE WOOD
Born in San Francisco, 1893

At sixteen Beatrice Wood rebelled against her staid and wealthy parents, threatening to run away, live in a garret, and become a painter. As a compromise, she was allowed to go to Paris with a chaperone, where she acted and danced. She then traveled to New York, where by chance she met Marcel Duchamp. He soon became her mentor and then her lover, encouraging her to draw imaginatively and introducing her to his avant-garde circle of friends. She contributed Dadaist drawings and watercolors to Duchamp's *Fountain* and edited the *Blindman* with Duchamp and Henri-Pierre Roché in 1917. In 1923 Wood joined the Theosophical Society and briefly followed the Indian philosopher Krishnamurti to Europe. Later she settled in Los Angeles, and then in Hollywood, where she studied ceramics from 1933. Wood developed a rich in-glaze luster that brought her international acclaim. In 1961 she visited India at the Indian government's request, traveling and lecturing on her ceramic work. Deeply influenced by Indian folk art, Wood continues to create whimsical clay figures and functional ceramic ware. J. R.

IL'IA MIKHAILOVICH ZDANEVICH
Born in Tiflis (Tbilisi), Georgian Republic, 1894
Died in Paris, 1975

Zdanevich, an artist and poet, began to study law at St. Petersburg University in 1911. At the same time, he started to establish himself in avant-garde circles. Zdanevich had several pseudonyms, including Varsanofi Parkin, Iliazd (from IL'YA ZDanevich), and Eli Eganbury, which he created by writing his name in Cyrillic script but reading it in Latin script. His play with words predates aspects of Dadaism, in which he later participated. In 1913 he developed the Futurist phenomenon *Vsechestvo* (Everythingism), which he described as an approach to art and its materials rather than a theory or a tendency. In March 1917, during the Revolution, along with Natan Al'tman, Sergei Isakov, Vladimir Maiakovskii, Vsevolod Meyerhold, Nikolai Punin, and Vladimir Tretyakov, Zdanevich helped to organize the Freedom to Art Association in Petrograd. From 1917 to 1919, he was also involved with the Georgian Futurist group 41°.

During 1918–19 Zdanevich apprenticed as a typographer, and in 1920 he moved to Paris after receiving a scholarship to study in France. Once in Paris, he became acquainted with the Dadaists and helped to organize the *Coeur à barbe* soiree. In 1923 he participated in a performance of Tristan Tzara's *La coeur à gaz.* Several of his books were included in the *Paris International Exhibition* of 1925. In the late 1920s and early 1930s, he directed fabric production for Coco Chanel, and by 1938 he had developed a close friendship with Pablo Picasso and produced a book containing six of Picasso's etchings. In the years 1939 to 1974 he created twenty illustrated works that included his own poetic texts. I. T.

PIET ZWART
Born in Zaandijk, the Netherlands, 1885
Died in Wassenaar, the Netherlands, 1977

Interior designer and graphic artist Piet Zwart studied at the Rijksschool voor Kunsthijverheld in Amsterdam from 1902 to 1906 and by 1911 was creating new designs for interiors and furniture. World War I cut short his studies at the Delft Technical College in 1914; five years later became acquainted with the De Stijl movement. For the next few years he worked with Vilmos Huszar and Jan Wils and through them was introduced to the architect H. P. Berlage, for whom he worked from 1921 to 1927. Zwart's signature style can be found in his typographic designs for the Dutch postal service and for the NKF cable company that were made during this period. The influence of such artists as El Lissitzky, Theo van Doesburg, and Kurt Schwitters is visible in his work, and in the late 1920s, his graphic design began to include photography. In 1938 he designed a kitchen for the Bruynzeel Company that modernized home interior design. I. B.

CHECKLIST OF THE EXHIBITION

EVA CHRISTINA KRAUS

1

plate 16

NATAN ISAEVICH AL'TMAN
Krasnyi student (Red student)
Design for journal cover, USSR, 1923
Ink, crayon, 15 3/8 x 11 1/2

2

fig. 1.18

JOHANNES BAADER
Reklame für mich: Dada Milchstrasse
(Advertisement for myself: Dada Milky Way)
Collage, Germany, 1919–20
Halftone photographs, printed letters, ink,
handwriting, paste, 19 5/8 x 13

3

fig. 1.19

JOHANNES BAADER AND RAOUL HAUSMANN
Dada Milchstrasse (Dada Milky Way)
Poster with letter, Germany, 1918
Lithograph with handwriting in ink, 19 5/8 x 12 1/8

4

GIACOMO BALLA
Exposition des peintres futuristes italiens
Leaflet, Italy, 1921
Letterpress, 9 1/4 x 6 7/8

5

plate 12

GIACOMO BALLA
TI TA TO One Step
Music sheet, Italy, 1918–20
Lithograph, 13 3/8 x 9 1/2

6

plate 44

OTTO BAUMBERGER
PKZ
Poster, Switzerland, 1923
Lithograph, 50 1/4 x 35 1/2

7

fig. 3.15

ATTRIBUTED TO WILLI BAUMEISTER
Die Wohnung (The dwelling)
Poster, Germany, 1927
Lithograph, 45 1/16 x 32 1/8

8

plate 33

HERBERT BAYER
Bart-Nasen-Herzensfest (Beard-Nose-Heart Festival)
Invitation, Germany, 1928
Letterpress, 5 13/16 x 16 5/8

9

plate 28

HERBERT BAYER
Ausstellung (Exhibition)
Design for Bauhaus exhibition sign, Germany, 1923
Pencil, ink, gouache, 12 x 3 3/4

10

plate 47

HERBERT BAYER
Glasmaler Kraus (Glass painter Kraus)
Design for illuminated roof sign, Germany, 1923
Pencil, ink, gouache, pasted paper, 11 1/4 x 8 3/8

11

HERBERT BAYER
Glasmaler Kraus (Glass painter Kraus)
Design for sign, Germany, 1923
Pencil, ink, gouache, 11 1/4 x 8 3/8

12

HERBERT BAYER
Glasmaler Kraus (Glass painter Kraus)
Design for sign, Germany, 1923
Pencil, ink, gouache, 11 1/4 x 8 1/2

13

HERBERT BAYER
Glasmaler Kraus (Glass painter Kraus)
Design for sign, Germany, 1923
Pencil, ink, gouache, 11 1/4 x 8 3/8

14

plate 29

HERBERT BAYER
Mural design for Bauhaus stairwell, Germany, 1923
Gouache, pencil, cut paper, 22 7/8 x 10 3/8

15

plate 27

HERBERT BAYER
Staatliches Bauhaus Ausstellung (Bauhaus exhibition)
Design for poster, Germany, 1923
Pencil, ink, gouache, 16 15/16 x 11 7/8

16

plate 48

HERBERT BAYER
Ventzky Ackergeräte
(Ventzky Agricultural Machinery)
Design for exhibition stand, Germany, 1928
Pencil, gouache, paste, halftone photograph
19 5/8 x 26 13/16

17

HERBERT BAYER
Werbeentwurf und Ausführung
(Advertising design and production)
Promotional card, Germany, 1928
Letterpress, 4 3/16 x 5 7/8

18

plate 74

LESTER BEALL
Cross Out Slums
Poster, USA, 1930s
Lithograph, 39 3/4 x 29 7/16

All measurements are in inches.

19
plate 107
LESTER BEALL
It Mustn't Happen Here
Design for poster, USA, 1930s
Gouache, gelatin silver prints,
pencil, cut paper, 27 1/2 x 19 1/2

20
plate 79
LESTER BEALL
It's Fine for Us
Poster, USA, 1930s
Silkscreen, lithograph, 40 x 29 7/8

21
fig. 3.14
plate 78
LESTER BEALL
Light
Poster, USA, 1937
Silkscreen, 39 7/8 x 30 1/8

22
plate 75
LESTER BEALL
Radio
Poster, USA, 1937
Silkscreen, 40 x 30 1/8

23
plate 77
LESTER BEALL
Running Water
Poster, USA, 1937
Silkscreen, 40 x 30 1/8

24
plate 58
LESTER BEALL
Rural Electrification Administration
Poster, USA, c. 1937
Silkscreen, lithograph, 40 x 30

25
plate 76
LESTER BEALL
Wash Day
Poster, USA, 1937
Silkscreen, 39 7/8 x 30 1/8

26
plate 24
HENRYK BERLEWI
1ᵃ *WYSTAWA PRAC MECHANO = Fakturowych*
(First exhibition of Mechano-Faktur works)
Design for poster, Poland, 1924
Gouache, 24 3/4 x 19 3/8

27
plate 26
HENRYK BERLEWI
Neo Faktur 23
Theoretical exercise, Germany, 1923
Gouache, pencil, 21 x 16 5/8

28
fig. 3.19
FRANCIS BERNARD
Arts ménagers (Domestic arts)
Poster, France, 1933
Lithograph, 61 3/4 x 46 1/16

29
fig. 3.5
FRANCIS BERNARD
Gaz
Poster, France, 1928
Lithograph, 63 x 47 1/4

30
plate 82
MARIANNE BRANDT
Les sports—le sport
Collage, Germany, 1928
Halftone photographs, printed letters, paste
19 x 12 1/4

31
plate 81
MARIANNE BRANDT
Nos soeurs d'Amérique (Our American sisters)
Collage, Germany
Halftone photographs, printed letters,
hand lettering, paste, 19 9/16 x 12 5/8

32
plate 66
MAX BURCHARTZ AND JOHANNIS CANIS
Bochumer Verein (Bochum Union)
Catalogue, Germany, 1929
Lithograph, 11 7/8 x 8 1/2

33
plate 67
MAX BURCHARTZ
Rotes Quadrat (Red square)
Collage, Germany
Gouache, halftone photograph, printed logo
20 3/8 x 13 7/8

34
MAX BURCHARTZ
Werbe-Bau (Advertising construction)
Promotional leaflet, Germany, 1925–26
Letterpress, 11 3/4 x 8 1/4

35
plate 45
JEAN-GEORGES-LEON CARLU
Disques Odéon
Poster, USA, 1929
Lithograph, 99 x 52

36
fig. 3.24
JEAN-GEORGES-LEON CARLU
Production
Poster, USA, 1941
Lithograph, 29 7/8 x 40 1/8

37

plate 51

CASSANDRE
L'Atlantique
Poster, France, 1931
Lithograph, 39 3/4 x 25

38

plate 72

CASSANDRE
L'Intransigéant
Poster, France, 1925
Lithograph, 35 3/8 x 63

39

fig. 3.30

CASSANDRE
Nicolas
Poster, France, 1935
Lithograph, 94 1/2 x 126

40

plate 50

CASSANDRE
Restaurez-vous au wagon-bar
(Refresh yourself at the wagon bar)
Poster, France, 1932
Lithograph, 39 1/2 x 24 1/2

41

fig. 3.25

CASSANDRE
Thomson
Poster, France, 1931
Lithograph, 46 15/16 x 31 1/2

42

plate 100

CHIAREL
Duce a noi (Il Duce for us)
Poster, Italy, 1930s
Lithograph, 12 5/16 x 37

43

CHARLES TOUCEY COINER
Give It Your Best!
Poster, USA, 1940s
Lithograph, 41 1/4 x 57 1/8

44

plate 106

CHARLES TOUCEY COINER
NRA. We Do Our Part.
Poster, USA, 1934
Silkscreen, 28 1/4 x 21

45

fig. 1.13

JEAN CROTTI
Poésie sentimentale
Painting with embossing, France, 1920
Gouache, ink, 21 1/8 x 17 3/8

46

fig. 1.14

JEAN CROTTI AND SUZANNE DUCHAMP
Exposition des oeuvres de Suzanne Duchamp et Jean Crotti
Poster, France, 1921
Lithograph, 46 1/2 x 31

47

plate 10

FORTUNATO DEPERO
Depero Futurista (Depero the Futurist)
Book, Italy, 1927
Letterpress, 9 5/8 x 11 5/8

48

plate 13

FORTUNATO DEPERO
Secolo XX (Twentieth century)
Magazine cover, Italy, 1929
Letterpress, 15 5/8 x 11 9/16

49

fig. 2.27

WALTER DEXEL
Fotografie der Gegenwart (Contemporary photography)
Poster, Germany, 1929
Linocut, 33 1/16 x 23 7/16

50

fig. 3.6

WALTER DEXEL
Gas zum kochen, backen, heizen, beleuchten
(Gas for cooking, baking, heating, and lighting)
Design for illuminated sign, Germany, 1924
Ink, gouache, pencil, pasted paper, hand lettering
19 3/4 x 13 3/8

51

fig. 3.26

WALTER DEXEL
Zigarren, Zigaretten (Cigars, cigarettes)
Design for advertising clock, Germany, 1927
Ink, gouache, pencil, 14 1/2 x 10 5/8

52

plate 2

THEO VAN DOESBURG
6e jaar, NB DeStijl, Dada, 1923
Postcard, Germany, 1923
Ink, watercolor, stamped and printed letters
3 1/4 x 5 3/8

53

*figs. 1.26,
3.17*

THEO VAN DOESBURG
Mécano No. Bleu, Blauw, Blau, Blue, 1922
Journal, Netherlands, 1922
Letterpress, 6 1/2 x 5 1/8

54

plate 40

THEO VAN DOESBURG
Prima Goudsche Kaas (Fine Gouda cheese)
Label, Netherlands, 1919
Lithograph, 7 3/8 diameter

70
JOHN HEARTFIELD
Upton Sinclair: Petroleum
plate 96   Book jacket, Germany, 1927
Letterpress, 7 7/16 x 18 3/8

71
JOHN HEARTFIELD, RAOUL HAUSMANN,
AND GEORGE GROSZ
fig. 1.16   *DER dADa 3*
Journal with reproduction of collage by Heartfield
Germany, 1920
Letterpress, 9 1/8 x 6 3/16

72
HANNAH HÖCH
dada
fig. 1.22   Collage, Germany, 1922
Printed letters, postage stamp, cut paper, paste
18 5/8 x 24 7/8

73
VILMOS HUSZAR
Miss Blanche Virginia Cigarettes
fig. 3.10   Poster, 1926
Lithograph, 11 3/4 x 7 1/2

74
VILMOS HUSZAR
Miss Blanche Virginia Cigarettes
plate 39   Display object, 1926
Lithograph, 9 1/4 x 6 5/8 x 3

75
VILMOS HUSZAR
Miss Blanche Virginia Cigarettes
plate 38   Halftone photograph of display cart, 1920s
Letterpress, 5 13/16 x 9

76
VILMOS HUSZAR
N. V. Hollandsche Deurenfabriek (Dutch Door Factory)
Letterhead and envelope, Netherlands, c. 1920
Letterpress; envelope 4 1/8 x 9 1/2;
letterhead 11 15/16 x 8 11/16

77
MARCEL JANCO
Galerie Corray
fig. 1.4   Poster, Switzerland, 1917
Linocut, 16 3/4 x 10 3/8

78
VASILII VASIL'EVICH KAMENSKII
Tango s korovami (Tango with cows)
plate 20   Book, Russia, 1914
Letterpress on wallpaper, 7 7/8 x 16 1/8 (open)

79
EDWARD MCKNIGHT KAUFFER
Power: The Nerve Centre of London's Underground
fig. 3.21   Poster, England, 1930
Lithograph, 39 13/16 x 24 3/4

80
EDWARD MCKNIGHT KAUFFER
Tea Drives Away the Droops
plate 4   Poster, England, 1936
Lithograph, 29 x 19

81
EDWARD MCKNIGHT KAUFFER
Vigil, the Pure Silk
plate 46   Poster, England, 1919
Lithograph, 31 5/8 x 23 1/8

82
EDWARD MCKNIGHT KAUFFER
Yugoslav People Led by Tito
plate 103   Poster, USA, 1940s
Lithograph, 24 3/4 x 19 1/4

83
GUSTAV GUSTAVOVICH KLUTSIS
Ekran (Screen)
fig. 3.7   Design for propaganda stand, USSR, 1922
Linocut, 9 1/16 x 4 7/16

84
GUSTAV GUSTAVOVICH KLUTSIS
Elektrifikatsiia vsei strany
(Electrification of the entire country)
plate 59   Design for poster, USSR, 1920
Ink, gouache, gelatin silver prints,
colored paper, pencil, printed letters, paste
18 1/8 x 10 3/4

85
GUSTAV GUSTAVOVICH KLUTSIS
K mirovomu oktiabriu (Toward a world October)
fig. 2.30   Design for poster, USSR, 1931
Gelatin silver prints, halftone photographs,
gouache, ink, paste, 11 1/8 x 8 1/8

86
GUSTAV GUSTAVOVICH KLUTSIS
Osnovanie (Fundamentals)
plate 21   Design for stand, USSR, c. 1926
Pencil, ink, gouache, 7 1/16 x 4 13/16

87

plate 70

GUSTAV GUSTAVOVICH KLUTSIS
Pod'niat proizvoditel'nost' truda
(Raise the productivity of labor)
Design for poster, USSR, 1933
Ink, pencil, gouache, gelatin silver prints,
hand lettering, handwriting, paste, 9 3/8 x 12

88

plate 91

GUSTAV GUSTAVOVICH KLUTSIS
Real'nost' nashei programmy
(The reality of our program)
Design for poster, USSR, 1931
Ink, pencil, gelatin silver prints, 10 x 14

89

plate 92

GUSTAV GUSTAVOVICH KLUTSIS
Real'nost' nashei programmy
(The reality of our program)
Design for poster, USSR, 1931
Photographs, ink, gouache, paste, photomechanically
reproduced letters, 9 1/2 x 6 1/2

90

plate 90

GUSTAV GUSTAVOVICH KLUTSIS
Real'nost' nashei programmy
(The reality of our program)
Poster, USSR, 1931
Lithograph, 56 3/8 x 40 3/4

91

plate 22

GUSTAV GUSTAVOVICH KLUTSIS
Smotri v vitrinu (Look in the shop window)
Design for window display, USSR
Pencil, ink, gouache, 10 1/8 x 7 7/16

92

plate 83

GUSTAV GUSTAVOVICH KLUTSIS
Spartakiada Moscow 1928
Design for poster, USSR, 1928
Halftone photographs, gelatin silver prints,
colored paper, paste, 23 3/4 x 27 1/2

93

fig. 2.29

GUSTAV GUSTAVOVICH KLUTSIS
Spartakiada Moscow 1928
Five postcards, USSR, 1928
Letterpress, approx. 6 x 4 1/2 each

94

plate 23

GUSTAV GUSTAVOVICH KLUTSIS
Workers of the World Unite
Design for propaganda stand, USSR, 1922
Linocut, 9 1/4 x 5 5/16

95

fig. 2.13

VLADIMIR IVANOVICH KOZLINSKII
Nesmotria na trekhletnie usiliia
(Despite three years of effort)
Poster, USSR, 1920
Linocut, 28 1/8 x 19 5/8

96

plate 63

VALENTINA NIKIFOROVNA KULAGINA
Stroim (We are building)
Design for poster, USSR, 1929
Watercolor, gouache, sandpaper,
halftone photographs, cut paper, paste
22 5/8 x 14 1/4

97

VALENTINA NIKIFOROVNA KULAGINA
Stroim (We are building)
Postcard, USSR, 1929
Letterpress, 5 3/4 x 4

98

plate 60

VLADIMIR VASIL'EVICH LEBEDEV
Soiuz derevni i goroda, rabochie i krest'iane
(The union of country and city,
workers and peasants)
Drawing, USSR, c. 1920
Ink, gouache, 10 1/2 x 8 5/16

99

plate 6

BART VAN DER LECK
Delftsche Slaolie (Delft Salad Oil)
Design for poster, Netherlands, 1919
Gouache, 34 1/4 x 23 1/8

100

plate 7

BART VAN DER LECK
Delftsche Slaolie (Delft Salad Oil)
Design for poster (state 1), Netherlands, 1919
Charcoal, pastel, 39 1/8 x 28 1/2

101

plate 8

BART VAN DER LECK
Delftsche Slaolie (Delft Salad Oil)
Design for poster (state 2), Netherlands, 1919
Gouache, pencil, charcoal, 34 1/4 x 23

102

plate 9

BART VAN DER LECK
Delftsche Slaolie (Delft Salad Oil)
Design for poster (state 3), Netherlands, 1919
Gouache, pencil, 39 1/8 x 28 3/4

103 ANDRE LHOTE AND
IL'IA MIKHAILOVICH ZDANEVICH
fig. 1.10 *Fête de nuit à Montparnasse, Bal costumé*
(Evening party at Montparnasse, costume ball)
Poster, France, 1922
Lithograph, 54 7/8 x 39 3/8

104 EL LISSITZKY
(LAZAR' MARKOVICH LISITSKII)
fig. 1.30 *Merz-Matinéen*
Broadside, Germany, 1923
Letterpress, 9 x 11 1/8

105 EL LISSITZKY
(LAZAR' MARKOVICH LISITSKII)
fig. 3.23 *Pelican Drawing Ink*
Advertisement, 1925
Lithograph, 12 3/4 x 17 3/8

106 EL LISSITZKY
(LAZAR' MARKOVICH LISITSKII)
plate 37 *Pelikan—Siegellack* (Pelikan Sealing Wax)
Package, c. 1925
Lithograph, 3 1/2 x 8 3/8 x 1 1/2

107 EL LISSITZKY
(LAZAR' MARKOVICH LISITSKII)
plate 37 *Pelikan—Siegellack* (Pelikan Sealing Wax)
Package, c. 1925
Lithograph, 4 x 9 5/8 x 1 1/16

108 EL LISSITZKY
(LAZAR' MARKOVICH LISITSKII)
plate 71 *Pressa Köln 1928*
Book, Germany, 1928
Rotogravure, 8 3/8 x 12
(c. 80 inches wide fully extended)

109 EL LISSITZKY
(LAZAR' MARKOVICH LISITSKII)
plate 57 *Russische Ausstellung* (Russian exhibition)
Poster, Switzerland, 1929
Rotogravure, 49 3/4 x 35 5/8

110 EL LISSITZKY
(LAZAR' MARKOVICH LISITSKII)
fig. 1.28 AND VLADIMIROVICH MAIAKOVSKII
Pro 2 kvadrata (Of two squares)
Book, Germany, designed 1920, published 1922
Letterpress, 11 1/8 x 8 7/8

111 EL LISSITZKY
(LAZAR' MARKOVICH LISITSKII)
figs. 1.29, AND VLADIMIR VLADIMIROVICH MAIAKOVSKII
2.15 *Dlia golosa* (For the voice)
Book, Germany, 1923
Letterpress, 7 7/16 x 10 1/4 (open)

112 HEINZ LOEW
Design for exhibition, Germany, 1929
plate 49 Gouache, halftone photographs, rotogravure, pencil
21 1/2 x 18

113 LEO MARFURT
Flying Scotsman
plate 53 Poster, Great Britain, 1928
Lithograph, 40 x 50 1/8

114 FILIPPO TOMMASO MARINETTI
Almanacco Italia veloce (Almanac of fast Italy)
plate 14 Cover, Italy
Letterpress with handwriting, 9 x 11 5/8

115 FILIPPO TOMMASO MARINETTI
Les mots en liberté futuristes (Futurist words in liberty)
figs. 1.3, Book, Italy, 1919
2.7 Letterpress, 7 9/16 x 5 1/8

116 FILIPPO TOMMASO MARINETTI
Parole in libertà (Words in liberty)
fig. 2.8 Journal, Italy, 1915
Letterpress, 13 5/8 x 9 3/4

117 VLADIMIR VLADIMIROVICH MAIAKOVSKII
Kto pobedit? (Who will win?)
Posters, USSR, 1921
Stencil prints with gouache
Twelve pieces, sizes vary

118
fig. 3.8

ROBERT MICHEL
Persil, für alle Wäsche
(Persil, for all your laundry)
Design for billboard, Germany, 1926
Colored ink, ink, pencil, 20 1/2 x 17 1/4

119
fig. 2.23

LASZLO MOHOLY-NAGY
14 Bauhausbücher
(Fourteen Bauhaus books)
Catalogue, Germany, 1927
Letterpress, 5 5/16 x 8 1/4

120

LASZLO MOHOLY-NAGY
Bauhausbücher (Bauhaus books)
Prospectus, Germany, 1924
Letterpress, 9 1/16 x 14 1/8 (open)

121
plate 32

LASZLO MOHOLY-NAGY
Fototek 1
Book, Germany, 1930
Letterpress, 9 13/16 x 6 13/16

122
plate 25

FARKAS MOLNAR
MA—Aktivista Folyoirat
Design for cover, Hungary, 1924
Gouache, ink, pencil, cut paper
12 1/16 x 12 1/8

123
plate 55

C. O. MÜLLER
Elisabeth Bergner in Donna Juana
Poster, Germany, 1920s
Letterpress, 47 5/8 x 34 5/8

124
fig. 1.11

FRANCIS PICABIA
Cinésketch
Poster, France, 1924
Lithograph with watercolor, 27 3/8 x 21

125
fig. 3.28

NATAL'IA SERGEEVNA PINUS-BUKHAROVA
Trudiashchiesia zhenshchiny—v riady . . . !
(Women workers—Into the ranks . . . !)
Poster, USSR
Lithograph, 38 5/8 x 28

126
plate 61

B. POPOV AND I. VILKOVIR
Luchshie udarniki (The best shockworkers)
Design for factory wall, USSR, 1931
Gouache, pencil, cut paper, halftone photographs,
paste, hand lettering, 9 1/4 x 33 9/16

127
plate 15

LIUBOV' SERGEEVNA POPOVA
Da zdravstvuet diktatura proletariata!
(Long live the dictatorship of the proletariat!)
Placard, USSR
Ink, watercolor, pencil, cut paper, paste
7 15/16 x 9 13/16

128
plate 16

LIUBOV' SERGEEVNA POPOVA
Prozodezhda aktera No. 7
(The magnanimous cuckold: Actor no. 7)
Costume design, USSR, 1921
Pencil, gouache, cut paper
13 1/2 x 9 11/16

129
plate 73

MAN RAY
Keeps London Going
Poster, England, 1932
Lithograph, 39 11/16 x 24 1/2

130
fig. 2.31

MIKHAIL IOSIFOVICH RAZULEVICH
Kabel' i ukhvaty (Cables and tongs)
Design for book cover, USSR
Gelatin silver prints, hand lettering,
gouache, ink, paste, tracing paper, colored paper, pencil
6 3/16 x 9 9/16

131
fig. 2.32

MIKHAIL IOSIFOVICH RAZULEVICH
Kabel' i ukhvaty (Cables and tongs)
Book cover, USSR
Letterpress, 8 1/2 x 13 1/4

132

MIKHAIL IOSIFOVICH RAZULEVICH
Noveishie navigatsionnye instrumenty
(The latest navigational instruments)
Design for book cover, USSR, 1934
Ink, gouache, watercolor, hand lettering,
cut paper, 12 7/16 x 8 3/8

133
MIKHAIL IOSIFOVICH RAZULEVICH
Shest' uslovii pobedy (Six conditions of victory)
plate 95 Design for book cover, USSR, 1932
Rotogravure photographs, gouache, cut paper, paste
14 3/4 x 11 5/8

134
MIKHAIL IOSIFOVICH RAZULEVICH
Sovetskaia vlast' plius elektrifikatsiia
plate 69 (Soviet power plus electrification)
Vintage photomontage, USSR
Photograph, 6 9/16 x 23

135
ALEKSANDR MIKHAILOVICH RODCHENKO
Kakao (Cocoa)
fig. 3.1 Design for poster, USSR, c. 1923–24
Pencil, gouache, 33 1/8 x 23 1/2

136
ALEKSANDR MIKHAILOVICH RODCHENKO
Kino Glaz (Kino eye)
fig. 2.1 Poster, USSR, 1924
Lithograph, 36 1/2 x 27 1/2

137
ALEKSANDR MIKHAILOVICH RODCHENKO
LEF No. 3
plate 68 Design for magazine cover, USSR, 1924
Halftone photograph, printed letters,
cut paper letters, hand lettering, pencil,
gouache, colored paper, paste, 9 1/8 x 6 1/8

138
ALEKSANDR MIKHAILOVICH RODCHENKO
Pechen'e 'Krasnyi aviator' ("Red Aviator" cookies)
fig. 3.13 Wrapper, USSR, 1923–24
Lithograph, 10 1/8 x 11 1/16

139
ALEKSANDR MIKHAILOVICH RODCHENKO
Pechen'e 'Zebra' ("Zebra" cookies)
plate 36 Wrapper, USSR, 1924
Lithograph, 13 7/8 x 5 11/16

140
ALEKSANDR MIKHAILOVICH RODCHENKO
SMOTRI (Look)
plate 35 Design for signboard, USSR, c. 1924
Gouache on cut board, 17 1/2 x 18 5/8 (irregular)

141
ALEKSANDR MIKHAILOVICH RODCHENKO
Stolovoe maslo (Vegetable oil)
fig. 2.18 Design for poster, USSR, c. 1923
Gouache, ink, pencil, cut paper, paste, 33 x 23

142
ALEKSANDR MIKHAILOVICH RODCHENKO
Stolovoe maslo (Vegetable oil)
fig. 3.3 Poster, USSR, 1923
Lithograph, 26 11/16 x 19 1/2

143
ALEKSANDR MIKHAILOVICH RODCHENKO
U.R.S.S. L'Art décoratif Moscou-Paris 1925
fig. 2.16 Book, USSR, 1925
Lithograph, 10 1/4 x 7 7/8

144
ALEKSANDR MIKHAILOVICH RODCHENKO
AND VLADIMIR VLADIMIROVICH MAIAKOVSKII
fig. 3.12 *Karamel' 'Nasha industriia'* ("Our Industry" candy)
Two wrappers, USSR, 1924
Letterpress, 3 1/4 x 3 each

145
ALEKSANDR MIKHAILOVICH RODCHENKO
AND VLADIMIR VLADIMIROVICH MAIAKOVSKII
plate 65 *Daite solntse noch'iu* (Give me sun at night)
Design for poster, USSR, 1923
Gouache, ink, pencil, gelatin silver print
4 3/8 x 11 3/16

146
ALEKSANDR MIKHAILOVICH RODCHENKO
AND VARVARA FEDOROVNA STEPANOVA
fig. 2.17 *LEF No. 2 Prospekt*
Prospectus for magazine, USSR, 1924
Letterpress, 9 1/8 x 6 1/8

147
VLADIMIR O. ROSKIN
GET (GET—State Electric Trust)
fig. 3.18 Design for poster, USSR, 1925–26
Gouache, ink, pencil, 8 1/2 x 11 3/16

148
VLADIMIR O. ROSKIN
NGSNKh
plate 64 (Commissariat of the National Economy)
Design for poster, USSR, 1925
Gouache, pencil, ink, hand lettering
13 1/2 x 10

149
XANTI SCHAWINSKY
1934—Year XII of the Fascist Era
fig. 2.6 Poster, Italy, 1934
Letterpress, 37 11/16 x 28 1/4

150

FRITZ SCHLEIFER
Staatliches Bauhaus Ausstellung (Bauhaus exhibition)
fig. 1.35   Poster, Germany, 1923
Lithograph, 39 3/8 x 28 3/4

151

OSKAR SCHLEMMER
Das Triadische Ballet (The triad ballet)
plate 34   Poster, Germany, 1921
Lithograph, 32 1/2 x 22 1/8

152

JOOST SCHMIDT
Das Neue Schachspiel (The new chess game)
plate 31   Design for poster, Germany, 1923
Ink, pencil, 15 3/4 x 16 3/16

153

JOOST SCHMIDT
Schach (Chess)
plate 30   Postcard, Germany, 1924
Lithograph, 4 11/16 x 5 7/8

154

JOOST SCHMIDT
Staatliches Bauhaus Ausstellung
(Bauhaus exhibition)
fig. 1.34   Poster, Germany, 1923
Lithograph, 27 x 19

155

PAUL SCHUITEMA
Centrale Bond 30.000 Transportarbeiders
(Central Union 30,000 transport workers)
plate 41   Poster, Netherland, 1930
Lithograph, 47 3/4 x 31 1/2

156

PAUL SCHUITEMA
Every Berkel Is a Proved Machine
fig. 1.32   Advertisement, Netherlands, 1926
Letterpress, 8 1/4 x 11 1/2

157

PAUL SCHUITEMA
Superior Dutch Ham
figs. 1.31,   Poster, Netherlands, c. 1925
3.27   Lithograph, 19 3/4 x 19 7/8

158

PAUL SCHUITEMA
Toledo Berkel 85000
fig. 1.33   Advertisement, Netherlands, 1926
Letterpress, 11 9/16 x 8 1/4

159

KURT SCHWITTERS
Die Neue Gestaltung in der Typographie
(The new design in typography)
fig. 2.11   Booklet, Germany, c. 1930
Letterpress, 5 7/8 x 8 3/8 (open)

160

KURT SCHWITTERS
Kurt Schwitters liest Märchen vor
(Kurt Schwitters reads fairy tales)
fig. 1.23   Collage, Germany, c. 1925
Printed letters, printed wrapper, handwriting,
cut paper, paste, 13 1/2 x 9 1/8

161

KURT SCHWITTERS AND THEO VAN DOESBURG
Kleine Dada soirée (Little Dada evening)
fig. 1.24   Poster, Germany, 1923
Lithograph, 11 7/8 x 11 3/4

162

ELENA VLADIMIROVNA SEMENOVA
Politicheskii sostav
(Central Committee personnel
at the Fourth Party Congress)
Design for chart, USSR
Ink, gouache, metallic paint, gelatin
silver prints, 4 3/4 x 4

163

SENCO
2e mostra della radio (Second radio exposition)
fig. 2.5   Promotional card, Italy, 1930
Lithograph, 9 1/2 x 6 3/4

164

OTIS SHEPARD
Wrigley's Spearmint Gum
fig. 3.2   Poster, USA, c. 1935
Lithograph, 39 3/4 x 26 3/8

165

ARDEGNO SOFFICI
BÏFŞZF+18, Simultaneità chimismi lirici
plate 11   (The simultaneity of lyrical chemical reactions)
Book, Italy, 1919
Letterpress, 7 3/4 x 11 3/8 (open)

166

VLADIMIR AVGUSTOVICH STENBERG
AND GEORGII AVGUSTOVICH STENBERG
fig. 3.29   *Chelovek s kinoapparatom* (Man with a movie camera)
Poster, USSR, 1926
Lithograph, 43 1/2 x 28

167   VLADIMIR AVGUSTOVICH STENBERG
         AND GEORGII AVGUSTOVICH STENBERG
plate 54   *Odinnadtsatyi* (The eleventh)
         Poster, USSR, 1928
         Lithograph, 37 7/8 x 26 3/4

168   ATTRIBUTED TO VLADIMIR AVGUSTOVICH STENBERG
         AND GEORGII AVGUSTOVICH STENBERG
fig. 3.31   *Poslednii polet* (The last flight)
         Poster, USSR, 1929
         Lithograph, in two pieces, 28 x 42 3/16 each

169   VLADIMIR AVGUSTOVICH STENBERG
         AND GEORGII AVGUSTOVICH STENBERG
fig. 3.20   *Simfoniia bol'shogo goroda* (Symphony of a great city)
         Poster, USSR, 1928
         Lithograph, 42 1/2 x 27 3/4

170   VARVARA FEDOROVNA STEPANOVA
         Goloi rukoi nas NE VOZMESH'
plate 93   (You won't take us with your bare hand)
         Book, USSR, c. 1932
         Letterpress, 9 9/16 x 17 1/4

171   VARVARA FEDOROVNA STEPANOVA
         (Photograph by IGNATOVITCH)
plate 94   *KREPI chem mozhesh' oboronu!*
         (Strengthen defense with whatever you can!)
         Design for poster, USSR
         Photograph pasted on red paper, 9 15/16 x 6 7/8

172   VARVARA FEDOROVNA STEPANOVA
         Smert' Tarelkina (The death of Tarelkin)
fig. 2.14   Poster, USSR, 1922
         Letterpress, 27 1/16 x 41 1/4

173   WLADYSLAW STRZEMINSKI
         Ż Ponad (From beyond)
plate 5   Book, Poland, 1930
         Letterpress, 8 1/2 x 7 1/2

174   LADISLAV SUTNAR
         Automobilista před z Ykonem (Motorist ahead of the law)
         Book cover, Czechoslovakia
         Letterpress, 8 9/16 x 6 1/2

175   LADISLAV SUTNAR
         Státni grafická škola v Praze
fig. 2.24   (Prague State School of Graphic Arts)
         Brochure, Czechoslovakia, 1933
         Letterpress, 8 1/4 x 5 7/8

176   LADISLAV SUTNAR
         Výstava harmonického domova
fig. 3.16   (Exhibition of the harmonious home)
         Poster, Czechoslovakia, 1930
         Lithograph, 37 1/2 x 23 15/16

177   SOLOMON BENEDIKTOVICH TELINGATER
         10 Posters of Exercise and Sports [cover of portfolio]
plate 84   Design for poster, USSR
         Halftone photographs, rotogravure photographs,
         gouache, colored paper, paste, hand lettering
         12 1/2 x 10 1/2

178   SOLOMON BENEDIKTOVICH TELINGATER
         10 Posters of Exercise and Sports
plate 85   [sports scene with motorcycle and car]
         Design for poster, USSR
         Halftone photographs, rotogravure photographs,
         gouache, colored paper, paste, 12 1/4 x 9 7/8

179   SOLOMON BENEDIKTOVICH TELINGATER
         10 Posters of Exercise and Sports
plate 86   [sports scene]
         Design for poster, USSR
         Halftone photographs, rotogravure photographs,
         gouache, colored paper, paste, 12 1/4 x 9 7/8

180   SOLOMON BENEDIKTOVICH TELINGATER
         10 Posters of Exercise and Sports
plate 87   [sports scene with motorcycle and airplane]
         Design for poster, USSR
         Halftone photographs, rotogravure photographs,
         gouache, pencil, colored paper, paste, 12 1/2 x 10 5/16

181   SOLOMON BENEDIKTOVICH TELINGATER
         Slovo predostavliaestsia Kirsanovu
plate 19   (Kirsanov has the floor)
         Book, USSR, 1930
         Letterpress, 8 x 3 1/8

182

plate 18

SOLOMON BENEDIKTOVICH TELINGATER
Vytiazhka (Stretching)
Collage, USSR, 1920s
Ink, watercolor, crayon, decorative paper,
halftone photographs, printed letters, printed
illustrations, paste, 13 3/4 x 9

183

SOLOMON BENEDIKTOVICH TELINGATER
AND SERGEI MIKHAILOVICH TRET'IAKOV
Dzhon Khartfil'd (John Heartfield)
Book, Russia, 1936
Case-binding with pasted paper
11 3/4 x 18 1/4 (open)

184

fig. 2.2

GEORG TRUMP
Ausstellung Kunstgewerbeschule Bielefeld
(Exhibition at the School of Applied Arts, Bielefeld)
Design for poster, Germany, 1927
Gelatin silver print, cut paper letters, pencil, paste
23 1/8 x 18

185

fig. 2.26

GEORG TRUMP
Das Lichtbild (The photographic image)
Poster, Germany, 1930
Lithograph with pasted paper correction
23 9/16 x 32

186

fig. 2.28

JAN TSCHICHOLD
Der Berufsphotograph (The professional photographer)
Poster, Germany, 1938
Letterpress, 25 1/8 x 35 13/16

187

plate 56

JAN TSCHICHOLD
Die Frau ohne Namen, Zweiter Teil
(The woman without a name, part two)
Poster, Germany
Lithograph, 48 3/4 x 34

188

fig. 2.12

JAN TSCHICHOLD
Die Neue Typographie (The new typography)
Book, Germany, 1928
Letterpress, 8 5/6 x 11 7/8 (open)

189

fig. 3.22

JAN TSCHICHOLD (photomontage by
EL LISSITZKY [LAZAR' MARKOVICH LISITSKII])
Foto-Auge: The Constructor
Prospectus, Germany, 1929
Letterpress, 5 3/8 x 4

190

figs. 1.5,
2.10

TRISTAN TZARA
Salon Dada, Exposition Internationale
Poster, France, 1921
Lithograph, 47 5/8 x 31 9/16

191

plate 101

JO VOSKUIL (photograph by CAS OORTHUYS)
De olympiade onder dictatuur
(The Olympics under dictatorship)
Poster, Netherlands, 1936
Rotogravure, letterpress, 22 5/8 x 16 1/4

192

plate 1

HENDRIK NICOLAAS WERKMAN
The Next Call, No. 1
Magazine, Netherlands, 1926
Letterpress, 16 1/4 x 16 7/8 (open)

193

HENDRIK NICOLAAS WERKMAN
The Next Call, No. 8
Magazine, Netherlands, 1927
Letterpress, 8 1/2 x 10 7/8

194

fig. 2.20

HENDRIKUS THEODORUS WIJDEVELD
Architectuur Tentoonstelling (Architecture exhibition)
Poster, Netherlands, 1931
Letterpress, 30 1/4 x 19 1/4

195

fig. 1.1

BEATRICE WOOD
The Blindman's Ball
Poster, USA, 1917
Letterpress, 28 x 10

196

fig. 1.7

IL'IA MIKHAILOVICH ZDANEVICH
Iliazd
Poster, France, 1922
Lithograph, 21 5/8 x 18 7/8

197

figs. 1.8,
2.4

IL'IA MIKHAILOVICH ZDANEVICH
AND TRISTAN TZARA
Le coeur à barbe (The bearded heart)
Journal, France, 1922
Letterpress, 5 5/8 x 9

198

figs. 1.9,
2.9

IL'IA MIKHAILOVICH ZDANEVICH
Soirée du coeur à barbe
(Evening of the bearded heart)
Poster, France, 1923
Letterpress, 10 1/4 x 8 1/8

CONTRIBUTORS

DEBORAH ROTHSCHILD is curator of exhibitions
at Williams College Museum of Art.

ELLEN LUPTON is adjunct curator of contemporary
design at Cooper-Hewitt, National Design Museum,
in New York and co-chair of graphic design at
Maryland Institute, College of Art, in Baltimore.

DARRA GOLDSTEIN is professor of Russian
at Williams College and a specialist in Russian
modernism, culture, and cuisine.

MAUD LAVIN teaches cultural criticism at the
University of Illinois, Chicago.

COLOPHON

Book designed by Ellen Lupton

Photography by Jim Frank

Cover designed by Ellen Lupton
and Eva Christina Kraus

Body text set in the Scala type family,
designed by Martin Majoor, 1990–95

Headlines set in Bureau Grotesque,
designed by David Berlow and
Font Bureau, Inc., 1989–93

Display headlines set in Airport Gothic,
designer unknown, printed letterpress at
The Dolphin Press, Maryland Institute,
College of Art, Baltimore

Printed in the United States of America
on 80 lb Mead Moistrite® Matte
by Thames Printing Company
Film by Gist Inc.